Assyrians Beyond the Fall of Nineveh

William M. Warda

Assyrians Beyond the Fall of Nineveh,

A 2,624 Years Journey

William M. Warda

Copyright © 2013 by William M. Warda

All rights reserved. No part of this book may be reproduced or transmitted in any form or by any means, electronic or mechanical, including photocopying, recording, or by any information storage and retrieval device, without permission in writing from the copyright owner, except in case of brief quotations cited in critical articles and reviews.

The cover image shows an illustration of a ninth century BC, ancient Assyrian relief, where King Ashurnasirpal II, is standing in reverence on the side of the Tree of Life. On the right, is a relief from the gate of the 4th century AD, Mar Behnam Monastery, in the Plain of Nineveh, where the cross is portrayed as the Tree of Life.

In praise of the Tree of Life, the fourth-century Mar Ephraim wrote: "while the Tree of Knowledge brought death to Adam and Eve, the Tree of Life, i.e. cross, restores life to humanity.

At the bottom of the illustration is a picture drawn by Henry Layard in mid-nineteenth century, showing his Christian Assyrian workers wearing their traditional conical hats that resemble the helmets worn by the ancient Assyrian soldiers. For comparison, the author has added to the side of the drawing, a photo of a relief showing an ancient Assyrian Calvary soldier wearing a metallic helmet.

DEDICATION

This book is dedicated to the memory of the countless Assyrian generations who despite being ruthlessly persecuted by others have strived to preserve their identity and heritage to this day. During the periods of wholesale massacres they often were forced to flee to other countries and return when the danger had subsided. It is also dedicated to my dear parents, who as young children, and young adults equally suffered during such hardships.

Leda's family fled to Russia in 1915, Babajon's family fled to Iraq, (Mesopotamia) in 1918. During the 1920's their families returned to their village in Urmia where the two married.

TABLE OF CONTENTS

Introduction..13
Chapter 1, Misconceptions..16
Assyrians and the Old Testament............................20
Facts Overlooked...22
Bias of archaeologists and writers...........................25
Confusing the 9th satrap with the fifth....................32
Chapter 2, Syrian/Suraye meant Assyrian................35
Even Dur Sharrukeen was remembered...................41
Weren't there Babylonians in Babylon?...................42
What did Beth Aramaye mean..................................43
Not everyone who spoke Aramaic was Aramean......44
Ancient Assyrians were also known as Syrians........45
Why they called themselves Suraye?.......................49
Vilification of the Assyrians......................................51
Chapter 3, The Genetics of the Assyrians.................53
Assyrians according to the Vatican archives............57
According to the Syriac writers................................58
According to Carmelites missionaries.....................50
Assyrians according to the Armenians....................62
According to the Persians and others.....................65
According to the Georgians.....................................65
Assyrians according to the Kurds............................66

Assyrians according to the Russians..........................67
Chapter 4, Assyrian Nationalism..............................68
Chaldean Assyrians...70
Nationalism among Jacobite Assyrians......................71
Rejection of Nationalism By Some Clergies..............73
References to Jacobites as Assyrians..........................76
Ancient Assyrians in Anatolia...................................77
Assyrians in Tur Abedin..79
Chapter 5, Ancient Assyrian Traditions.....................82
Ancient Assyrian New Year in Edessa.......................83
Ancient Burial Practice..85
Ancient and Christian Icons......................................86
 Syriac Dispute Poems...89
Assyrians in Syriac Literature....................................90
The Legend of Mar Behnam......................................92
The Legend of Ahikar..94
Hats Worn by the Highland Assyrians.......................96
Head Ornaments of the Assyrian Women...................98
Surnames of the Christian Assyrians........................100
Assyrian Surnames on the Facebook........................101
Homeland of the Assyrians......................................105
Chapter 6, Nineveh After the Fall............................107
Bishops of Nineveh..113
Reports of Travelers...113
Assyrian Fast of Nineveh...117
Chapter 7, Survival of the Assyrian Cities...............125
Assyrian Survival in Harran.....................................128
Arbil Adiabene..132
Assyrian City of Nisibin..133
Assyrians and Silk Manufacturing...........................135
Assyrian Survival in Other Places...........................137
Chapter 8, Archaeological Discoveries....................139
Discovery at Eski Mosul Dam Basin........................140
Assyrian City of Ashur..140
Assyrians at the City of Hatra..................................143
Chapter 9, Assyrians in the Plain of Nineveh...........146

Town of Alkosh..148
Town of Ankawa...149
Town of Baghdida...150
Ba Nuhadra, The Plain of Nineveh........................150
Village of Baqof..151
Town of Bartella...152
Town of Karmales..152
Town of Telkaif...154
Town of Zakho..154
Struggle for Survival...155
Nader shah's Destruction......................................158
Part II, After the Fall of Nineveh...........................158
Persian Achamenid Domination............................161
The Seleucid Dynasty.......................................165
The Parthian Rule..166
Chapter 11, Assyrian Christianity...........................168
Conversion of Abgar O' Kama................................169
Legend of the Wise-men..170
Chapter 12, The Sassanian Rule............................172
Persecutions of Shapur II......................................173
New School in Edessa/Urhay.................................176
Theological Disputes...180
The second School in Nisibin................................184
The Rule of Khosro Anushirwan............................186
Rescue of the Persian Troops.................................186
Assyrians and the Jundi-Shapur Academy.............190
Translations into the Pahlavi Language................192
The Rule of Khosro Parviz....................................193
War against Syria..194
Defeat of Persia Near Nineveh..............................195
Chapter 13, Arab Conquest of Mesopotamia...........197
The Oldest Church in Karbala...............................199
The Oldest Christian Cemetery in Najaf................200
The Founding of Baghdad.....................................201
Mesopotamia During the Arab Rule......................202
Assyrian Contribution to Islamic civilization..........204

Most Influential Assyrian Scholars..........206
Translation into Arabic..........207
Yuhanna ibn-Masawayah..........209
Hunayn ibn Ishaq..........210
Hunayn Master Translator..........211
Harranian School of Beth Qarah..........214
Prominence of the Christian Doctors..........216
The Philosophers..........217
Chapter 14, End of the Golden Age..........219
Struggle for survival..........221
The Mongol's Rule..........222
Massacre in Arbil..........226
The Onslaught of Tamure..........226
Ottoman Turks' Genocide..........227
World War I Massacre of the Assyrians..........228
Turks and Kurd's Attack on Urmia..........230
Massacre in Urmia..........231
Massacre of the Highland Assyrians..........236
Highland Assyrians in Persia..........242
All-out Attack against Assyrians..........246
Departure of the Russian Troops..........245
Murder of Mar Benjamin..........247
Exodus From Urmia..........251
The Last Assyrians in Urmia..........253
From Hamadan to Baquba..........256
The Mosul Affair..........258
1933 Semail Massacre..........266
Saddam's Rule..........274
2003 U.S. Invasion of Iraq..........276
Assyrians Today..........277

ACKNOWLEDGEMENT

The success of any project depends largely on the encouragement and guidelines of many others. I take this opportunity to express my gratitude to Dr. Robert Paulissian, and Vladimir Bid David, who provided me with needed sources of information for research. To Melis Lachin who read the book and gave suggestion about how to improve it. To my Sister Frieda Warda, and my brother Victor Warda, for their moral support and encouragement. I would like to express Special thanks to Mr. Atour Bejan who assisted in indexing the book. I wish to thank all the Assyrians who were asking about the book long before it was published, this kept me motivated. All Assyrians owe a debt of gratitude to the Assyiralogist, Simo Parpola, who unlike others has been willing to honestly explore and write about archaeological evidences that atteat to the survival of the ancient Assyrians after their defeat.

Preface

In the introduction of a book by Yusuf Malek, titled; "British Betrayal of the Assyrians," Wigram wrote the following which *is also relevant to this book.*

"There is no type of mankind that has had a history more interesting, and few lengthier than the Assyrian nationality to which he belongs. Reaching back as they do through the ages when Babylon and Assyria were producing the dawn of civilization in the lands where civilization had one of its very earliest beginning. They have seen the rise and fall of the Persian Empire in its early form, have seen the struggle between Parthia and Rome, and finally found in Christianity the religion that they could take to themselves, in the days when the latter empire of Persia was beginning a development that lasted till Islam spread a new faith and a new culture over all the near and central east...

Readers will find here description and history of every one of these aspects of the people written by one of themselves, with a knowledge and sympathy that no foreigner, no matter what his experience, can really hope to attain.

The work appears at a moment that the fortune of the people seem to be at their very darkest, and may serve to attract to those who have suffered more severely and more undeservedly than almost any other nation in the war, some of the sympathy and help that is their just due."

Wigram, D.D. – Wells, Somerset – November 1933

Introduction

Today's Assyrians belong to a unique culture that has survived for thousands of years; they are a distinct ethnic group who trace their origin to the ancient Assyrians. Due to persecution in their homeland they presently are scattered in many countries, including, Iraq, Syria, Iran, the United States, and the continent of Europe.

The Assyrian Empire is well known to the readers of the Old Testament and the students of the ancient history. It started as a small country located in Northern Mesopotamia, today's northern Iraq, and gradually expanded into a great empire. From about 1000 to 600 BC, it became the greatest power in the ancient world. It dominated a vast area that stretched from Iran to the Eastern Mediterranean, from the Taurus Mountains to Southern Turkey and down to the Persian Gulf.

Later empires such as the Persian, and Roman, owed much to the Assyrian Empire's military and administrative legacy. However, aside from the archaeological and ancient history journals, information about what happened to the ancient Assyrians after the fall Nineveh is scarcely reported. This has led to the erroneous assumption, outside the Christian Assyrian community, that the ancient Assyrians were defeated into extinction by the Babylonians and Medes in 612 BC.

Absence of information about the ancient Assyrians, after their defeat, is primarily due to the fact that Greek historians, who wrote about them, called them Surios (Syrians). At the same time, they gave the name Syria to the region west of Euphrates, which, for as long as they could remember had been part of the Assyrian Empire. All references to Syrians afterward were presumed to mean citizens of Syria, despite the fact that the Greek and Roman historians wrote about Assyrians as an existing people during their life time.

Some contemporary Authors, such as John Joseph have claimed that Christian Assyrians who claim to be the descendants of the ancient Assyrians did not identify themselves as such, nor they were known as Assyrians before the 19th century British archaeologist Austen Henry Layard after discovering the ruins of Nineveh declared them to be *"as much the remains of Nineveh and Assyria as the rude heaps and ruined palaces."* However, evidences attest to the fact that Christian Assyrian writers, since early Christianity have identified their people as Assyrians, as have writers of other nationalities.

The first part of this book includes rarely published, amazing facts and historical evidences about the survival of the ancient Assyrians and the progression of their descendants into the modern age.

The second part starts with the defeat of the ancient Assyrians by the Medes and the Babylonians; and continues to narrate the history of the descendants of the Assyrians during the rule of other nations who invaded their homeland. This format may sound odd to some readers who expected the book to start after the fall of Nineveh and continue into the Christian era, however, because of existing misinformation about the history and identity of the Christian Assyrians, it is important to set the record straight by answering questions that have been raised by some writers to cast doubt about the relation between the contemporary Assyrians and the ancient Assyrians.

This is not a history of the Nestorians, Jacobites, or Chaldeans; it is the story of a people who otherwise have shared a common language, homeland, culture, religion, history, ancestry, and destiny. Unfortunately they have been divided by theological conflicts and denominational animosities that have resulted in their decline and have undermined their survival.

In addition to narrating history of the Christian Assyrians, this book also describes their encounters with nations that since have ruled them or have come in contact with them, including the Persians, Greeks, Romans, Parthians, Arabs, Turks, Mongols, and Kurds. Christian Assyrians have also suffered because of Western countries' military adventures in their Muslim-dominated homeland.

References to the Nestorians, Jacobites, and Chaldeans throughout this book have been used out of necessity because these labels have been used in the West to define them based on their relationship with the Roman Catholic Church. It is important to note that for the sake of consistency throughout this book, the term Atturaye has been used as the English transliteration for the word Assyrian, as it is pronounced in the Syriac language, the Christian Assyrians speak.

Chapter 1

Misconceptions

Academic texts seldom acknowledge the existence of a Syriac speaking people known as Assyrians who have been inhabitants of Mesopotamia, i.e., today's Iraq and southeast Turkey since before the dawn of Christianity, therefore, it should not surprise us that, with few exceptions, most of the information published in the West about who the Christian Assyrians remains incomplete and misleading due to the superficial knowledge of their writers.

For example there has been little mention in the West of the World War massacre of the Christian Assyrians by the Ottoman Turks, who obliterated three-fourths of their population. Nonetheless, Western writers who lack complete knowledge of their history have no problem making judgment about their identity. Walker T. Joel writes:

"In the early nineteenth century, European and British travelers who visited Mesopotamia described its landscape through the lens of the Greco-Roman historians they had studied in school . . . after Layard's excavations at Nimrod and the decipherment of cuneiform tablets, the next generation of travelers learned that the city of Arbela, today's Arbil, had been the sacred city of Assyria, where kings Sennacherib and Ashurbanipal prayed for the goddess Ishtar to help ensure their

victory." (Walker, 1968, 2).

Though they had employed local Christian guides and interpreters, judging by the statement of a British historian who in 1482 wrote: *"Of the character of the Christians in that part of Asia, the little we know of, is not very favorable."* In other words, they were not even eager to learn about them.

The Europeans' interest in Christian Assyrians peaked in mid-nineteenth century, primarily because they were informed about extensive massacres of the Christians in the highlands northwest of Arbela. Even then, they only knew them as Nestorians, a derogatory nickname that was given to them by the Roman Catholic Church to define them as heretic. According to Jenkins, Western writers have not only mischaracterized the Assyrian Church of the East as less than Christian, they have also distorted the mental map of Christianity by omitting a thousand years of its story and several million miles of the territory where it flourished. Jenkins contends that Christianity thrived in northern and southern Mesopotamia well into the Middle Ages, In cities of Nisibin, Edessa, and Jundi-Shapur, where Assyrian scholars kept alive the culture and science of the ancient world and passed on the Greco-Roman scholarship first to the Persians and later to the Arabs—it was this knowledge that arrived in Europe in mid-thirteenth century to ignite the Renaissance (Jenkins Philip, 2008, 7).

Jenkins also writes: *"Over the past thirty years, scholars have rediscovered the many spiritual currents that characterized the earliest church, the various lost or forgotten Christianities that were remembered, if at all, as heretical byways of the faith"* (Jenkins Philip, 2008, 8).

He further contends that Mesopotamia or Iraq possessed a robust Christian culture, at least up to the thirteenth century.

"In terms of the number and splendor of its churches and monasteries, its vast scholarship and dazzling spirituality, Iraq was through the late Middle Ages at least as much a cultural and spiritual heartland of Christianity as was France or Germany, or

indeed Ireland" (Jenkins Philip, 2008, 6)

Some of the Assyrian churches and monasteries in the Plain of Nineveh such as Mar Mattay and Mar Behnam that date back to the early Christian centuries have survived to this day, though in poor state of disrepair.

In addition to distorting the map of Christianity by omitting a thousand years of its story, and several millions miles of the territory where it flourished, some Western writers have also gone out of their way to insist that Christian Assyrians should not be called Assyrian, but be known as Nestorian or Jacobite, labels that were imposed on them by their detractors after the fifth century theological conflicts within the Roman Catholic church. These nicknames imply that they did not exist as people of unique culture, heritage, and history before the fifth century AD.

The use of such terms in reference to the Christian Assyrians has given an excuse to the extremist Turk, Kurd, and Arab nationalists to question their ancient history and identity by claiming that they are not the indigenous people of their homeland, where they and their forefathers have lived since before the dawn of Christianity and the rise of Islam. In retaliation of the American invasion of Iraq in 2003, Christians in that country were kidnapped, imprisoned, wrongly arrested, beaten, and murdered -- not because of anything they have done, but simply because they were Christians which is suposedly the religion of the people in the United States more than a thousand Assyrians have been murdered, some seventy of their churches have been bombed, and half a million Christian Assyrians of all denominations have been driven out of that country by the Islamic extremists.

During the Saddam Hussein's rule, in addition to bombing the Assyrian villages in northern Iraq, various other nonviolent means of ethnic and religious cleansing were used to force them to define themselves as Christian Arabs. The school textbooks were modified to claim that the ancient Assyrians and Babylonians were Arabs. When there was a complaint in the United Nations about the persecution of the Assyrians in Iraq,

Saddam Hussein's representative contended that there were no Assyrians in Iraq. Other methods were also used to prevent the Christian Assyrian students from learning about their history and identity. Suha Rassam in her book "Christianity in Iraq" writes:

"Although we were taught some of the ancient history of Mesopotamia in school, the emphasis was on Arab history and Muslim achievements. There was no mention of the presence of Christians on Iraqi soil before Islam, nor was their role in the emergence of the Arab Abbasid civilization that was established in Iraq ever raised. This created in me and in many other Christians a reaction against the Islamic history and culture which were taught more than once during our intermediary and secondary education. It caused in us Christians a feeling of tension regarding our Iraqi identity.

During my second visit to England in 1990, searching for my roots became an obsession, and I started to investigate the history of Iraq and my Christian background. I was astonished at the paucity of material available on our churches, whether in English or in Arabic. This led me to serious research on the subject, which took me to scholarly books and to undertake an MA in Eastern Christianity at the School of Oriental and African Studies in London" (Rassam, Suha, 2006, 4-5).

In response to the denial of the Assyrian identity of the Christian Assyrians by the Western writers, Arian Ishaya wrote:

"Assyrians call themselves Assyrians for a very simple and convincing reason: they are the age-old inhabitants of ancient Assyria. It is their homeland. They have churches there that date as far back as third and fourth century AD and still others such as St. Mary at Kharput and St. Mary at Urmia that are of apostolic foundation. That is sufficient and says it all. There is no need to engage in the inconclusive argument of racial and cultural purity. When any nation says that it is what it is, it is that because its forefathers inhabited that region since time immemorial. The Assyrians say they are Assyrians because their forefathers inhabited Assyria and the French say that France is

their homeland because they have lived there for many centuries. One claim is as valid as the other. What makes the French claim more respectable and that of the Assyrians questionable isn't science, it is politics pure and simple" (Ishaya, Arian, Nineveh Magazine, Vol. 6 No. 4, 1983).

The abbreviation of the Assyrian into Syrian, by the Greek historians, led to the erroneous assumption that ancient Assyrians no longer existed after their 612 BC defeat. Also, due to the fifth-century theological conflicts, within the Roman Catholic Church, members of the Church of the East were called by the derogatory nickname Nestorian and members of the Syrian Orthodox church were labeled Jacobite. During the last 1,500 years the Eurocentric and Western writers have used the two terms indiscriminately, both as the religious, as well as the ethnic identity of the Christian Assyrians. Christian Assyrians have been also known as Syrian, a term used by the classical Greek historians for the ancient Assyrians, but the later writers seldom associated the use of this term during the Christian era with its ancient meaning. Furthermore, in 1552 when a faction of the Church of the East joined the Roman Catholic Church and was given the name "Chaldean Catholic Church," its people were called Chaldeans, to distinguish them from the members of the other two denominations. Ironically these nicknames have been often cited as evidence that Christian Assyrians are not related to the ancient Assyrians. Those who do so clearly seem to be incapable of distinguishing between the religious affiliation and the ethnic identity of the Christian Assyrians.

Assyrians and the Old Testament

As if that wasn't enough, for the last 2,000 years the Old Testament was the only source of information about what happened to the ancient Assyrians. Those who read the book of Nahum were wrongly led to believe that Assyrians and their cities were completely destroyed by God, and Assyrians no longer existed.

Though people of ancient Mesopotamia contributed greatly to human civilization—by inventing the wheel, the plow, the first form of writing, as well as building the first cities and the first schools,__ they developed the twelve-month calendar and a code of law—the most popular image representing Assyrians and Babylonians in the West, until recently, was the half-ruined, mythical Tower of Babel. It was supposedly destroyed by God to punish mankind who had allegedly rose to challenge his authority. Inspired by the depiction of the Nineveh and ancient Assyrians as the oppressors of Israel and Judah, poets such as Byron wrote poems to define them as cruel: *"The Assyrian came down like the wolf on the fold."*

Likewise, the artists were busy painting pictures showing how the angels of God killed 85,000 Assyrians overnight when King Sennacherib's besieged Jerusalem in 701 BC. As D.J. McIntosh puts it:

"Lord Byron sealed the reputation of the Assyrians with just two lines of poetry: 'The Assyrian came down like a wolf on the fold, / And his cohorts were gleaming in purple and gold;' The Assyrian empire comes off even worse in the Bible. Written by the descendants of the empire's Judaic victims, the Bible has heavily influenced what people know of the Assyrians . . . " (McIntosh D.J. Historical Friction).

The discovery of the Assyrian cuneiform tablets have provided detailed information about the ancient Assyrians and Babylonians that readers of the Old Testament knew nothing about. Martha Roth, editor-in-charge of the Assyrian Dictionary project of the University of Chicago's Oriental Institute, revealed that by reading the ancient tablets,

" We began to see entire civilizations that had been thriving, flourishing for 3,000 years and more. The writings gave us the histories that went into forming who we are, they told, a creation story, older than the Hebrew creation story, told a flood story that preceded the Noah story, and described a code of laws that predated Moses." (News.blogs.cnn.com/2011/06/10)

Therefore, it is not surprising that the knowledge in the West about the Assyrians and ancient Mesopotamia, up to the twenty-first century, has been no more than what people remember from the sermons of the hellfire-and-brimstone preachers who recited Nahum's account of Nineveh's destruction, to show how even the mightiest nations can be obliterated by God, but no one paid attention to the section where Nahum wrote, *"O king of Assyria, your nobles slumber, Your people are scattered on the mountains with none to gather them"* (Nahum 3:18, ESV). Even the readers who noticed this did not care if any Assyrians had survived, because, by presenting Assyrians as the enemy of God, the Old Testament had taught its readers to hate them.

Facts Overlooked

Christian Assyrians who lived at or near Nineveh and other ancient Assyrian cities had no doubt that they were the descendants of the ancient Assyrians. They could not believe that Nineveh was destroyed by God and was uninhabitable, because they were its inhabitants and were absolutely certain that ancient Assyrians were not defeated into extinction. Instead of celebrating the book of Nahum as the rest of the Christian world did, they believed in the book of Jonah, which refutes the popular assumption that God destroyed Nineveh and its inhabitants. Though historical accounts attest to the fact that Babylonians and the Mede destroyed most Assyrian cities, killed thousands, and took many as prisoners, evidence suggests that ancient Assyrians survived their defeat into Christianity.

Historian Stephanie Dalley in her "Nineveh After 612 BC," questions the often repeated statement that when Xenophon, and his army, in 401 BC, marched past the abandoned Nineveh, he did not recognize it, because it was in ruin. She writes, the source is not as accurate as is sometimes claimed, because he did not enter the city, but passed below its walls. She cites the Book of Jonah as evidence. She writes:

"The Prophet Jonah is barely known historical figure of the eighth century [BC], but the composition dates to around the

fourth c. B C. when Nineveh should long have been abandoned. Nahum, prophesying in mid-seventh century, had proclaimed that God was working through history to destroy Nineveh, so that she would be "empty, void and waste", and this theme was taken up by other prophets." (Dalley, Stephanie, 1993, 134) She also states: *"As Hitzig (1881, 174-6) pointed out, the purpose of the book of Jonah is to explain why the early prophecies were not fulfilled. Jonah's humiliation implies that Nineveh was flourishing in the fourth c. B.C."*

In other words, if Nineveh did not exist at the Fourth century BC it would have been irrational to include the Book of Jonah in the Old Testament. The fact that the 5th century Xenophon makes no mention of the ruins inside the walls of Nineveh suggests that he may have seen only the exterior of the city. Otherwise, it would have been impossible for him to not have seen the two-story-high colossal Winged Bulls guarding the Assyrian places, which according to Layard were still standing when he discovered them.

The Barber geographer Ibne-Battuta who visited the site of Nineveh in the thirteenth century attested to the fact that walls encircling the city were still visible. He also wrote: *"the position of the gates that were in them could be seen."* Ironically, about the end of his book, Xenophon mentions the arrival of the "Assyrian hoplite" employed by the Persian King coming to the rescue of an Iranian land holder, whose fortress Xenophon and his three hundred soldiers were about to storm. (Warner Rex, 1972, 350) In fact, Assyrian soldiers known for their combat skills, along with the Lydians constituted the main heavy infantry of the Achaemenid empire's military.

(http://en.wikipedia.org/wiki/Achaemenid_Assyria)
Archaeological discoveries refute the assumption that the Assyrian Heartland was in ruin during the Achaemenid Period (239-254), or when Xenophon passed through it. Amélie Kuhrt, writes:

"New archaeological finds at Seh Hamad lead to a correction of a view (often thought to be supported by evidence in X.'s

Anabasis*) of the Assyrian state as 'a hollow state which collapsed on itself, leaving little trace.' Apparently the old Assyrian city-sites were not as deserted and in ruins as has been thought in accordance with X.'s description of the area, and the Neo-Babylonian (and afterwards the Persian) state had taking over surviving Assyrian physical and institutional structures."* (Pierre Briant, 1995, 302)

According to David Oates: "*By the late fourth century BC the villages that dotted the countryside between Nineveh and the upper Tigris must have been in moderately prosperous condition when Xenophon and his 10,000 man army marched by them . . . He always comments on the plentiful supplies that were available. Since the Greeks must still have numbered close to 10,000 men, this argues a considerable production of grain.*" (Oates, David, 1968, 61). One must also add, a considerable population to grow and harvest the fields.

To underscore the fact that God had not destroyed Nineveh and its inhabitants, as described in the Book of Nahum of the Old Testament, Christian Assyrians, who considered themselves as their descendants, initiated a yearly fast during the early centuries of Christianity similar to the one their forefathers had observed, as mentioned in the Book of Jonah. They called it 'Baoota d' Ninevaye' or "the Wish of the Ninevites." This Fast is still observed by the members of the Church of the East, the Syrian Orthodox Church, and the Chaldean Church. What the readers of the Old Testament didn't know was that Nahum was neither a prophet nor a witness to what happened at Nineveh.

"J.M.P. Smith describes Nahum as an enthusiastic and optimistic patriot. K. Spronk thinks that the Book of Nahum was written in Jerusalem, by a talented, faithful royal scribe, who used the pseudonym Nahum as an indication of his purpose: *"to encourage the people of Judah groaning under the yoke of Assyrian tyranny"* (Pinker, Aaron, Jewish Bible Quarterly, 2005). In fact, Nahum or Nachum in Hebrew means relief/ resting/ comport. According to R.H. Pfeiffer: *"Nahum was a poet . . . There is nothing specifically religious in this exultant outburst of joy over the inevitable downfall of the Assyrian Empire"* (Pinker).

Nahum is described as "the Alkoshite" to imply that he lived in the Assyrian city of Alkosh, to make believe that he had first hand knowledge of what happened in 612 BC. While the Old Testament readers had no problem accepting the book of Nahum as the Gospel of truth, they knew nothing about the fact that the ancient Assyrian city of Alkosh was resettled after the fall and has survived to this day along with its inhabitants, who consider themselves Assyrians. However, because they have been wrongly labeled as Nestorians or Jacobites for the last 1,500 years, and Chaldeans in later centuries, their Assyrian identity has been totally ignored. The same is true about inhabitants of the other Christian Assyrian towns, in the plain of Nineveh, in northern Iraq.

Bias of Archaeologists and Writers

Judging by how often the early archaeologists quoted the Old Testament prophecies in their writing, one can conclude that they had come to believe that God had indeed destroyed the Assyrians for daring to invade Israel and for the exiling of Israel's Ten Tribes. Most of these scholars were educated in the religious schools; their interest in the ancient Assyrian history and antiquity was driven primarily by a desire to prove the infallibility of the Old Testament and to bolster its divine origin. Proving that God had utterly destroyed the mighty Assyrians was a good way to show that everything described in the Old Testament is scientifically provable.

While it is true that the major Assyrian cities were destroyed, their population partially massacred, and other inhabitants carried into captivity, as often happened in the ancient wars, there is no reason to believe that Assyrians were wiped out during a relatively short period of time. It is a known fact that nations have survived despite all attempts to destroy them. Neither the English nor the French became extinct during what is know as The Hundred Years' War, beginning in 1337 and ending in 1453. Fifty million dead during World War II did not cause the extinction of any nation. The persecution, including wholesale massacres, of the Jews during more than two thousand years of their history did not wipe them out.

The Syriac speaking Christians of Mesopotamia, (Assyrians) of Iraq, Turkey, and Northwest Iran survived 2,000 years of persecutions, including repeated massacres by the Sassanian Persians, Arabs, Mongols, Tatars, Kurds, and Turks. Two-thirds of the Assyrian population was murdered or forced into Islam between 1914 and 1919 by the combined military forces of the Kurds, Turks, and Persians in an all out attempt to wipe them out, but they survived, despite their relatively small number and concentration in a small geographic area. The Armenians lost 1.5 million of their population at that time, but they are still here.

As more historical information and archaeological discoveries have become available since the nineteenth century, Assyriologists such as H.W. F., Saggs, Robert D. Diggs, Giorgi Tsereteli, Simon Parpola, and Iranologists like Richard Nelson Frye have come to believe that the ancient Assyrians survived beyond their seventh-century BC defeat, and that their descendants continued into Christianity.

H.W.F. Saggs, the author of several books about the history of Mesopotamia including "The Greatness that was Babylon," and "The Might That Was Assyria, wrote:

"The destruction of the Assyrian empire did not wipe out its population. They were predominantly peasant farmers, and since Assyria contains some of the best wheat land in the Near East, descendants of the Assyrian peasants would, as opportunity permitted, build new villages over the old cities and carry on with agricultural life, remembering traditions of the former cities. After seven or eight centuries and various vicissitudes, these people became Christians." (Saggs, H.W.F., 1989, 290)

Simo Parpola writes: "Assyria was a vast and densely populated country, and outside the few urban centers life went on as usual." (Parpola, Simo, JAAS Vol. XIII No. 2, 1999) Xenophon, who with ten thousand Greeks passed through the rural Assyria in 401 BC, confirms these facts. He wrote:

". . . there was an abundance of corn in the villages, and

found a palace, with many villages round about it... In these villages they remained for three days, not only for the sake of the wounded, but likewise because they had provisions in abundance—flour, wine, and great stores of barley that had been collected for horses, all these supplies having been gathered together by the acting satrap of the district." (Anabasis, book III.IV., 24-32)

Due to misinterpretation of the Old Testament, Christian writers in the West have been vociferous in claiming, or implying, that ancient Assyrians were defeated into extinction because they had mistreated the Jews. They wrongly conclude that the people who later lived in the ancient Assyrian homeland were Arameans, not Assyrian, but provide no justification for such presumption and ignore all the historical and archaeological facts that prove otherwise.

Kelley L. Ross, a teacher at the Los Angeles Valley College, in an article posted on the Internet, intended to rebuke his students who identified themselves as Assyrians wrote:

"it might strike one as unseemly, that Christians should be at pains to get too excited over descent from a people who not only were not Christians, but whose terror and brutality were a byword in the ancient world, and who were actually responsible for the disappearance or even extermination of the Ten Tribes of Israel, (or who, ironically, could claim to be their descendants."

It seems that Ross has no use for historical facts, he can not make up his mined if the Ten Tribes were exterminated or survived to call themselves Assyrians, as if 27,000 members of the Ten Tribes were more likely to survive than hundreds of thousands, or perhaps millions, of Assyrians in their own homeland. He naively thinks that Assyrians were the only nation that treated their enemy unkindly. Furthermore, various communities recently have been identified in India, and elsewhere, that claim to be the descendants of the Ten Tribes of Israel. In all cases, they contend that they migrated from Assyria to the far away places on their own.

Ross is profoundly upset about what happened 2,500 years ago, but does not shed tears about the cruelty and inhumanity that killed millions in the wars of the previous century. Furthermore, a people's identity is not something that can be discarded like yesterday's underwear. Most older nations trace their history and identity to the pre-Christian era; therefore, according to him, they are committing an unforgivable sin.

In a speech at the Assyrian American Association of Southern California in 2009, Dr. Yona Sabar, a Jewish scholar and professor of the Middle Eastern cultures and languages at UCLA, spoke about his childhood in the town of Zakho in northern Iraq, where Assyrians and Jews lived in friendship. He traces the Jews' arrival in Mesopotamia to 721 BC when Assyrian King Sargon II exiled 27,290 Samaritan Jews and settled them by the River of Khabor, where the town of Zakho is located. In fact, there is an inscription by King Sargon II that attests to this fact. Dr. Sabar believes that he and other Jews in that region may be the descendants of the exiled Samaritans. As for Christian Assyrians, he believes there is no reason to doubt their discordance from the ancient Assyrians. He said: *"Nations have been defeated, empires have disappeared, but their people have survived."*

Writers such as Jean Fiey and John Joseph have questioned the Assyrian identity of the Christian Assyrians by misinterpreting the known historical evidences that corroborate the survival of the ancient Assyrians after their defeat. Jean Fiey for instance, who in his previous book titled "Assyrian Christian Contribution to the Study of History and Geography of Ecclesiastical and Monastic Northern Iraq" and other books, referred to the Christian Assyrians as Assyrians in a later article titled " 'Assyriens' ou 'Aramaens'?" (Assyrians or Arameans), has strived to prove that they are Arameans. He writes: *"Since before Christianity, Greek and Latin authors seem to have used the names 'Assyrian's and 'Syrians' indifferently. Linguists explain that the second is an abbreviated form of the first, by omission of the prefix "a."* However he goes on to say: *"If one wants to make a distinction between the two names, Greek specialists would rather think that the Surioi represented non-Assyrians tribes of the Assyrian Empire, and among those, the Arameans held a predominant position."* (Fiey, J. M., 1965, 1)

Fiey seems to think that Herodotus Surioi meant Syrian, which he equates with Aramean. He overlooks the fact that Greek historians such as Herodotus and Strabo have specifically stated that by Syrian they meant no other than Assyrians. Greeks gave the name Syria to the region west of Euphrates, because for as long as they could remember it had been part of the Assyrian Empire. It did not have a common national name; it was known to the Assyrians, Babylonians and later Persians as Ebar-Nahra, meaning Beyond the River. The faulty assumption that all references to Syrians by the Greek and Roman historians meant citizens of Syria gained momentum when the Greek Seleucid dynasty, (312 BCE–63 BC) ruled Mesopotamia and called them collectively Syria. (Britannica, *Seleucid kingdom*, 2008, O.Ed.)

Persians, who were in a perfect position to know the correct nationality of soldiers serving in their military undoubtedly informed Herodotus that the troops he mentions were Assyrians and Babylonians. However, The later historians routinely ignored or misinterpreted this important testament to the survival of the ancient Assyrians after their defeat. They did not want such facts to interfere with their long-standing prejudices. Herodotus wrote:

"The Assyrians went to the war with helmets upon their heads, made of brass, and plaited in a strange fashion which is not easy to describe. They carried shields, lances, and daggers, very much like the Egyptian; but in addition, they had wooden clubs knotted with iron, and linen corselets. This people, whom the Hellenes called Syrians, are called Assyrians by the barbarians." He even gives the names and the lineage of the Persian commander who led them into war. *"They had for commander Otaspes, the son of Artachaeus."* (Herodotus,1942, [7.63]) The Persian kings who ruled Mesopotamia from 539 to 330 BC, mention Assyria and Assyrians, in their inscriptions, among countries and people that were part of their empire.

Babylonian king Nabonaid (555–539) who wished to rebuild the temple of Sin in Harran could not do it before driving the Medes out of northern Mesopotamia, which they had occupied since 610 BC. To solve the problem, he made an alliance with the Persian king Cyrus to rise against the Medes, which led to the occupation of the median capital, Ecbatana, by the Persians in (550 BC), and allowed Nabonaid to capture Harran while the Median Army was kept busy at home. After defeating the Medes Cyrus also conquered Babylonian, in 539 BC. In an inscription, he wrote:

"From [. . .] to Ashur and Susa, Agade, Eshnunak, Zamban, Meturnu, Deri, with the territory of the land of Qutu, the cities on the other side of the Tigris, whose sites were of ancient foundation—the gods, who resided in them, I brought back to their places, and caused them to dwell in a residence for all time. And the gods of Sumer and Akkad—whom Nabonidus, to the anger of the lord of the gods, had brought into Babylon—by the command of Marduk, the great lord, I caused them to take up their dwelling in residences that gladdened the heart. May all the gods, whom I brought into their cities pray daily before Bêl and Nabû for long life for me." (Pritchard, Editor, 1950, 208)

This indicates that the city of Ashur was inhabited after the fall of Nineveh and Nebunaid had transferred the Statue of Ashur to Babylon for protection. An inscription by Darius (512–48) at the Nagshe Rostam, which lists the national types of the Persian Empire, includes an Assyrians. A reference to him reads: "Iyam Atturyah," 'This is an Assyrian.' (Sukumar Sen, 1941, 107) In an inscription by Darius about a palace that he built in Susa and the people who contributed to its building, Assyrians are mentioned as the people who brought the cedar timber from a mountain in Lebanon. The text reads: *"The Assyrian people, it brought it to Babylon; from Babylon, the Carians and the Ionians brought it to Susa.*

"Proclaims Xerxes, the King: "By the favor of Ahura Mazda; these are the people/countries which I was king of . . ." The list includes Babylonia and Assyria. (Wiesehofer, Josef, 1969, 60)

Assyrians and Babylonians are listed among workers and

artisans brought from the fourteen countries of the Persian Empire to work at the king's palace. They were grouped according to traditional categories such as men, women, boys and girls. According to Yale Babylonian texts (TBT 16813) Egyptians and Assyrians were placed to work together. (Yana George Bibla, 2008, 26) The Zoroastrian religious book of "Zand-i Vohuman Yasht" in the Pahlavi language, in one section accuses the Greeks (Yunan) who ruled in Asuristan (330–145 BC) of slaying the [Asori] Assyrian people and destroying their abode. "Zand-i Vohuman Yasht, CHAPTER 3."
www.avesta.org/pahlavi/vohuman3.html (2007)

Influence of the Assyrian art on the Achaemenid architecture is readily evident throughout the Persian Apadana palace at Persepolis, developed by the Persian king Darius I, starting in 518 BC. Many of its builders and artists came from Assyria, they brought with them the style of Art, and Architecture of their people, which they used in the building of the Persian palaces. (www.ahuramazda.com/wingedbull .htm)

A century after the fall of Nineveh, slightly modified Assyrian winged bulls with human head guarded the entrance of the Apadana Hall, its floor was paved by a carpet-like pattern similar to those at the Assyrian palaces. The bas-reliefs of tribute bearers, from various nations, along the staircase walls of the Apadana hall, are reminiscent of their Assyrian predecessors. The image of Ahuramazda; the Persian supreme deity complete with wings and holding a ring in his right hand is an obvious copy of the Disk of Ashur. A bas-relief of King Cyrus the Great in Pasargadae, engraved upon a stone-slab, depicts him as a four-winged genius similar to those that decorated the interior walls of the northwest palace of King Ashurnasirpal II, at Nimrud. The relief showing King Darius I, stabbing a lion with sword, is a copy of similar stele at the Ashurbanipal's palace. A century after the fall of Nineveh the bas-reliefs of King Darius I depict him wearing long braided beard, as did the Assyrian king.
(wikipedia.org/wiki/Achaemenid_architecture)

The presence of the Assyrian troops in the Xerxes army is

also attested to, by a bronze conical shaped Assyrian helmet from the 490 BC Battle of Marathon which in 2006 was on display at the Onassis Cultural Center in Greece. (Associated Press, Dec. 5, 2006)

Confusing the 9th satrap with the fifth

Fiey also overlooks the fact that Herodotus was writing about the people of the ninth Persian taxation province (Satrap), which included the Assyrians, and Babylonians, who paid 1,000 talents of silver tribute annually and contributed five infantry contingents to the Empire's military. (Burn, Robert, 1962, 336) Perhaps in response to such misconception, Edwin Guest writes:

"Herodotus represents Surioi as the name given by the Greeks to the people whom the Barbarians called Assurioi; and though this statement has been questioned, I see no reason for doubting its correctness." (Guest, Edwin, 1971, 119) He further adds: *"It would seem that Surioi was the name that was current among the Greek for the various subjects of the Assyrian empire, and when the travels of Herodotus had made him acquainted with a more perfect form of the word, educated Greeks, following his example appropriated Assurioi as the name of the Assyrians proper, and continued to use Surioi or suroi for the name of the races on the Mediterranean who were more familiar to them."*

The first Century AD Strabo corroborated this when he wrote: *"[T]he city of Nineveh was destroyed immediately upon the overthrow of the Syrians,"* he left no doubt that Greeks' Syrians meant Assyrians." He further states: "When those who have written histories about the Syrian empire say that the Medes were overthrown by the Persians and the Syrians by the Medes, they mean by the Syrian no other people than those who built the royal palaces in Babylon and Ninus; and of these Syrians, Ninus was the man who founded Ninus [Nineveh], in Atturia. [Assyria]." (Jones H.L, 1916, Vol. VIII, 195)

Fiey's attempt to define Surioi to mean Aramean is intended

to prove that Assyrians in their homeland were defeated into extinction, but not the Arameans who lived there. This is practically impossible because there would have been no way for the enemy, in the heat of war, to distinguish between Assyrians and Arameans.

Those who have argued that the troops mentioned by Herodotus were probably Syrian overlook the fact that they belonged to the ninth Persian taxation province, which included Babylon and Assyria. Xerxes had attached Ebar-Nahra, to the fifth taxation province in 482 BC, which already included Phoenicia, Palestine, and Cyprus. Due to repeated revolts in Babylon, he not only punished the city by tearing down its fortifications and melting down the golden statue of Marduk, also dissolved the Babylonian Satrap and annexed Babylon to the 9th Assyrian taxation province. The very name of Babylonia was officially under ban, according to Olmstead. (Olmstead 1970, 245) This accounts for the fact that the Greeks often presented Babylon as part of Assyria. The later Parthian and Sassanian documents described it as Asorestan. The list of the Persian satraps provided by Herodotus shows that the fifth taxation province did not have troops serving in the Persian army. (Burn, Robert, 1962, 336) Another indication that the Greek's Syrian meant Assyrian comes in Herodotus book VII, where he credits the Athenians for having saved Greece from being conquered by Xerxes. While other Greek cities had lost hope, Athenians were determent to fight. They had sent an envoy to Delphi and waited for an advice oracle from him, so that they could decide to stay and fight, or give up and run. The envoy returned with a discouraging oracle:

"Go, bid the people to flee,
nor let them lag
Quit the wheel-shaped city [Athens] and its crag
And in a distant land, seek a safe retreat,
Lo neither the head remains, nor the feet,
The trunk, the arms, and midriff, all are gone:
Fire and the spiteful war-god hurl them down.
 Not yours alone, but towers near and far,
  He [Xerxes] shall destroy, urging his Syrian car, . . ."

On a side note, the translator writes: *"The Greeks believed that the war chariot was an Assyrian invention."* (Carter, Harry 1958, 453) This comes to reason, because Assyrians were renowned for their superior military technology, but not the Arameans. Syriac documents of early Christianity attest to the fact that Christianity in Mesopotamia began among the Assyrians. The existence of the Assyrian communities in the city of Ashur and Hatra until the third century AD refutes the assumption that Assyrians were defeated into extinction. In the city of Ashur the temple dedicated to Ashur, the national god of the Assyrians, was rebuilt over its previous location, which indicates the continued occupation of the city by ethnic Assyrians. Assyrians in the two cities worshiped the ancient Assyrian religion, took pride in their Assyrian identity and heritage. They gave their children the ancient Assyrian names. The Aramaic language they spoke had gradually replaced the Akkadian language, even before the fall of the empire, yet they showed no interest in considering themselves as Aramean. Parpola writes:

"As late as third century AD, personal names in Ashur and Hatra were still completely in line with Neo-Assyrian onomastic... gods Ashur, Shrua, Ishtar, Bel, Nabu, and Nergal continued to be worshiped in Ashur at least until the early third century AD; the temple of Ashur was faithfully restored in the second century AD; the local cultic calendar was that of the imperial period; and the stele of local rulers resemble those of Assyrian kings in imperial period." (Parpola Simo, Jaas, 2004, 20)

Even the ancient Assyrian Akitu New Year festival, which included a procession from the Ashur temple to the Akitu House, was celebrated. (Potts T. editor, 2012, 1015} Though the city of Ashur was destroyed by the Persian king Shapur I (241-272 AD), evidence indicates that it was reoccupied *by* the Assyrians during the Islamic period until the 14th century Tamerlane onslaught, when Christian Assyrians were massacred.
www.islamic-architecture.info/WA-IQ/WA-IQ-026.htm

Chapter 2

Syrian/Suraye meant Assyrian

Because Christian Assyrians have been known as Syrian and have identified themselves as Suraye/Suryoye; John Joseph, in his first book, titled "Nestorians and Their Muslim Neighbors," contends that: "Nestorians had never called themselves Assyrian, nor were known as such, before the nineteenth century." Joseph fails to realize that Nestorian was a derogatory nickname given to the members of the Church of the East by their detractors, to demean their Christianity. It had noting to do with their ethnic identity. Furthermore, evidence shows that Assyrian writers since the early century of Christianity have equated the terms Syrian/Suraye with Atturaye, meaning Assyrians, For example, Michael the Great, the twelfth-century patriarch of the Syrian Orthodox Church, wrote:

"Inhabitants of the land to the west of Euphrates were properly called Syrians, and by analogy, all those who speak the same language, which he calls Aramaic, both east and west of Euphrates to the borders of Persia, are called Syrians. He continues that the basis of the Syriac language, i.e., Aramaic, is from Edessa (Urha). Even more interesting is his remark, (Vol. I, p. 32) where he gives the name of people who possessed writing, among them are '[A]Twraye d' hywn Swryy,' i.e., "Assyrians, who are "Syrians," by which presumably he means the ancient Assyrians, whom he identifies with his contemporary speakers of Syriac." (Frye Richard, JASS, Vol. XI, 2, 1997, 33)

When confronted with such facts, Joseph responded with a statement by Jean Fiey, where he tries to devalue the meaning of Michael the Great's statement. Fiey writes:

"By Atturaye, the renowned Patriarch undoubtedly meant the inhabitants in and around Mosul. As has been pointed out by many before, someone with the surname Atturaya means simply that the person hails from the city of Attur, the name by which the city of Mosul and its province were known during the pre-Islamic period. Christians continued to use the geographical designation Atturaya as a surname, a common practice in the Middle East, where a surname identifies a person with the name of his birthplace." (Joseph, John, JAAs 11, 2, 37-43)

Fiey and Joseph overlook the fact that Nineveh had been the capital city of the Ancient Assyrians, and Mosul was its offshoot. The fact that the people who lived in the two cities were eager to proclaim their Assyrian identity was because they were proud of their ancient heritage. If they believed they were Arameans, they would not have been happy to call themselves Atturaye. It comes to reason that they could have easily changed the name of their city to something that better defined their identity.

Furthermore, the self-designation of Atturaye by the Christian Assyrians was not restricted to the inhabitants of Mosul and Nineveh. Timothy I, the patriarch of the church of the East (780 to 823), who was born in in Hedayab or Adiabene and lived in Baghdad, in a letter to the monks of Mar Maroon, wrote: *"Babylonia, Persia, Assyria, and all countries of the East, including India and China were under his ecclesiastic jurisdiction."* (Young, William G., 1974, 152)

For him, Assyria was not restricted to Mosul or Nineveh. He considered Assyria as a country in par with Persia and other countries of that time. If by Assyria he meant only Mosul and Nineveh, he would have disowned other ecclesiastical provinces in Mesopotamia that he led. The fourth-century Ephraim the Great and the fifth-century Narsai (the harp of soul) did not live in Mosul or Nineveh; they were not born in these cities, yet they took pride in the fact that the three Wise- Men who visited Christ upon his birth were Assyrians. (Odisho Ghivargis Malco, JAAS, 2002, 82) When the thirteenth-century Ghiwargis Warda Arbillaya [from Arbil], who was not born in Mosul or Nineveh and did not live there, wrote that the Syriac speaking people of Mesopotamia are Assyrians and Babylonians, he was not writing about the inhabitants of Mosul and Nineveh.

In other cases, John Joseph, like Fiey, has strived to minimize or misinterpret all references to the Assyrians during the Christian era by claiming they were not intended to denote ethnic identity. For example, in commenting about the second-century Tatian, who in his address to the Greeks wrote, *"I was born in the land of the Assyrians ..."* Joseph contends, that he did not claim to be an Assyrian. He further states, scholars point out that he was not even born in lands to the East of Euphrates. According to Joseph: *"Tatian (Greek Tatianos), writes Millar, no more came from geographical Assyria 'than did that other "Assyrian" with a Latin name, Lucian (Greek Lucianos) of Samosata.' "* Millar explains simply that the term Assyria and Assyrians were common terms then for geographic Syria and its inhabitants.

Parpola writes that there is no reason to doubt the Assyrian identity of writers and philosophers who were born in Roman Syria who identified themselves as Assyrians. He cites, *"the second-century belletrist, Lucian of Samosata, who introduces himself as 'an Assyrian... still barbarous in speech and almost wearing a jacket in the Assyrian style ..."* In a footnote in his "Assyrians After Assyria," Parpola writes: *"Despite Millar, the name Tatian is not 'in origin Latin' but a Grecized form of Aramaic Tat!, well attested already in Assyrian imperial sources . . . Similarly, the name Lucian can also can be traced back to Aramaic Luqu, not necessarily to Latin Lucius!"* (www.betnahrain.net/1History/Parpola1.htm)

Tatian, in his address, calls the Greeks, "you men of Greek." By Joseph's logic, Tatian was also denying the Greek identity of the Greeks. We don't know why Millar assumed that Tatian was not born in Assyria; other writers have stated otherwise. What is well known is that he returned to Adiabene /Assyria. If he were not born in Assyria, there would have been no reason for him to leave the comfort of Rome and Greece, or the cosmopolitan lifestyle in Syria to go to Assyria, which was far less affluent. About Tatian,

McCullough writes:

"The second-century Tatian was a pagan from 'Assyria,' which probably means, either Northern Mesopotamia or Adiabene, and like his contemporary, Lucian of Samosata, he journeyed westward in pursuit of a Greek education . . . He further adds: *"The most important contribution of Tatian to the Syriac Christianity was his Diatessaron, it included the four, or perhaps five gospels, that had existed separately, he compiled into a continuous form.* (McCullough W. Stewart, 1982, 31)

According to Samuel Moffet:

"The Syriac version of the five gospels allowed the native population in Mesopotamia and Syria's cities access to the scripture in their own language. Consequently Syriac, instead of Palestinians Aramaic, became the ecclesiastical language of the Eastern Churches, comparable to Latin in the Western Church." (Moffett Samuel Hugh, 1992, 74)

The fact that Diatessaron was written in Syriac, the language of Adiabene and Edessa, instead of Palestinian indicates that Tatian was born in Assyria. Segal writes: *"Adiabene, from where Tatian originated, and where the Diatessaron may have been written, had close ties with the Christian community of Edessa."* (Segal J.B., 1970, 165)

It is interesting how Joseph and Fiey always manage to find quotes from writers who agree with their premise that no Assyrians had survived after the fall of Nineveh.

The nineteenth-century editor of Lucian's book, who also felt more qualified to decide Lucian's nationality wrote in a footnote: "Confusion between Assyrian and Syrian is not peculiar to this piece nor to Lucian. It goes back to Herodotus who says that 'Syrian' is a Greek equivalent of Barbarian 'Assyrian'." It is important to note that some Greek and Roman writers, as Herodotus, equated the term Syrian, in reference to the inhabitants of Mesopotamia, with Assyrian, but such facts have been overlooked by the cynics.

It is preposterous to assume that Lucian was incapable of knowing his own nationality and could not tell the difference between Assyrians and the citizens of Syria who by then were mostly Greeks, Romans, Jews, Arabs, Arameans and Assyrians. In his "Goddess of Syria," Lucian rightly distinguishes between people who lived on the east and the west banks of Euphrates. Another Assyrian called Prepon, who was Marcian's student, was known to have introduced a new theological philosophy based on a work by Bardaisan, who claimed the world is managed by good and evil. Lucian's birthplace, Samosata, located on the eastern side of the river, a short distance north of Harran, had been part of Assyria for more than a millennium. In 64 BC the Roman Emperor Pompeii annexed Samosata to Syria. Seven ruined temples dedicated to the Assyro-Babylonian gods were discovered in Samosata above the hills to the west and northwest that was known as the "Sacred Hill." The temples represented the seven planets associated with the Assyro-Babylonian deities.

Thea Halo, author of "Not Even My Name," whose father was an Assyrian of the Syrian Orthodox Church, wrote: when she and her siblings attended public school in New York City, they were often asked about their national identity, and their answer was "Assyrian," but their teachers embarrassed them by stating that there was no such nationality. To avoid future humiliation, the children resolved to identify themselves as Egyptian which resulted in their being admired as the descendants of a great civilization. Facts did not seem to matter much in this case.

Deniers of the contemporary Assyrians' identity often claim that only during the last 150 years they have identified themselves by that name. However copious references to the Christian Assyrians as "Assyrian", by the Assyrian and non-Assyrian writers, since early centuries of Christianity prove otherwise. No other people than Assyrians would have continued to preserve the memory of Assyria, and the ancient Assyrians, for more than two thousand years after the fall of Nineveh, certainly not the Arameans! Arabs who built their capital near the ancient city in Southern Mesopotamia did not call their country Babylon. Kurds, who recently declared northern Iraq as their semi-independent state did not call it Iraq, a name Arabs had given to the region, nor did they call it Assyria; they called it Kurdistan, to tell the world that they are Kurds and this is their country. Some of the cities and towns in northern Iraq and Southwest Turkey still bear the names that the ancient Assyrians had given them—Arbil: Assyrian Arabaillu; Tikrit: Assyrian Tikriti; Kirkuk: Assyrian 'Kirkha d' beit

Suluk' or Arrapha; Nineveh: Assyrian Nineveh; Harran: Assyrian Harranu; Nisibin: Assyrian Nisibini; Alqoush: Assyrian Alquoushtu; Karmales: Assyrian Kar; Mullissi: Mosul, Mespilla. Not even in Iran so many cities are still known by their ancient names. Cities in southern Mesopotamia were given Arabic names after the seventh century Arab invasion. Greeks had given new names to the cities of central Assyria, but these names were rejected by their inhabitants in favor of their ancient identity, according to the Amenius Marcelenius.

Why would have Arameans cared to preserve the ancient Assyrian names of these cities instead of giving them names that were relevant to their ethnicity, especially, if they were as determent to wipe out all traces of the Assyrian survival after their defeat, as John Joseph and Fiey seem to be. The Parthians changed the name of central Assyria to Adiabene. In 61 AD the Armenian king Tigranes, who briefly invaded northern Mesopotamia, changed Adiabene to Norshirakan in hope of annexing it to the Armenian region in northwest Iran, known by that name. Among the lands and provinces ruled by Shapur I (240–270 AD), central Assyria is mentioned as Nod-Ardakhshiragan, meaning ruled by prince Ardakhshir, and southern Mesopotamia is listed as Asorestan. (Wiesehofer Josepef, 1996, 185)

When Arabs invaded Mesopotamia they changed the name of the entire region to Iraq. Assyrian writers however continued to identify their homeland as Assyria. Given the fact that Christian Assyrians did not have a sovereign government, nor an army to protect their homeland, it is remarkable that despite the turns and twists of history, and vilification of their forefthers, they have managed to preserve their Assyrian identity for such a long time. Ironically, Fiey at the end of his " 'Assyriens' ou 'Araméens'? " writes: *"Encyclopedia Britannica (1965 edition) has applied the term 'Nestorian' to the modern Assyrians, and the Oxford Dictionary of the Christian Church concludes: 'The name Assyrian, despite W.A. Wigram, is almost certainly a misnomer.'*

With all due respect to the Oxford Dictionary and all other reference books that mindlessly copy each other, they are obviously oblivious to all the other historical sources, before and since the dawn of Christianity, that have attested to the survival of Assyrians to this day. At the conclusion of his article Fiey writes:

"I wouldn't go that far, because an exhaustive scientific study of all the aspects of the problem does not yet exist, at least to my knowledge. It might be time for such a study to replace moving speeches and passionate affirmations. As to me, I do not want to draw conclusions; the poor 'Assyrians' have already lost so many things, for us now to also dispute their name. Maybe we should simply realize one thing: It is through a very tortuous path that this name has come to them, or as they say, has returned to them." (Fiey, J. M., 1965, 12) Too bad Fiey didn't follow his own advice before coming to such a conclusion, or perhaps he made this statement to soothe his guilty conscious.

Even Dur-Sharrukin Was Remembered

Dur-Sharrukin, the fortress city of Sargon II, was the Assyrian capital during his rule. (722–705). According to Layard, it was mentioned as "Khorsabad, or Khistabad, by the early Arab geographers, but the villagers who occupied the site called it 'Saraoun' or 'Saraghoun.' " (Layard Austin Henry, 1852 107)

The village is located fifteen kilometers northeast of Mosul and is still inhabited by the Christian Assyrians. According to Yakut, soon after the Arab conquest, considerable treasures were found among its ruins. This information led M. Botta to excavate the site during the nineteenth century; unfortunately, the valuable items unearthed by him ended up at the bottom of the river, when the boat transporting them capsized. While Christian Assyrians called the site Saraghoun, Persians may have called it "Khosro Abad," meaning "Built by Khosro." This seems to have been corrupted by the Arabs into Khorsabad. Arabs also gave the name Nimrud to the ancient Assyrian city of Kalhu, in reference to its Assyrian origin. Such facts show that Christian Assyrians were far more aware of their history and identity than Western scholars are willing to give them credit for. However, Joseph further wrote:

"The assumption that the Nestorians were the descendants of the ancient Assyrians found a great advocate in the missionary William Ainger Wigram, who, in his post-World War I books [The

Assyrians and Their Neighbors, and Our Smallest Ally] *popularized the name Assyrian and familiarized the world with the tragedy that had befallen these 'descendants of Shalmaneser.'* (Joseph John, 1961, 15)

The above statement implies that Assyrians were waiting for someone, to bestow on them any ethnic identity, so they would blindly accept it and use it thereafter. This means if Layard and Wigram had told them they were Chinese, they would have believed it, and would have called themselves accordingly. In fact, more than a decade before Layard discovered the ruins of Nineveh, a certain Marie-Therese who was an Assyrian nun in France, at the St. Lawrence Monastery, was known as "princess Marie-Therese of Assyria," "a noble from Nineveh," and so-forth. She was from the Assyrian town of Tell-Kaiff, located fifteen kilometers from Mosul, and died in Paris in 1870. (Yana George, 2005, 73)

Weren't There Babylonians in Babylon?

Fiey continues with another sweeping claim to prove that not only were no Assyrians in Assyria, neither were there Babylonians in Babylon. He writes:

"Meanwhile, whatever political names used, the Christians have always held to the name of Beth Aramaye for Babylonia, and have always reserved the name of Attur for classical Assyria. "But here a remark needs to be made which I believe to be important and which derives from the morphological comparison of the two appellations, Beth Aramaye and Attur. The first comprises an ethnicity; it is the district where Arameans live; the second is a purely historical survival of the past of the glorious Ashur, and I have never encountered the appellation Beth Atturaye." (Fiey, J. M., 1965, 2) Here Again, Fiey is misrepresenting the known facts, without offering historical evidence, to support his opinion. In fact, this issue underscores the Assyrian identity of the Christian Assyrians rather than disproving it. The ancient Assyrians called their country Ashur; it was the geographic region, or heartland of the empire, and where Assyrian people lived. Parpola, in his "Assyrian

Identity In the "Ancient Times and Today" writes;

> *Due to a sound shift in early second millennium BC, the pronunciation of Aššur changed to Attur. Aššūrāyu which defined the national identity of an Assyrian was derived from Aššur plus the gentilic suffix-āyu. [Its plural] was later pronounced Atturaye, equivalent to Aššūrāye."* (www.nineveh.com/parpola_eng.pdf 2012)

The above facts show continuation of an ancient Assyrian tradition, which dates back to the Akkadian language, and has survived in the Syriac language. It describes the ethnic identity of all nations by adding "aye" after the name of their homeland. For example, in Syriac, Egypt is called Misser, Egyptians are Misraye, Persia is called Parsa, its people are Parsaye, France is known as Fransa, and French people are called Fransaye.

What Did Beth Aramaye Mean?

The use of Beth in front of a region's name is a throwback to when Arameans were nomads and had several small tribal states; each was identified by the name of its chief with a prefix of Beth to designate their geographic location. It was intended to distinguish the territories ruled by their different chiefs from each other. This was also the case with the Chaldean sheikhs. Joan Oates writes: *"Each Chaldean Bitu ('house') was under the leadership of a Sheikh, who at times called himself a 'king'. But the tribal regions were ill-defined and the political strength of each individual Sheikh was largely a matter of personal ability and prestige."* (Joan Oates, 1979,112)

This clearly refutes Fiey's claim that the term Beth in front of a name is indication of ethnic identity. One can argue that Beth Aramaye means the house of the Arameans, i.e., where they live, rather than the country of the Arameans, which would have been, "Atra d' Aramaye".

There were many places, before and during the Christian era, whose name started with Beth. For example, Beth Garmye was where Alexander the great defeated the Persian army in the winter of 331 BC, at Gaugamela, near the Assyrian town of Karmales. The dead Persian soldiers remained unburied there, and their bones littered the field, consequently, the place was called Beth Garmye, i.e, 'the house of bones.' There were other regions such as Beth Ardashir, Beth Raman, Beth Seri, and so forth. The fact that a place was called Beth Ardashir (where Ardashir ruled) did not mean that its inhabitants had a common ethnicity or were in any way related to Ardashir. Another reason which contributed to the use of Beth Aramaye as the identity of Southern Mesopotamia was because Persian kings, who, in the course of their wars with the Romans, transferred tens of thousands of Syriac speaking prisoners from Syria to that region, to replace the Christians that had been killed during persecutions, or had fled from Syria. The term Beth Aramaye was to signify the presence of the new comers to the region. (Arsanos Benjamin, 1953, 54)

Georges Roux write, starting in the eighth century BC the Aramaic began to replace the Akkadian language, the latter continued to be used by the Babylonian priests and astronomers in Cuneiform text until AD 74-75.

He further adds: *"It is quite possible...[that] they continued] for several generations to write in Aramaic on Papyrus or parchment, but no work of this kind is likely to be found."* Meanwhile the ancient temples were restored and the cult of Nabu in Barsippa continued until, perhaps the fourth century AD." (Roux Georges, 1992, 20)

One can also argue that the reason the name Beth Aramaye was given to Southern Mesopotamia had more to do with the transformation of the Akkadian language into Aramaic than the displacement of the entire Babylonian population by the Arameans. A parallel example of this happened in Southern America. After the Spaniards' conquest of the region, the conversion of the natives to Christianity, directed by the Spanish clergies, required the learning of the Spanish language, which gradually replaced their tongues. This however did not transform the South American natives into

Spaniards. Today they identify themselves as Hispanics or Latino to acknowledge the Latin-based languages they speak, but that does not mean they are no longer related to the Aztecs, the Mayans, or the Incas.

Not all Aramaic speakers Were Aramean

Christian Assyrians speak a language related to the Aramaic, but it is called Syriac. It is classified as the Northwestern branch of the Semitic family of languages that evolved in Mesopotamia among members of the Church of the East and the Syrian Orthodox Church. It has a coherent form, style, and grammar that is different than the Old Eastern Aramaic dialects. By the second century AD Syriac became the language of Christian worship in central Assyria and Edessa. This was the time when Tatian, who was known as Assyrian, compiled into a continuous form, the four or five gospels of the New Testament, this is known as Diatessaron. The fact that Assyrians call their language Lishana Suryaya or Suryoyo, i.e., Syriac language, indicates that they considered it a different language than the Aramaic.

Not everybody who spoke a language related to Aramaic was Aramean. Ancient Assyrian chancelleries adopted the Aramaic language as an international means of communication, because people west of the Euphrates did not speak the Akkadian language, nor they could read its cumbersome cuneiform writing. Dominance of the Neo Assyrian Empire over the Abar-nahra region, the homeland of the Arameans, known also as Aram, led to the establishment of the Aramaic as the lingua Franca of the empire, during the 8th century, Tighlath-Pileser's rule. This was continued by the Babylonians and the Persians in later centuries. Aramaic was an easy language to learn by the Assyrians and Babylonians because it shared a great number of words with the Akkadian. The change of language expedited inter-empire communication and facilitated trade. The Akkadian influence over the Assyrian and Babylonian Aramaic is well attested to. From 700 BC on Aramaic spread to Levant and Egypt. Around 600 BCE, Adon, a Canaanite king, used Aramaic to correspond with the Egyptian Pharaoh.

According to Geoffrey Khan, Cambridge professor of Semitic languages:

"Another way in which the morphology of the infinitive forms differ from Syriac in the modern Assyrian dialect is in the modern Assyrian dialect is in the vowel pattern. For example, in most dialects, there is the vowel "o," in the infinitive of some of the verbal conjugations. Where, in [literary] Syriac, this is not found. This feature of the modern dialects, which distinguishes them from literary Syriac may have developed in antiquity due to contact with Akkadian. Since Akkadian, especially the northern Assyrian dialect of Akkadian had similar vowel patterns in infinitives."

The change of language in these countries did result in transformation of their population into Arameans. European nations such as Italian, French, Spaniards, and Portuguese before the fifteenth century abandoned the Latin language, but it did not mean they relinquished their identity. Christian Assyrians had every opportunity to call themselves Aramaye because, unlike the ancient Assyrians who were vilified in the Old Testament, the Arameans were treated with great respect. Assyrians continued to call themselves Suraye and Atturaye though they take pride in the fact that Jesus spoke the Aramaic language.

Ancient Assyrians were also known as Surai/Syrian

The fact that Christian Assyrians have called themselves Suraye and Suryoye has confused many to think that it means something other than Assyrian, but recent historical and archaeological evidences prove that Surai is a corrupted form for Asurai, which means Assyrian. Simo Parpola acknowledged this when he wrote:

"Modern Assyrian Suraya/Surai, perfectly agrees with Neo-Assyrian Surau, while Suryoyo displays an intrusive yod, which it shares with Greek Surios and Suria. This intrusive yod is due to the

Greek influence, since in classical Syriac the word also occurs in the form Suroyo, in perfect agreement with the Modern Assyrian Suraya. It is worth noting that Suraya is reported to have a variant with initial A-, but this is avoided in careful speech, since it instinctively sounds incorrect in view of the classical Syriac. Since omission of initial vowel is not a feature of Aramaic phonology, the lack of A- in Suraya/Suryoyo can not be due to internal Aramaic development but must go back directly to Neo Assyrian." (Parpola Simo, Jaas, 2004, 18)

According to Robert Rollinger of the Leopold-Franzens University of Austria, an archaeological discovery of a Hieroglyphic Luwian, and Phoenician bilingual inscription, found in Turkey, reveals that Luwians used *"Surai"* or (Syrian) as a variant for "Asura/i" meaning Assyrians. This Term was used in southern Anatolia as early as the eighth century BC, long before Greeks began to use it. In the Luwian inscription, King Warikas/Urikki, who was an ally of the Assyrian kings Tiglath-pileser III (744–727) and Sargon II (721–705), proclaims: "An Assyrian king (su+ra/i-wa/i-ni-sa (URBS)) and the whole Assyrian "House" (su+ra/i-wa/i-za-ha (URBS)) were made a father and a mother for me." (Rollinger Robert 2006, 283-287)

Fiey contends that*"Greek usage of the terms 'Assyria' and 'Syria' was applied almost interchangeably for the area that roughly covered the Assyrian Empire."* Fiey, however, provides another explanation to undermine such interpretation, he wrote: *"When the word 'Assyrian' or 'Syrian' came to signify 'Christian,' it didn't have any proper ethnic reference but more and more it became synonymous with 'Aramean.'* (Fiey, 1965, 3)

Fiey does not provide any evidence to prove such possibility other than revealing his own bias. There is no doubt, that in the following statement Timothy I, (770–823), the patriarch of the Church of the East, uses the term "Assyrians" as an ethnic identity. He wrote: *"The Persians and Assyrians don't do this, he argued, and nor do the churches of the countries of sunrise,"* such as India, China, and so forth.
(Jenkins Philip, 2008, 11)

While speaking about Christianity, in the above statement,

Timothy describes the ethnic identity of his people as Assyrian, comparable to the national identity of the Persian Christians, Indians, and other people. There would have been no reason for him to write one thing but mean something else. There is no justification for Fiey and Joseph to assign different meaning to the written words, to win arguments. A century before Timothy, Mar Ishoyahab III, patriarch of the Church of the East (647-657) wrote: *"I will be delayed for a few days until I visit those scattered people of Assyria outside this territory."* (Dual R., 1962, 102, 106)

No matter how one misinterprets the phrase "people of Assyria," it means Assyrians. The idea that Assyrian writers used Atturaye to mean Arameans is silly and has been refuted by other classical, Assyrian writers. Ghiwargis Warda of Arbil wrote a famous hymn, that has been recited in the Assyrian churches on the Wednesday during the Ninevite Fast. He asks the Lord to accept the rogation and fasting of the Babylonians and Assyrians, which he considers the national identity of his people.

"Lord, heed to the rogation of Babylonians and Assyrians,
Now that the church leadership is in confused order . . .
Lord, heed the rogation of the poor people of our country,
That glorify your Godliness, and a ask for your forgiveness."
(Odisho Ghivargis Malco, 2000, 84) The fourteenth-century Assyrian Writer Sleewa bar Yohanna describes the duties of the Church of the East patriarch, after its separation from the Church of Antioch, as follows:

"The administration of the affairs of the flock, the ordination of the Heads in the Eastern Borders, in Attur (Assyria), Media and Persia: all these sees shall be subject to him, shall submit to his authority, listen to his orders and his bidding ..." (Werda Joel, E, 1924, 231-233)

The very fact, that Assyrian authors continued to call their country Assyria, validates the notion that they considered their people to be Assyrian. Sleewa's use of Attur (Assyria) 2000 years after the fall of Nineveh was not only in reference to Mosul or Nineveh but to Mesopotamia, the homeland of the ancient and Christian Assyrians. Arab Geographers such as the eleventh century Abu Alfoda, the thirteenth century Yaqut, and Ibn Saeid, used the term Attur, not only in reference, to Mosul, and Nineveh which were the heartland of Assyria, also to Mesopotamia, and the cities of Kalkh, i.e. Nimrud, and Ashur, which they wrote about. This clearly contradicts the notion that the term Attur meant only Nineveh and Mosul. (Rassam Hormuzd, 1897, 176)

Since the early centuries of Christianity, the right word for Christians has been kristyônê, or Kristyane,. In fact, even at the present time the word for Christians is Krastyani, in the Eastern Assyrian dialect, and Kristyônê, in the Western dialect. A fourth-century AD Persian inscription also refers to Christians as Nazzarene. In later Syriac documents it is also evident that 'Suryaya' and 'Suryoyo' were not intended to mean Christian. The eleventh-century Odisho Bar Brikha in the introduction to his "Paradise of Eden" refers to himself as 'Allila Suryaya,' i.e., "obscure As(syrian)," and 'Mkhila 'd Mshikhayee,' " feeble of the Christians." (Benjamin Yoab, Jaas Vol. VIII, NO.1, 1994, 57) Since "Mkhila 'd Mshikhaye," was enough to describe his Christianity, his distinction between that and 'Allila Suryaya', indicates that Suryaya did not mean Christian or Aramean.

Why They Called Themselves Suraye?

Several issues undoubtedly discouraged Assyrians from identifying themselves as Assyrians. During early Christianity, believers were told that their new religion was their new nation. Christians were described by Bardaisan as: *The 'new people . . . that the Messiah has caused to arise in every place and in all climates by his coming (BLC 58–60). They are called by one name, Christians (kristyônê) after the Messiah (BLC 60, 1–2); on the first day of the week 'we gather together' (BLC 60, 2–3); on appointed days we fast (BLC 60, 3–4). There follows a list of instances in which Christians do not conform to national customs . . .'* (Drijvers H. J. W., 1967, 127-165)

However, a common religion did not mean that all nations abandoned their language, culture, and heritage and melted into each other. For example, Assyrians and Armenians have lived side by side since before Christianity, but both have preserved their separate language, culture, heritage, and independence to this day. The ardent followers of the new religion had dedicated their life to the kingdom of heaven and not to a sovereign state ruled by kings, queens, nations, or military institutions. They were to a great extent abiding by the Biblical passages which promoted Christianity as substitute for nationalism. Several verses in the New Testament such as Gal 3: 26-29 underscore such conviction. Galatians 3:28 states: *"There does not exist among you Jew or Greek, slave or freeman, male or female. All are one in Christ Jesus."*

Right after converting to Christianity, Assyrians had to be careful not to suggest that they were still worshipping the ancient deities such as Ashur, Ishtar, or Nergal; therefore, the Christian friendly terms Suraye and Suryoye served to solve this problem. These terms also bonded them religiously to the Christians of Syria, especially since the Patriarch of Antioch, residing in Syria, served as the spiritual leader of the Christians of Syria as well as Mesopotamia during the first five centuries of Christianity. By the end of the ninth century, there was a shift in what constituted national identity. In the beginning, Islam was intended to be the religion of the Arabs in Arabia, but after conquering the neighboring countries, Arabs instituted a taxation policy that served to transfer wealth from the non-Arabs to the people of Arab ancestry. This resulted in conversion of non-Arabs to Islam to escape the grinding taxation and the social degradation, and to receive stipend and be entitled to power and prestige. Eventually, the converts were recognized as Arabs, and benefited from the above privileges. (Armajani Yahya, 1970, 58) Ethnic identity, which until then was based on language, ancestry, culture, and heritage was now turned upside down. Since religion became an important indication of a persons ethnic identity, Christian families had to be careful to call themselves Suraye and Suryoye to set themselves apart from their relatives who had converted to Islam.

Vilification of the Ancient Assyrians

Another issue that may have discouraged Christian Assyrians from publically proclaiming their Assyrian identity were the Mishnah myths propagated by the Jewish community in Mesopotamia. These stories portrayed the mythical Nimrod, the supposed founder of Assyria and Assyrians, to have waged wars against the Prophet Abraham to stop him from preaching Monotheism. Mica 5:6; The proliferation of such myths were undoubtedly aimed at shaming the Christian Assyrians by claiming that their supposed king was the enemy of not only the Jewish faith but also, of Christianity and Islam. What made such vilifications especially dangerous is that Abraham (Ibrahim) is considered as the father of monotheism not only by the Jews and Christians but as well by Muslims who honor him as a prophet; therefore, his name is mentioned in the Quran sixty-nine times in sixty-three verses (ayahs).

Mishnah's call for violence against Assyria and Assyrians is evident in quotes like this: *"They will shepherd the land of Assyria with the sword, the land of Nimrod with a drawn blade. So He will rescue us from Assyria when it invades our land, when it marches against our territory."*

Information about Nimrod in the Old Testament makes no mention of any meeting between Nimrod and Abraham. In fact, they are not described as contemporaries. The Old Testament suggests a gap of seven generations between the two; furthermore, there is no historical evidence that such king ever existed. The Old Testament describes Nimrod as follows:

"Cush became the father of Nimrod. He began to be a warrior on the earth. He was a mighty hunter before the Lord. Therefore it is said "Like Nimrod a mighty hunter before the Lord." The beginning of his kingdom was Babylon, Erech, and Accad. All of them in the land of Shinar. From that land he went into Assyria and built Nineveh, Rehoboth-Ir, Calah, and Resin between Nineveh and

Calah —that is the great city." (Genesis 10:6-12)

What made the Mishnah stories even more dangerous for the Assyrians was that they were translated into Arabic. In one version of these myths, Nimrod supposedly ordered the killing of all children upon hearing that Abraham was born. Wholesale killing of newborns in the Jewish stories is a common attribute of villains. In another story, the ten-year-old Abraham leaves the cave where his family lived and declares war against the ungodly king. And yet another tale tells of how Abraham was captured and thrown into a furnace by king Nimrod, but with God's help the fire was turned into water, the wood was changed into fish, and Abraham walked away unhurt. Being thrown into a furnace and surviving the flames is familiar to those who have read the book of Daniel in the Old Testament. Later, most of these legends found their way into the Islamic folklore and are repeated into the Several Mesopotamian ruins were given the name Nimrod by the Arabs.

As Layard was ready to excavate the ancient Assyrian city of Calah, called Nimrod by the Arabs, he met an Arab Bedouin in its vicinity who told him that *"The place was built by Attur,* [Syriac for Assyrian] *the Kiayah, or the lieutenant of Nimrod. Here the holy Abraham, 'peace be with him,' cast down and broke in pieces the idols which were worshiped by the unbeliever. The impious Nimrod sought to slay Abraham and waged war against him. But the prophet prayed to God and said, "Deliver me, O God, from this man who worships stones and boasts himself to be the lord of all beings . . . and he [God] sent a gnat which vexed Nimrod day and night."* (Layard Henry Austen, 1969, 76)

Supposedly the gnat entered into his brain through his ear and tormented him for four hundred years. Layard wrote: *"these traditions are called "Kusset el Nimrod' or 'stories of Nimrod' and are told by the villagers near the ruins of the ancient city."* The very fact that these stories were told indicates an awareness that Christians of Mesopotamia were identifying themselves as Assyrian, and where their homeland was known as Assyria, also by the Jews and Arabs .

Chater 3

The Genetics of Modern Assyrians, Their Relationship to Other People of the Middle East

Evidences presented in this book prove that Christian Assyrians are a homogeneous group of people, distinct from others in the Middle East, and elsewhere. They undoubtedly inherited such qualities from their pre-Christian forefathers. Following are some highlights from an article titled *"The Genetics of Modern Assyrians and their relationship to Other People of the Middle East,"* by Dr. Joel J. Elias, Professor (Emeritus) University of California School of Medicine, San Francisco, who presents detailed information about the extensive research by Prof. L.L. Cavalli-Sforza, Professor of Genetics and the preeminent human population geneticists in the world, who has worked in this field for over forty years.

"His findings were published in 1994 under the title "The History and Geography of Human Genes I. After eight years of collecting this massive information, the authors spent several more years doing the genetic and statistical analyses using sophisticated computer methods. The objective was nothing less than to define the

genetic variations in the entire human population of the world and, from that information, to trace the origin and migration of modern humans to their present locations on the planet (hence the "History and Geography" in the title)." Information provided here has been quoted verbatim to maintain its authenticity and the original intent. Due to this research *"it became possible to determine not only the genetic makeup of a people and the genetic relationships of different groups to each other, but also to measure the "genetic distance" between them. The analyses showed that there were sufficient data to provide statistically significant information on the genetic characteristics of **491** different human populations. Assyrians were one of them, 3-6. In this article we will focus on the knowledge that has been gained about Assyrians and the genetic relationships between Assyrians and their neighbors, with the hope that it will lead to better understanding between the people of the Middle East."* (Joel, J. Elias, http://www.atour.com)

"Members of a specific human population, for example an ethnic group, identify with each other by a shared language and also by cultural, religious, social, geographic, and other features which are held in common. They distinguish themselves from other groups by the same criteria. What are "hidden" from external view are genetically determined attributes of the type that are only brought into the light by scientific methods such as those described in this book, and they reveal a very important component of a group—its genetic character. This can provide both a genetic definition of a group and also its relationships to other groups that would not be apparent otherwise. The use of language along with genetics to define groups is very useful, but linguistic change can occur much faster than genetic change and "languages are sometimes replaced by others of totally different origin in a very short time", as will be pointed out later in this article. As the authors state, "Only genes almost always have the degree of permanence necessary for discussing" the changes in populations that took place in the history of our species.

Analysis of the Assyrians [genetic markers] shows that **they have a distinct genetic profile that distinguishes their population from any other population."** My Emphasis. *"It is important to understand that this applies to the population as a whole, not to any* *one individual. Each individual can have a variety of genetic features, but it is when all the data for the individuals are assembled together that the population can become distinctive."* The conclusion of the study was that ***"The Assyrians are a fairly homogeneous group of people, believed to originate from the land of old Assyria in northern Iraq,"*** *and* ***"they are Christians and are possibly bona fide descendants of their namesakes."*** My Emphasis.

The main research paper on Assyrians is that of Akbari et al, who states: *" the Assyrians are a group of Christians with a long history in the Middle East. From historical and archeological evidence, it is thought that their ancestors formed part of the Mesopotamian civilization." Akbari et al. examined some 500 members of Christian communities in Iran (Armenians and Assyrians from six localities) from whom specimens were obtained and examined for a number of blood group, red cell enzyme and serum protein systems. In the case of Assyrians, the researchers studied 18 different gene sites with a total of 47 different forms of those genes (alleles) in Assyrians in two regions of Iran - Urmia and Tehran. The particular gene frequencies of those 47 genes in the population formed the basis, along with the other two studies (4, 5), for establishing the distinctive genetic character of the Assyrians. A major finding of the study is that Assyrians, especially those in Urmia (their home area in Iran), are genetically homogeneous to a high degree. That is, an individual Assyrian's genetic makeup is relatively close to that of the Assyrian population as a whole. "The results indicate the relatively closed nature of the [Assyrian] community as a whole," and "due to their religious and cultural traditions, there has been little intermixture with other populations." The small size of the population is also a factor. The genetic data are compatible with historical data that religion played a major role in maintaining the Assyrian population's separate identity during the Christian era.* ***For most of that period Assyrians existed as a Christian minority in non-Christian majority populations, and adherence to their religion, abundantly documented in the historical record, would have provided a "genetic barrier" to gene flow from external groups."*** My Emphasis.

"In analyzing other groups in similar situations, Cavalli-Sforza et al. arrived at this opinion: The important conclusion is that the genetic origin of groups that have been surrounded for a long time by populations of different genetic type can be recognized as different only if they have maintained a fairly rigid endogamy [marriage within the group] for most or all the period in which they have been in contact with other groups," although genes contributed by external groups ("gene flow") can be tolerated for many centuries or even millennia by a population, provided they are not on a large scale. Later in this article we will see an analogous situation with Jews, where a religious difference allowed them to maintain their genetic characteristics as a minority over many centuries while living among non-Jewish majority populations. In any case, the data provide unequivocal evidence that Assyrians as a people are distinguishable from all other population groups in their genetic characteristics and are not a part of any other population. Also standing at the dawn of the new millennium are the Assyrians—on the brink of extinction. For over 1900 years, since they accepted Christianity and established the Church of the East, the Assyrians in the Middle East have survived for the most part as a religious and language minority. While this preserved their identity and kept them from disappearing, it came at a terrible price. The history of the Assyrians reads like one long unbroken story of massacre, persecution and indescribable horror, culminating in the twentieth century with genocide and diaspora, followed by even more persecution and massacre. Was it just a coincidence that the first fratricide occurred in the Middle East, when Cain murdered his brother Abel? Will we ever be free of the curse of Cain?"

"In the seventh century AD, after the conversion to Islam, the Arabs of the Arabian Peninsula conquered large areas, including Mesopotamia and adjacent regions. Arabic became the major language of the region and an Arab nation was established there under Islam. But again, the pre-existing indigenous population, mainly Christian (including Assyrians), did not physically disappear, and the majority must have become part of the Arab population. Looking at the figure, one sees a very large genetic separation between the Arabs of the South—Saudis, Yemenites - and those in the region of Mesopotamia—Jordanian, Iraqi." The results of these scientific studies lead to the startling realization that Turks,

Iranians, Kurds, Iraqis, Jordanians, Lebanese are more closely related genetically to Assyrians than they are to other members of their own respective language families in Asia."

This undoubtedly was possible due to the extensive assimilation of the Christian Assyrians into these other communities. Dr. Joel J. Elias concludes; *"Will the younger generations of the Middle East release their souls from the dark forces of the past?"*

Assyrians According to the Vatican Archives

During the sixteenth century, when the Catholic missionaries succeeded in uniting a disaffected segment of the Church of the East with the Roman Catholic Church, the new church was given the name Chaldean by the Pope Julius III. However, its Patriarchs according to the Vatican archives were known as Assyrian, their homeland was termed Assyria, and their people were called Assyrians.

On February 19, 1562, Cardinal Amolius in a codex to the committee of the cardinals in Tredando introduced Sulaga's successor Patriarch Odisho Bar Yohannan Bet Maron (1555–1570) as *"The Patriarch of the Assyrians who has been elected by the clergies and approved by their people."* (Jammo Sarhad, 1996, 196)

Mons. Cesare Gloneno, who for a short time was the secretary of the Pope Pius IV (1555–1565), reported that Mar' Abraham Archbishop of "Angamalensend" in India says, he was sent [to that country] by *"Abdisho Patriarch of Assyria." Venerabili Fratri, Abdisho Patriarchae Assyriorum sive de Muzal Pius Papa Quartus."*

XI. (=XXII) In 1578 Chief men of Syrio Malabar Christians wrote to Pope Gregory XIII (1572–1585) that they previously "received their Bishops and Archbishops from the "Assyrians of the East and that they had the orders of priesthood and deaconates from the same" they asked that he should order the Patriarch of the Assyrians or Chaldeans without delay to send them Bishops according to the ancient customs. (Gamin Samuel, (Vatican archives, 1902, 69–100; 604–610. XII).

XIV. (=XXXV) Mar Elia the Archbishop of Amedia in 1580 presented a report to the Pope about the state of the "Chaldean Church in Assyria" and in Malabar. In the same year, he traveled to Rome as representative of the Chaldeans (members of the Chaldean Church) to get mar Simon Dinha confirmed as the Patriarch of the Church and to receive the sacred Pallium for him

In a letter to Cardinal Carafa in 1580, Mar Elia implored him to obtain an order from the Holy See to abolish the practice of addressing the Syro-Chaldeans as Nestorians. The Pope Eugnius IV reminded the cardinals that the "Chaldeans of Assyria" and Malabar are Catholic living in perfect submission to the Holy See that this order should be published throughout the Christendom (Vide Patronatus Porugallee Tom. II page 241)

XV. (=XXXVI) In 1584 Mar Abraham asks the Pope Gregory XIII to confirm the election of the Archdeacon, George of Christ as Bishop of Palur, Coadjutor and successor to him. According to his letter, this election was made by the power granted him by the "Assyrian Patriarch." [Odisho Bar Yohannan Bet Maron]. (Vatican archives 1902) It is important to note that the sixteenth-century references by the Vatican to the Christian Assyrians and their homeland, Assyria, were made long before Layard discovered the ruins of Nineveh and the Anglican missionaries arrived in the Middle East.

Assyrians According to the Syriac Writers

Ancient Syriac documents about the establishment of Christianity in Edessa and Adiabene testify to the fact that Assyrians were among the first people to accept Christianity. The fourth-century Eusebius of Caesarea in his Acts of Addaeus, where he describes the arrival of Christianity in Edessa, also asserts that: *"people of the East, in the guise of Merchants, passed over into the territory of Romans that they might see the signs which Addaeus did. And such as became disciples, received from him ordination to the priesthood, and in their own country of the Assyrians they instructed the people of their nation, and erected houses of prayer . . ."* (Roberts Alexander, 1869, 25) In the following hymn, the fourth-century Ephraim the Great, imagines a Lullaby that the Virgin

Mary may have sang to the baby Jesus, after the Wisemans, whom he believed were Assyrians, departed. This again contradicts the notion that Christian Assyrians did not consider themselves descendants of the ancient Assyrians until Layard declared them as such.

"My little boy:
Jews in slavery were taken to Assyria and Babylon.
Their temple was plundered.
In return [now] Assyrians brought back what was taken;
they brought gifts to you my son Jesus.
See my son the once mighty Assyrians
Today they bring gifts and worship you
The sons of the mighty, now put down king's crowns at your feet."
(Mar-Emmanuel E.J., 2003, 33)

How can any one doubt that Atturaye in the above statement means anything other than a national identity? Patriarch Timothy I, in a letter to bishop Sarkis of Eilam wrote:

"To our brothers Khnanishu and IshoSawran we have written twice, and this by the law of God's word. Even if they do not wish to come, the Assyrians will honor them."

In another letter to the monks of Mar Maroon, he declared that Assyria, Babylonia, Persia and the other oriental countries such as India and China were all under his ecclesiastical jurisdiction. (Young William G., p.152) For Timothy and the thirteenth-century Givargis Arbillaya the fact that Arabs had changed the name of their country to Iraq did not matter. As far as they were concerned, their homeland still was called Babylonia and Assyria. In 790 AD Nestorius, the Metropolitan of Arbil in the synod of Timothy, signed his title as "Metropolitan of Assyria.(f iey "L'OrientChre'tienne" vo X, p. 70)

The ninth-century Thomas of Maraga in his 'The Book of Governors' writes: *"When there was a famine in Adiabene, Metropolitan Marnameh came to the Assyrian city of Arbil to provide assistance and leadership to the people."* (Thomas of Maraga, 1893, 186) The tenth-century writer Bar Shahree Emanoil wrote:

"The twin cities of the Seleucia (Salek) and Ctisphoon, where the patriarchs of the Church of the East resided, until the eighth century, were not only the capital cities of the Persians (Sassanian), they also were the ecclesiastical centers of the Assyrians." (Ghiwargis Malco, 2000, 23) The twin cities were located near Baghdad, on the border between Iran and Iraq.

Assyrians and The Carmelite Missionaries

Carmelite Missionaries who arrived in Persia as Pope Paul V ambassadors and settled in the city of Isfahan in 1608, reported in a book titled "A Chronicle of the Carmelites in Persia," about their contacts with the Assyrian individuals and communities of both the Church of the East and the Syrian Orthodox Church (Jacobites), whom they encountered in Isfahan, Northwest Persia, Southern Iraq, and the Plain of Nineveh.

In a letter dated Nov. 3, 1612, to the Persian king Shah Abbas I, Pope Paul V pleads with the Shah to take pity on *"Those in particular who are called Assyrians or Jacobites and inhabit Isfahan, who will be compelled to sell their very children in order to pay the heavy tax you have imposed on them, unless You take pity on their misfortune. This matter grieves our spirit exceedingly, the more so, because the after said Assyrians as we have been informed, having rejected and abhorred their ancient (Doctrinal) errors, have returned to the bosom of the Holy Roman Church. On this account, trusting in your exceptional good will toward us, demonstrated to us by so many and such manifest signs, we ask your highness pressingly for our sake to be good as to give order that our beloved sons the Assyrians, especially those of Isfahan, are treated more leniently."* (Eyre & Spottiswoode, 198-199)

The Carmelite historian, Fr. Eusebius gives greater preference to using the name Chaldean when he encounters Assyrians, but he often uses the two names as synonymous. For example when fourteen Chaldeans, meaning Assyrians, heads of their community, arrived from Tabriz in Isfahan, the Carmelites learned about their community that lived about six days journey from Tabriz round the shores of Lake Urmia, and were eager *"to get into relations with these Assyrians,"* to work and reconcile relationships with them. On the 22 of May, 1652, Fr. Dionysius (a Belgian by race) was sent to find them and convert them from their schism. When he arrived in Tabriz, Dionysius learned that their patriarch, whom he identifies as Mar Simeon (Shimon) and is also known as Patriarch Eshuyow Shimun XIII, (1653–1690), had fled Kurdistan for fear of his life and was living in the village of Khosroabad in the district of Sa-la-mas.

The patriarch was reminded of how a hundred years earlier John Sulakka had come into communion with the Catholic Church at the time of Pope Julius III, and he (Eshuyow Shimon) was a successor of that line. However, the last candidate for that position, Elia Shimun XII (1600–1653), had not been able to travel to Rome to become consecrated and had established a new hereditary branch of the Church of the East in the Hakkari mountains of Kurdistan. Patriarch Eshuyow Shimon XIII was encouraged to write a letter to the Pope, in June of 1654, in hope that his people would join the Catholic Church. All the priests and the Rais' "(i.e., headmen) of the districts of Salamas, Urmia, Arsenouk, Solduz, and Maraga signed the letter from the Patriarch to the Pope, but by the time it arrived, Pope Innocent X had died. Dionysius' estimate of the Assyrians under Mar Shimon within the Persian frontier did not exceed 1,000 households in the whole of Azerbaijan, but might have included collateral families." However, he presided over 40,000 households in the Hakkari Mountains and Urmia. Dionysius was told that about 5,000 Assyrian families lived in hundred villages round the Lake Urmia at that time, and there were few other Assyrian villages in the provinces of Maraga and Solduz. They were very poor because of constant oppression suffered from their Muslim neighbors. They subsisted primarily from agriculture. One reason they were eager to join the Catholic Church was because of *"the great fear they have of ill-treatment by the Muhammadan governors who seized on any pretext and occasion to ill-treat them, and extort money from them."* (Eyre & Spottiswoode, 1939, 388–392)

In another report from Baghdad, Fr. Dinoysius describes his travel to the Plain of Nineveh in 1653, and his visit with Mar Eliya

VIII Shimon [1617-1660] the patriarch of the original Church of the East.

"I went to look for the patriarch of Babylon, whom they call Mar Ilyas (Elias)—it is true that this journey only served to make it clear that this man has no inclination or desire for union with the Holy Church. His ordinary residence is at a place called Alkush (Algoch) two days journey away from Nineveh in the monastery which they call Rabban Hurmmuz; but seven months ago, because of persecution by the Kurds he withdrew to a village called Til Kaif, some three leagues distant from the town (Mausil), and there I went to find him." (Ibid)

It was not until 1830 that John Hurmizd, the last descendant of the Bar Mama Patriarchal family of Mosul, in the Plain of Nineveh, united his church with the Roman Catholic Church, and his people became to be known as Chaldean.

Assyrians According to the Armenians

John Joseph has consistently misrepresented facts about the Assyrian identity of the Christian Assyrians. For example, he wrote: *"It has often been argued that the neighbors of the Nestorians, especially Armenians, have always referred to their Christian brethren as Assyrians; namely by the Armenian word phonetically rendered, Asori. Investigations indicate, however, that the Armenian word Asori, like Syriac Suryaya means Syrian and not Assyrian."* (Joseph John, 1961, 15)

He goes on to say that the right Armenian word for Assyrian is Asorrestantji. It has to be noted that in his second book, he has changed this word to Asorestansi. Joseph's claim that Asori means Syrian is contradicted by the classical and the modern Armenian sources. In a correspondence with George Yana, the author of "Ancient and Modern Assyrians," Dr. Joseph Melik-Hosepian, together with Dr. Hyk Madoian, a graduate in theology and history from Armenia, disagreed with John Joseph's claim for the following reasons:

First, during the ancient times, Armenians considered Syria as part of Assyria, therefore they did not have a separate identity for it. Second, since the third century AD, the Armenian name for Assyria has been Assoric, and Assory has been for Assyrians. Third, after the Islamic Arab conquests, the suffix "tan" was added to the names of the countries in the Armenian language. For example, Persia was called Parskastan, Armenia became Hayastan, and Assyria became Assorestan. However, the names "Assoric" for Assyria, and "Assori" for Assyrian are still valid. In conclusion, the gentlemen stated that the term "Asorestansi," contrary to Joseph's claim means, "from Assyria." (Yana George, 2008, 95) Furthermore, in a 1698 AD manuscript known as the Armenian version of the story of Ahikar, titled, 'Wisdom of Khikar' (Ahikar), Assyria is identified as Aorestan, and the ancient Assyrians are called "Asores." As in "the land of Asores," "the king of Asores," the "cowherds of the Asores." In the contemporary Armenian dictionaries such as Shirak's, English-Armenian Dictionary with Transliteration, Assyrian is rendered Asori, and Assyrians are Asoreren. The word for Syriac language is Asoragan. It means belonging to Assyria, the term for Syria is souria, the word for Syrian is souriastsi. (Ohannes and Sossie, Hannessian, 1999, 406)

In a Persian language 2002 pamphlet, titled Historical Relations between Armenians and Assyrians, published in Los Angeles, California Vahahn Karapetian, a contemporary Armenian writer, has identified the ancient and the contemporary Assyrians by the Armenian word 'Asori'.

He writes: *"Though Christianity was declared in 301 AD as the state religion of Armenia but because Armenians did not have their own Alphabet all their religious books were in the Assyrian (Asori) language and it continued as such, up to 420 AD, until Hesrop Mashtots created the Armenian alphabet."*
(Seibt W. "The Creation of the Caucasian Alphabets." 2011)

The following Armenian document, perhaps the earliest original writing in Classical Armenian, taken from Books V and VI, describes how the Armenian alphabet was invented:

[Armenian bishops] *"having devoted themselves to a great examination of experiment and investigation, and having endured great labors, they then made an announcement of their own searching, to the king of the Armenians, whose name was called Vramshapuh. Then the king told them about a certain man called Daniel by name, an Assyrian bishop of noble origin, who had elsewhere devised letters of the alphabet for the Armenian language. And when the king about the writing related this to them from Daniel, they prompted the king to take care according to their needs. And by decree he sent someone, Vahrich by name, to an elderly man whose name they called Habel, who was an acquaintance of the Assyrian bishop Daniel."* (Richard Diebold Center for Indo-European Language and Culture)

As it turned out the 22 letters invented by the Assyrian bishop Daniel did not remedy the needs of the sounds necessary for the Armenian language. According to the biography of St.Mashtots Vardapet, written by his pupil Koriun Vardapet, in order to find letters that were proper for the Armenian Language Mashtots with the authorization of the Armenian King Vramshapouh, together with his students traveled *"to the region of Arami [i.e. Syria], to two Assyrian cities, one of which was called Edessa [present Urfa in Turkey], and the other, Amid [present Diarbekir]. There he presented himself to two bishops, one of whom was called Babilas, and the other, Akakios. And they, clergy and nobles of the city, received the visitors with due honors and solicitude, in keeping with the custom of Christians. The dedicated teacher then divided his pupils into two groups, assigning one group to the [Syrian Orthodox], Assyrian school in the city of Edessa, and the other to the Hellenic school in Samosata."*

www.vehi.net/istoriya/armenia/korun/english/02.html)

As St.Mashtots was praying, and traveling to various places in search of the right letters for the Armenian language, he had a vision that helped him to invent the needed 36 Armenian alphabet letters in 404-406 AD. Two other letters were added to the alphabet in the 12th century. Karapetian cites various Armenian sources for his research, including a thirteen volume collection of the Armenian History published in 1974 in Eiravan, a book written by the fifth-century Hesro p Mashtots printed in Eiravan in 1972, plus works by other classical Armenian writers including the fifth-century Koriun, Gazar Parpetze, and Moses Khrenatzi. The Armenians acknowledge that the first Armenian New Testament was created from Syriac, not Greek, but after the Council of Ephesus between AD 433 and 436 a second translation was made from Greek. http://www.syriac.talktalk.net/chron_tab4.html)

According to the Persians, and Others

Persians, like the Armenians, have called Assyrians Asuri, or Ashuri. The Persian plural for Asuri is Asurian. To account for the fact that the Greeks and the Europeans dropped the Beginning 'A' in Assyrian, as did the Christian Assyrians, Persians used Surrian to mean Christian Assyrians. Later a possessive pronoun 'I' was added to it to make it Suriani which has been often used in reference to the Jacobite Assyrians. The Persian term for Syria is Suriyeh. The people of Syria are called 'Ahleh Suriyeh,' or Suriyehei.

The tenth century Arab scholar, Abu al-Faraj Muhammad Ibn Ishaq al-Nadim, in his index titled Fihrist al-Nadim, gives a definition of the word Ashuriyun (Arabic for Assyrians) as follows: "Their master and chief is named Ibn Siqtiri Ibn Ashuri. They collect revenues and profits. In some things they agree with the Jews, and about other things they disagree with them. They appear to be a sect of Jesus." (Budge, E.A., (1976)

Assyrians According to the Georgians

"*Assyrians in Georgia were first mentioned in the 6th century A.D. It was at that time that 13 Assyrian monks from the city of Urhai (Edessa, Mesopotamia) came to Georgia. History knows them as 13 saint Assyrian fathers. Later scholars likened their contribution to the enlightenment of the newly*

Christianized Georgia to what Saint Nino had done to convert the pagans. The monasteries and churches they founded are still standing." www.aina.org/reports/tykaaog.pdf

Konstantin Tesereteli: mentions other references to Assyrians by the Georgians in various centuries. A document prepared by the court of Irakli II in 1769 reported: *"Millions of Assyrians live in the mountains and Valley which straddle Persia and the Ottoman Empire."* Georgian court documents reveal that in the past Assyrian clergymen, bishops, priests, and Maliks had petitioned the court for permission to migrate to Georgia. *"It was our wish to rescue those Assyrians living the nearest to us. While providing other forms of assistance to those more distantly located."* As postscript to the translation of a letter sent to Irakli II in July 1770, King wrote: *"This is the copy of the letter sent to us by the Assyrian Catholicos whose bishop (Isaia) has visited us."* (Tsereteli Konstantin, 1944, 4-11)

Assyrians According to the Kurds

The sixteenth-century Kurdish writer Shraf Khan Al-Bidlisi in his Sharafnameh identifies the Nestorians of Hakkari as *"Christian infidels called 'Asuri'."* (Sharaf Khan Al Bidlisi, 1596, 130-132) In the Arabic version of the same book we read: *"During the time of Hassan Beg Aq-Qwinlo (the fifteenth century) there were Christians in Zur district (Hakkari) known as "Asuri"* The book further asserts that *"Tamerlane rewarded the Kurdish leader Izz Eddine Shir by giving him part of Hakkari as reward for his slaughtering of the Assyrians and the Armenians . . ."* (Sharaf Khan Al Bidlisi, 1953) The sixteenth-century Kurdish Historian Ali Sidi Al-Gorani contends that *"The Nestorians in Azerbaijan and Urmia are the descendants of the Assyrians—and those of Tiara and Hakkari are the indigenous people of that region since more than twenty-five centuries ago."* (Al-Gorani Ali Sidi, 146, 155, 204)

Assyrians According to the Russians

In a letter dated May 26, 1784, The Russian Colonel Stephan D. Burnashev to the Russian General Paul S. Potemkin states that *"There are 100 villages inhabited by Assyrians in the domain of the Khan of Urmiya, in addition, some 20,000 families reside within the borders of Turkey."* (Bournoutian George, 1998, 578) It is important to note that all the above references to the Christian Assyrians, as Assyrian during the Christian centuries by various nationalities were made before the nineteenth century.

Chapter 4

Resurgence of the Assyrian Nationalism

According to the Assyrian writer Robert William, D' Kalaita, the rise of nationalism among the Assyrians was due to their knowledge of history. He writes that it was

"the Western-educated elite, including priests and bishops such as the French educated Mar Tuma Oddo, the Chaldean bishop of Urmia, that the espousal of nationhood took place, in 1890s. It is Mar Tuma Oddo's accession to the seat of Chaldean bishop of Urmia, in the 1982, that marks the beginning of nationalist awareness. As a prominent member of Urmi's community, he advocated returning to the name Aturaya/ Assyrian instead of using the term Suryaya."

D' Kelaita cites Heinrichs "The Modern Assyrians Name and Nation" in Semetica, where he asserts that the Assyrian national movement began in 1890s by the French educated Mar Tuma Odo. (De Kelaita Robert W., Jaas, Vol. VIII No.1, 1994, 9)

The above facts refute John Joseph's claim that Christian Assyrians identified themselves by that name because Layard or

Wigram told them that Assyrian was their identity. D'Kelaita, further writes, Kukhwa (the Star), a biweekly newspaper that was being published in the area of Urmia, from June 1906 during the First World War to autumn of 1914 and later, again from 1917–1918, played an important role in spreading the message of nationalism among the Assyrians. This also refutes the implication that Wigram's post-World War I books were instrumental in promoting Assyrian nationalism among the Nestorians. It is important to note that most Assyrians at that time had no access to what Layard or Wigram wrote, and could not read the English language. D'Kelaita further writes:

"though other periodicals were published in Urmia, 'Kukhwa' [the Star] was not only the first publication that was not sponsored by the Western missions, It was also the first to carry overt nationalistic messages. It included local news from diaspora, lessons in history, essays on denominationalism that had flourished among Nestorians by the Western missions, each trying to propagate its own brand of Christianity." (D'Kelaita Robert William, 1994, 9)

The mission of Kukhwa, as published in the first issue of the newsletter, was to espouse national unity and loyalty, condemn factionalism, to encourage standardization in education and communication, work for the advancement of education and culture, and elevate the ethics of the community. It is important to note that Assyrians once more were massacred during World War I, and three-quarters of their population was murdered or forced to convert to Islam. Survivors were driven out of their homeland from the Plain of Urmia, the mountains north of Mosul, and the cities of Turkey.

They consequently lost their homes, farms, schools, books, publications, and everything they owned. The massacres of world War I were a great blow to the Assyrian national identity. Not only a great percentage of their population was massacred, they were also uprooted from the cities and villages where they had lived for generations, and were scattered into other countries. Great number of Assyrians who lived in Urmia and highlands of Kurdistan fled to Russia, Armenia, and Georgia—the rest went to Iraq. Since then, most have migrated to the West. Surviving Assyrians of the Syrian

Orthodox Church and the Chaldean Church, who lived in cities and villages of Turkey, took refuge in Syria, Jordan, Lebanon, or migrated to the West.

Catholic Assyrians are Called Chaldean

Another issue that has contributed to the confusion about the Christian Assyrian history and identity has been a tendency by some clergies and members of the Chaldean Church, as well as Syrian Orthodox Church, to deny their Assyrian identity for religious and political reasons.

According the Canons, of the Church of the East, dating back to the fifth century, the patriarch had to be elected and consecrated by five specific Metropolitan Archbishops, which included those of "Beit Lapat" (Jundi shapour), "Maishan" (the region around Basra), cities of Arbil, Nisibin, and Kirkuk, plus the Bishop of "Kashkar" (southern Babylon) acting as an alternate. However, after the Tamerlane's onsaught in 1401, the sees of Bait Lapat, Maishan, and Kashkar had ceased to exist altogether, and the other three were vacant which made the Canons unenforceable. Consequently Patriarch Shimon IV Basidi, 1403 - 1407 changed the rules and made the patriarchal office hereditary in his own family. (Wigram W.A., 1929, 158-159)

In 1552 AD because of a disagreement over whether the Patriarch should be elected or inherit his post, a group of dissenting clergies elected John Sulakka as their leader, who with the help of the Catholic missionaries was sent to Rome to be consecrated as the patriarch of a new Catholic Church. Sulakka on Feb. 20, 1553, was first proclaimed patriarch of "Mosul and Attur" by Pope Julius III. (Rabban, 1967, 427-28) Other Roman Catholic documents refer to Sulakka as the elected patriarch of "the Assyrian Nation." (Xavier Koodapuzha, 1982, 59) The Chronicle of the Carmelites states that Sulakka was first proclaimed "Patriarch of the Eastern Assyrians," but on April 19, 1553, he was redefined as the "Patriarch of the Chaldeans." (Yana George. 2000, 80) The change of the name to Chaldean, was perhaps intended to distinguish the members of the new church and its clergies from their brethren who remained loyal to the old denomination. Or, maybe for bureaucratic reasons, it was deemed necessary to link the new Catholics with the Nestorians of Cyprus who were labeled Chaldeans by Pope Eugene IV on August 7, 1445, when they joined the Roman Catholic Church. (Yana George 2000, Ibid) In later centuries, the name Chaldean was promoted by the Roman Catholic Church not only as the name of a new religious denomination, but also as their ethnic identity. This was intended to alienate members of the Chaldean Church not only from their former denomination but also to ethnically disassociate them from their brothers of the Church of the East. The remaining members of the church of the East were often terrorized to force them to join the new denomination. Hormuzd Rassam, whose family belonged to the Chaldean church wrote:

"It is extraordinary to state that the delegates of the Roman Church have not succeeded in converting the Nestorians of Sheikh to their dogmas, though so near a Turkish town, where former possess so much power under the protection of the French Government. The Roman Church often used the influence of the French government to encourage the Ottoman and the Kurds to terrorize those who refused to join the Chaldean church. . . . the Nestorians of Sheikh told me that the Chaldean Catholics of Jezeerah, who were their co-religionist, had always tried through their influence with the local authorities to bully them into submission to the Pope." (Rassam Hormuzd, 1897, 389)

Nationalism among the Jacobite Assyrians

Before World War I, there was also national awakening among the Assyrians of the Syrian Orthodox Church. Dr. Ashur S. Youssef (1858–1915), was a prominent nationalists, he was a professor at the Euphrates College, and published a periodical called "Murshid Atturyiyeen," meaning "Assyrians Spiritual Leader" (1908–1914). Ashur and his brother Donabed along with other Assyrian leaders from the village of Harput were arrested on April 19, 1915 and were all later hanged. In a letter to his brother, Hanna Yousif in America, before he was killed, wrote:

"*Yesterday on Sunday morning April 19th 1915 when we had heard that the Turks were crazed with the anger of beastly slaughter, sparing neither man woman or child we became terrified. Especially when the news came of the arrests of my comrades, I began to shiver, and during the course of preparing a hiding place, I myself was arrested and brought to this cell. This is a good opportunity that I am enjoying to write you my last letter, for I know we will be cut to pieces when we leave here, though I do not know when and where. Do not worry over my death-it is God's will- I am going to heaven to protect the rights of the Assyrians at the presence of the biggest and greatest Judge. The books and the work I had started about our nation's education remains unfinished.*"
http://en.wikipedia.org/wiki/Ashur_Yousif

Another prominent nationalist, member of the Syrian Orthodox Church, was Naum Elias Yaqub Palakh (1868 –1930), known also as Naum Faig. He was a teacher and writer, who wrote several books about the Syriac language and published a newspaper called *'Kawkab Madnho'* ("Star of the East"). After arrival in the United States in 1912 he established other news papers, including *Beth-Nahrin* in 1916, later he served as the editor of the *Huyodo*, (unity), a magazine that is still being published by the Assyrian Federation in Sweden. Following is one of many Nationalistic poems that he has written.

"*Awake, son of Assyria,
Awake and see the world how enlightened.
...The chance is fleeing from us
And time is running out
Awake son of Assyria, Awake!
In vengeance you will take refuge.
Rise up and band together to strengthen.
And if one does not awake we have lost our chance
Without a purpose, misfortune will befall our land*"

See online: http://www.aina.org/books/oadoan.htm
The Origins and Development of Assyrian Nationalism

Rejection of Nationalism by Some Clergies

After World War I, for a brief period, clergies of the Syrian Orthodox Church and Chaldean clergies were willing to work with the Church of the East, in hope that the league of Nations would provide them collectively with a homeland, where they could live in peace, but that was not meant to be. After the 1933 massacre of the members of the Church of the East, by the Iraqi army, due to a conflict between the government and the patriarch of the Church of the East, clergies of the other two denominations shied away from advertising their Assyrian identity. Because. they attributed the massacre to the Assyrian nationalism of the Church of the East patriarch, and its members. Ephriam Shapira writes:

"The Syriac Orthodox Church's documents and memorial evidences show that nearly all its clergies who were born in the northern part of Iraq (Assyria) proudly titled their names or surname by "The Assyrian"—Al Atturaye—including the Patriarch who was known as Mar Ephraim Barsoum Al Atturaye. But sadly, after the [1933] Semail massacre . . . all clergies began to delete the title of Assyrian from their names including Mar Ephrim Barsoum."

In fact, due to political expediency, Ephraim Barsoum, who ascended to the Patriarchal See [in 1933] became the most fervent anti-Assyrian, and attacked anyone who claimed to be Assyrian. According to Metropolitan Mar Ishaq Saka Ephraim began to promote Arabism and was known as "The Priest of Pan Arabism" among Arab nationalists. (Mar Saka Ishaq, 1983, 145) On December 2, 1952, by a decree Ephriam Barsoum, the Patriarch of the Syrian Orthodox Church gave orders that the name Assyrian should no longer be used as the identity of his church or its members. He stated that it was historically incorrect because it was contrary to the traditions of fathers, in reference to his church. *"Furthermore, the use of Assyrian, according to him, created ambiguity about the identity of the church which is historically known as Syrian in India and the homeland."* He also added that the name Assyrian came to be used by the Anglican missionaries for the Nestorians. (Aydin Edip May 8, 2000) As it has been proven in this book, Christians of Mesopotamia were known as Assyrians since before the dawn of Christianity.

Barsoum asserted that the correct term for his Church and its people was Syrian, but since it was in use by the Rum Orthodox (Antiochian) Church in North America, he suggested that Aramean should be used instead, and the language they speak known historically as Syriac should be called Aramaic. Patriarch Ephraim Barsoum's justification for changing his people's identity was disingenuous. When he was the Archbishop of the Syrian Orthodox Church, he represented his people as Assyrians in the 1919–20 Paris Peace Conference. His petition read as follows:

"We have the honor of bringing before the Peace Conference the information that H.B. the Syrian Patriarch of Antioch has entrusted me with the task of laying before the Conference the suffering and the wishes of our ancient Assyrian nation who resides mostly in the upper valleys of Tigris and Euphrates in Mesopotamia." (http://christiansofiraq.com/reply2.html)

Ephraim Barsoum had also identified himself and his people as Assyrian before and after 1920. The Worcester Telegram and Gazette published an interview with him in 1927 about the "Historic Significance of the Syrian Orthodox Church of Antioch." It stated:

"His Eminence has given lectures on the psychology of the Assyrian people in the United States. His mission has been to create an understanding of the Assyrian people by Americans, because most of them, although well-educated in Assyria, have been forced by a changed atmosphere into menial occupations." The article concluded by mentioning Archbishop's participation in the 1919 Peace Conference in Paris, *"where he appeared to demand indemnity for the Assyrian churches sacked during the World War One."* http://christiansofiraq.com/joseph/reply2.html

Mar Barsoum assigned the Job of ridding the Syrian Orthodox Church from its Assyrian identity to Archbishop Athanasius Yeshue Samuel, he previously was Metropolitan of the Saint Mark's Convent in Jerusalem, which was also known as the "Assyrian Convent," according to a street sign leading to it. Like Ephraim Barsoum, he also had proudly identified himself and his people as Assyrians. In a letter to the editor of the Syrian Orthodox magazine "Beth-Nahreen" dated 6 June, 1947, he wrote: *"May the Almighty confer upon you, your staff, the readers of the issue and the Assyrian community all over the world his blessings and benedictions."* Upon arriving in the United States, on the letterhead of a notice he sent to his Parishioners, dated August 12, 1952, he identified himself as the "Assyrian Orthodox Archbishop to the United States and Canada." He asked for the *"cooperation of every Assyrian who has the love of his church and nation at heart."* (Ibid)

However, a year or so later, through court orders, he succeeded in removing the Assyrian name from most Syrian Orthodox Church properties despite strong opposition by the parishioners. Members of the "Assyrian Apostolic Church of the Virgin Mary" in Worcester, Massachusetts, and another in Paramus, New Jersey, refused to comply with the identity change. They succeeded in keeping the Assyrian name by registering their parishes under a trustee group. Though, Archbishop Cyril Ephraim Karim succeeded in removing the name Assyrian from the Virgin Mary church in Worcester, he failed to do so with the church in Paramus, and Worcester, Massachusetts. To justify the name change, Ephraim Barsoum published a book in 1953, titled "The Syrian Church of Antioch in Name and History" where he rejected the Assyrian identity of the Syrian Orthodox Church and its members. He wrote:

"The 'Assyrian' name is the English Protestant invention going back to 1900 AD. It was bequeathed to the Nestorians in the regions of Mosul 1919–1920 A.D. for a malicious, political purpose, so that the English politicians might create for themselves out of the Nestorian youth a militia they named 'Assyrian' aiming at the realization of their political plan in Iraq, a plan which failed in 1933 and resulted in the exile of the Catholikos of the Nestorians and his exile from the country with his followers."

Mr. Mattay Mousa who translated Ephraim Barsoum's book into English has admitted on various occasions that he was sent by Ephraim Barsoum to all Jacobite churches in Iraq, and Turkey to order their clergies to promote Aramean as the identity of their people, and to denounce their Assyrian identity. This clearly shows that Aramean was not the identity of the Syrian Orthodox Church prior to 1953. Mar Barsoum's efforts to remove the name Assyrian from his church and its members has resulted in dividing his people into two antagonistic groups, One faction continues to identify itself as Assyrian, and the other that claims to be Aramean is strongly hostile toward the other.

References to Jacobites as Assyrians

The twelfth-century Michael the Great, the Patriarch of the Syrian Orthodox Church, in his chronicle equated the term Syrian with Assyrian. Horatio Southgate who visited the Syrian Orthodox communities of Turkey in 1844 reported that members of the Syrian Orthodox Church identified themselves as Assyrians, i.e., "Suryoyo Atturoyo" He further wrote that they consider themselves *"Sons of Assour (Ashur) who 'out of the land of Shinar went forth, and build Nineveh, and the city Rehoboth, and Calah, and Resin between Nineveh and Calah; the same is a great city."* (Horatio Southgate, 1844, 80)

About fifty years later, Anglican Bishop O.H. Parry in his book, "Six Months in a Syrian Monastery" wrote: that members of the Jacobite church used the term Syrian interchangeably *with the 'Assyrian.'* (Perry, O.H. 1895)

After the 1885–86 massacres in Diarbekir and other cities in Turkey, members of the Syrian Orthodox community began their migration to the United States and Canada. They brought with them their pride in their Assyrian identity. The first organization established by them in the United States was called the "Assyrian National School Association of America," which was later renamed the "Assyrian National School Association." Among its commendable achievements was the establishment of an orphanage in 1921 in Adana Turkey to take care of the children that were orphaned during Turkey's massacre of the Syrian Orthodox community during World War I. It was closed due to the governmental orders, and it was reopened in Beirut, Lebanon, where it still exists, thanks to the struggle of the said organization. Starting in 1923, The Assyrian National School Association was also instrumental in publishing and distributing the "Assyrian New Beth-Nahreen" magazine. (Ibid, Aydin Edip Aydin, 2000)

In 1901 A women's organization called "The Assyrian Ladies Aid" was established. It succeeded in raising enough funds to build the first Syrian Orthodox Church in North America, completed in April 1927. It was consecrated as the "Assyrian Apostolic Church of the Virgin Mary" by no other than Archbishop Ephraim Barsoum. (Ibid, Aydin)

Ancient Assyrians in Anatolia

Ancient Assyrians' presence in Anatolia dates back to the second millennium BC, when their merchants arrived from Ashur. Between 2000 BC and 1750 BC, they established a series of trading colonies, the largest of them was in Neša. Perhaps due to the importance of the Assyrian trade network at this location, the language of Neša became the official language of the Hittite Empire. Assyrian merchants traded tin, textiles, gold, silver, and copper. The Assyrian military domination of Anatolia began when King Thiglatpileser III (745–727), defeated the Urartu army and incorporated a small kingdom that consisted of the city of Edessa, also known as Urhay in Syriac and Urfa in Turkish, plus the nearby regions. In 882 BCE he chose the city of Tushan to build a palace, and made it an Assyrian military and administrative center. In an inscription, Ashurnasirpal II wrote:

"I approached the city of Tushan. I took Tushan in hand for renovation. I cleared away its old wall, delineated its area, reached its foundation pit, and built, completed, and decorated in splendid fashion a new wall from top to bottom. A palace for my loyal residence I founded inside . . . I brought back the enfeebled Assyrians who because of hunger and famine had gone up to other lands to the land of Subr., I settled them in the city of Tushan." (MacGinnis John, JAAS, vol. 23 no. 1, 2009, 7)

The importation of Assyrians from the land of Suburu, who were given grants in the surrounding area, undoubtedly to was an important aspect of the Assyrianization of the region. Archeological discoveries indicate extensive Assyrian presence in the area of Mardin, Diyarbakir, and Urhay. By the reign of Sargon, Tushan had become the most important Assyrian political, economic, and military center in the upper Tigris. The evidence of agricultural sites in the region indicates that the Assyrian policy of agricultural colonization contributed to the prosperity of the region. Small Towns and villages sprung up around Assyrian centers near the bank of the Tigris, wherever sufficiently wide flood plains were available that made agriculture profitable. An Assyrian stamp indicates that about the eighth century BC docile bees were imported from the Taurus Mountains of Anatolia into Israel, which made beekeeping in that country possible.

A Neo-Assyrian governor's palace dating back to the ninth to seventh century BCE was found among the ruins on Ziyaret Tepee. Within its courtyard, cremation pits were found in addition to a rare treasure trove of more than twenty bronze vessels under the paving stones. Other items discovered included: ivory receptacles, carved ivory objects, seals and beads, plus about twenty embossed bronze vessels similar to those found in the Assyrian capitals of Ashur and Kalhu. A clay tablet found during the excavation of Tushan includes a desperate call by Assyrian official Mannu-ki-Libbalias for reinforcements at 630 BC, when the enemy was getting ready to invade the city. The city temples and palaces were pillaged and were torn down or set aflame by the invaders. (www.timesonline.co.uk, August 6, 2009)

Assyrians in Tur Abedin

Historical evidences reveal that Assyria during the neo-Assyrian period consisted; not only of the region known today as Northern Iraq, but also Tur Abedin, in southeast Turkey, which includes cities of Nisibin, Harran, Edessa [Urhay], Mardin, and Diyarbakir. On August 12, 2009, according to the UPI, a team led by University of Toronto archaeology department reported that a number of cuneiform tablets were found in a 2,700-year-old Assyrian temple in southeastern Turkey. The tablets date to the

Iron Age period between 1,200 BC and 600 BC. The archive is expected to lead to new insights about the religious dimension of Assyrian imperial ideology. (UPI, Iron Age cunieform,12, 2009)

Archaeology professor Timothy Harrison, wrote, *"The tablets, and the information they contain, may possibly highlight the imperial ambitions of one of the great powers of the ancient world, and its lasting influence on the political culture of the Middle East."* (blog.bibleplaces.com/labels/Turkey.html)

In an article by Afram Bar-yakoub, titled: "The Assyrian Identity of Tur Abedin." published on the aina.org, the author provides historical information to prove that Tur Abedin, which has been historically inhabited by the Christian Assyrians was as much the heartland of the ancient Assyria as was Nineveh. (www.aina.org/ata/20100111165243.htm)

He bases this conclusion on a study by the historian Karen Radner; titled "How to reach the upper Tigris, The Route Through the Tur Abdin." Karen Radner is also the author of "The Oxford Handbook of Cuneiform writing." which examines the Ancient Middle East, through the lens of cuneiform texts. The first mention of Tur Abdin in the Assyrian annals dates back to the reign of King Adad Nirari I, (1307–1275 BC.), it was called "Kashieri" a name that Hurrians, who had dominated the region, from 1300 B.C to 1200 BC, had given it. Assyrians took over Kashieri as well as Gozarto located south of it, traces of the Aramean settlers in the area existed parallel to the Assyrian takeover of the region. (Radner Karen, Volume XV (2006)

The names given by the ancient Assyrians to some places in Tur Abedin are still in use. For example, the name "Mardiane" today is pronounced Mardin, also Shura, first was mentioned during the reign of King Adad Nerari III (810-738), is believed to be the modern town of Sawro. Shumma-Ilani, the governor of Arkahu, according to one tablet, was involved in a civil case in a court. An Assyrian village in Tur Abedin still bears the name Arkah that is abbreviated form of Arkahu. "The ancient name "Kapar-Tatu," is recognized by Radner in todays Assyrian language as "Kfartutho." The prefix "Kapar," means village in ancient Assyrian. The word has transformed into "Kfar" in classical Assyrian and is found as a prefix in Assyrian names such as Kfarburan, Kfarze and Kfarbe."

During the first century of their settlement, Arameans of Kashieri posed no threat to the Assyrian rule, but as their population increased, starting during the reign of the Assyrian King Ashur Bel Kala, (1073-1056 BC,) they often revolted. Ashurnasirpal III's six day war campaign in 879 BC succeeded in subduing rebellions in Turabdin, and capture the city of "Matiatu," todays Midyat, on the second day of his campaign, where he erected a victory stele of himself in the town, but like the other Assyrian artifacts, that astrologists believe are hidden under the Tur Abedin's soil, this stele has not been found yet. However an inscription by Shalmansir III declares: *"In my fifth regal year, I ascended to Kashieri and captured eleven fortified cities."* After this event, there is no mention in the Assyrian royal archives, of battles in Kashieri. This leads to the conclusion that the Assyrian control over the region was firmly established. Radner believes that Arameans were eventually integrated into the Assyrian empire. Assyriologist, Simo Parpola, attributes their assimilation to the effective policies of the Assyrian kings.

At the end of her study, Radner mentions in passing, an attack by the inhabitants of Izalla, in Tur Abedin, in 609 BC against the Babylonian troops of King Nabopalassar, which forced them to halt and crush the rebellion before moving on. Though Radner does not give a reason for the action of Izalla's inhabitants, Bar-yakoub contends that attack on the Babylonian army was intended to stop it from joining the Medes to drive the Assyrian troops, who after the fall of Nineveh had retreated to the nearby Harran to regroup. According to him, this indicates that the inhabitants of Izalla or Tur Abedin considered themselves Assyrians; otherwise there would have been no reason for them to stand in the way of the powerful Babylonian army.

There was always awareness by the Syriac speaking people in the Southeastern Turkey of their Assyrian heritage, especially at the Tur Abedin region. The classical Syriac writers have directly and indirectly attested to this fact. In a commentary on Genesis, Mar Ephraim wrote that Nimrod ruled Erekh, which is

Urhay/Edessa. According to Yagoo Urhaya, Nimrod was Ninus son of Belus, the mythical founder of Nineveh. It is possible that Urhay at one time was called Urh or Urkh according to Seagal. Several sites in Urhay were specifically associated with Nimrod during the Christian era, including the "Throne of Nimrod" on which a Citadel stands. The site where once the Dair Yakup [Monastery] was located was known as the "hills of Nimrod." (Segal, 1970, fn2, 2) Until World War I, Assyrians lived primarily in a triangular-shape region with its western angle at southeast Turkey, going east to the shores of lake Urmia in northwest Iran, and south to the plain of Nineveh, in northern Iraq. Since then, due to repeated persecutions, a majority of their people was forced to take refuge in other Middle Eastern countries or to immigrate to Russia, Western Europe, United States, Canada, and Australia.

Chapter 5

Ancient Assyrian Traditions During the Christian Era

There is a false presumption that Christian Assyrian have nothing to show that links them back to the ancient Assyrians. It is a well-known fact that nations that converted to Christianity did their best to distance themselves from their pagan forefathers, and the Assyrians were no exception. However, despite such efforts, traces of ancient Assyrian art, literature, and traditions survived into Christianity, but due to lack of careful research, they have been difficult to recognize. Following are few examples of such legacies that have been identified.

In addition to language, history, geography, and ancestry, religion and culture have played important roles in shaping the ethnicity of all people in the Middle East. Historical evidence indicates that the ancient Assyrian religion was worshiped in the city of Edessa/Urhay in northern Mesopotamia during the early centuries of Christianity. According to "The Teachings of Addaeus," a fourth-century Syriac language document, when the Apostle Addai preached about Christianity in Edessa, even the priests of the house (temples) of Nebu and Bel honored the Christian apostle.

"Shavida, moreover, and Ebed-nebu (servant of Nebu), chiefs of the priests of this town, together with Piroz and Dilsu, their

companions, threw down the altars on which they were accustomed to sacrifice before Nebu and Bel, their gods, except the great altar which was in the middle of the town; and they cried out and said: Verily this is the disciple of that eminent and glorious Master, concerning whom we have heard all that He did in the country of Palestine." Segal tells us that the Altar in the middle of Edessa was still there until the fifth century AD. (Segal J.B., 1970, 70)

Assyrian New Year Celebration in Edessa

Jacob of Edessa and other Syriac writers believed that; the city of Edessa, known as Urhay in the Syriac language, was founded by Nimrod, also known as Ninus son of Belus, the founder of Nineveh. *"Basil cited by Michael the Syrian declares: 'After the flood, in the time of Noah, Nimrod...built Orhay. He called it "Ur", that is, "town"...'* (Segal, 1970, footnotes, 1,1- 2,2)

According to an early Christian, Syriac document, known as the "Acts of Sharbil," a festival was being celebrated on the eighth day of Nisan, in 115 AD, which has elements of the ancient Assyrian New Year called the Akkitu Spring Festival. The gathering of all gods, on the eighth day of the ancient Assyrian New Year was intended to elect Bel, (Ashur in Assyria, Marduk in Babylon), to fight and vanquish the forces of chaos, as told by the Assyro-Babylonian Creation Story. The following description about what went on in Urhay/Edessa during the New Year celebration has similarity to how it was celebrated by the ancient Assyrians.

"There was a great festival on the eighth of Nisan, on the third day of the week (115 AD). The whole city was gathered together by the great altar, which was in the middle of the town opposite the Record office. All the gods having been brought together and decorated and sitting in honor, both Nebu and Bel together with their fellows. And the priests were offering incense of spices and libations, and an odor of sweetness was diffusing itself around, and sheep and oxen were being slaughtered, and the sound of the harp and the drum was heard in the whole town. And Sharbil was chief, and ruler of all the priests; and he was honored above all his fellows, and was clad in splendid and magnificent vestments; and a headband embossed with figures of gold was set upon his head; and

at the bidding of his word everything that he ordered was done. And Abgar the king, son of the gods, was standing at the head of the people. And they obeyed Sharbil, because he drew nearer to all the gods than any of his fellows, and as being the one who according to that which he had heard from the gods returned an answer to every man." (Carcton W., 1864, 41)

At the ancient Assyrian period, during the New Year festival, the Creation Story was enacted. On the seventh day of the New Year, Nebu [son and savior of Marduk in Babylon and Ashur in Assyria] together with other gods succeeds in liberating assembled in the Chamber of Destinies (Ubshu ukkinna), to bestow their combined strength upon the lord, to prepare him for war against the forces of chaos and give him the right to determine destinies; to renew fruitfulness and life during the forthcoming year. While holding his scepter in his hand, the king also went to the great hall to receive a fresh outpouring of divine power. Then he participated in the procession by grasping the hand of the great lord Ashur, and went along with other gods to the Festival House (Bit Akitu), at the outskirts of the city. At the conclusion, a banquet was held to celebrate the triumph of Ashur and the well being of the country. Assyrian king Sennacherib has depicted the victorious armies of the gods in conflict with Tiamat, on the copper doors of the Bit Akitu in Nineveh. (www.mindspring.com/~mysticgryphon/bitakitu.hm)

The participation of the king in the New Year celebration was an important part of the Assyro-Babylonian celebrations. The presence of the Edessan King Abgar in this event shows that the New Year in Edessa/Urhay was based on the important elements of the ancient Assyrian Creation Story, and the New Year. Sharbil, or Sharbel, is also known as (Sarbelus) of Edessa who eventually converted to Christianity. The Syrian Orthodox Church has a St. Sharbil Monastery, in Tur Abedin and his name has survived among the Assyrians of the Syrian Orthodox Church and the Maronites. According to Segal the celebration of the Nisan festival in year, to the dismay of Christians continued to be celebrated in in Edessa continued until the 6th century AD, as did the worship of the ancient Assyrian gods; Nebu Bel, Sin, Shamash, and Nergal. (Segal, 1970, 52-53) On approximately March 165 AD the Roman armies occupied Edessa and put an end to the dynasty of kings that had ruled the kingdom of Osrhoene since 139 BC.

Ancient Burial Practice Among Highland Assyrians

According to Olmstead, the Persian king Darius (521–486), in one of his inscriptions, reports that his forces defeated one of his enemies *"in the district Autiyara in the mountains of Tiyari, a short distance form Nineveh, where until our own day the Assyrian Christians maintained a precarious independence."* (Olmstead, 1970, 114) He further writes: *"the hard to access northern mountains range during war times served as place of refuge for these Assyrians during most of the Christian era."* (Ibid)

Surma D'bait-Mar-Shimoun writes about a caring-for-the-dead tradition among the Thumnaye Assyrians, who like the Tyarai lived in the highlands north of Mosul, which is similar to that of the ancient Assyrians. About the burial customs of the ancient Assyrians, Olmstead writes: *"always the lamp was left in a niche, and even the smoke can still be seen. A large water jar, a jug, and several dishes formed the remainder of the equipment needed for the after-life . . ."* (Olmsted, 1968, 625) Surma writes: *"In some districts, Tkhuma, for instance—food is also placed on the graves, and in this valley the graves are often made with a little niche in the side of them, both for this purpose, and for the putting of the light."* Surma adds: *"on the morning of the resurrection day, before day light, Assyrians in the highland visited the grave of their loved ones before dawn and lighted tapers on their resting site. The usual greeting at this time was 'light to your departed'."* (Beit-Mar Shimon Surma, 1983, 40) This was undoubtedly why the pre-Christian Assyrians left a lamp in a niche at the side of their beloveds' graves. They believed that the underworld was a dark and frightening place, as it was described in the Epic of Gilgamesh.

"To the house from which who enters never goes forth:
On the Road whose path does not lead back;
To the house whose occupants are bereft of light;
Where dust is their food and clay their sustenance;
. . . Where they see no light and dwell in darkness."

Ancient and Christian Assyrian icons

Other elements of the ancient Assyrian cultures have survived among the Christian Assyrians that are not readily obvious. The following Christian Assyrian religious icons seem to have derived from the ancient Assyrian predecessors.

Cross replaced the tree of life

Cross was often portrayed as the Tree of Life by the early Christian Assyrians, as depicted on the front cover. The fourth-century Mar Ephraim wrote, *"the Tree of Knowledge brought death to Adam and Eve, the Tree of Life, i.e. cross, restores life to humanity."* The Christian Assyrian engraving, on the right shows angels praying to the cross, as the cherubim venerated the Tree of Life on this ancient relief. www.christiansofiraq.com/monastery.html
Relief engravings at the 4th century AD Mar Behnam Monastery in the Plain of Nineveh indicate the survival of the ancient Assyrian bas-relief carving art into the Christian period. Even the Rosette emblem which was a common feature in most ancient Assyrian bas-reliefs can be seen in the engravings at the Mar Behnam Monastery as shown on the right hand

Notice on this page, the uncanny similarity between the ninth-century BC ancient Assyrian relief where Ashurnasirpal, is pointing to the standard of Ashur, and on the left where prophet Joshua is pointing to the Judeo-Christian God in similar fashion, in an illustration in a sixth or seventh century Syriac Bible.

The following pictures show the survival of the emblem of the ancient Assyrian Ninurta as a Christian cross

The first image to the left is of a 6000 year-old, Sumerian Ninurta cross, next to it is the tree of life, the second image is of a cross at an old Syrian Orthodox church in Tur-abedin, the third cross is carved on the altar of a newly built St. Mary's Church, belonging to the Syrian Orthodox Church in Paris. Courtesy of the journalist Augin Kurt and the Assyriantimes.com

To the left, the ancient Assyrian king Shamshi Adad V (823-811 BC) is wearing the cross of Ninurta on his chest. To the right Raphael Bedavid (1922-2003), the Patriarch of the Chaldean Church is holding a Christian cross similar to the Ninurta emblem.

Parpola writes, *"in the Assyrian empire, the cross as an emblem belonged to the crown prince and his heavenly image, the savior god Ninurta/Nabû, who was elevated to his father's right hand and omnipotence after his victory over death and the forces of evil and became the proprietor of the "book of life".*
Without doubt, this symbolism of the cross, along with many other Assyrian symbols and religious beliefs such as the tree of life, were later adapted by Christianity, which in fact grew on Assyrian ground. A good part of the Assyrian perceptions dates of course back to the Sumerian period.
(Parpola http://www.forumbiodiversity.com Sons-of-God-The-Ideology-of-Assyrian-Kingship)

In other words, cross for the Christian Assyrians symbolized resurrection of the Son of God as did the Ninurta emblem to the ancient Assyrians.

Syriac Dispute Poem's Genre; Legacy of Sumerians and Akkadians

In an article titled "Syriac Dialogue – An Example from the Past," Professor Sebastian Brock, Oxford University, writes:

"The distinctive Syriac genre of the dispute poem, where two characters conduct an argument in alternating verses, has its roots in the ancient Mesopotamian precedence disputes, composed in Sumerian and Akkadian and going back to late third and the second millennium BC."

He contends that *"the earliest examples of such poems are found in the writings of St. Ephraim,"* and cites examples by other writers, such as the dispute between Nestorius and Cyril, where two historical figures are presented as arguing. In most other of such dialogue soghyatha, the pairs are biblical personalities, (such as Cain and Abel, Mary and Joseph, John the Baptist and Christ). A number of the soghyatha are attributed to Mar Narsai, but modern scholars dispute such possibility because several of them were also known in the Syrian Orthodox manuscript tradition, or seem to have been written in later centuries. (Brock Sebastian, Jaas, Vol. 18, no. 1, 2004, 57-70)

The survival of the Sumerian and Akkadian (Assyro-Babylonian language) literary tradition into Christianity would have been only possible if the same people who lived in ancient Assyria and survived after its defeat, especially since the earliest examples of such genre in the Syriac language comes from the early Christian writers who lived in northern and central Mesopotamia.

Assyrians in the Syriac Literature;

the Legend of Mar Qardagh

The legend of Mar Qardagh (i.e., "Saint") is a heroic story by an anonymous seventh-century Syriac [Assyrian] writer. In the beginning of the legend the hero is introduced as:

"the holy Mar Qardagh [who] was from a great people, from the stock of the kingdom of Assyrians ('Atturaye'). His father was descended from the renowned lineage of the house of Nimrod, and his mother from the renowned lineage of the house of Sennacherib II, and he was born of pagan parents, lost in in the error of Magianism..."

The fact that twelve centuries after the fall of Nineveh a writer will choose an Assyrian as the hero of his story indicates that he and his readers were aware of their Assyrian ancestry, otherwise he could have described him as Aramean, Persian, Kurd, or whatever he believed his readers would have enjoyed reading about. Walker describes the legend of Qardagh as "Christian heroism," but there is no reason to believe that its author was not also promoting Assyrian nationalism as the Persian and Armenian writers did in writing about the heroes of their nations. The introduction of Mar Qardagh as Assyrian by the writer of the story was not only intended to appeal to the "Christian pride"; it was also meant to please the patriotism of its Assyrian readers.

Though the legend of Mar Qardagh introduces him as *"a powerful hero of royal Assyrian lineage,"* Walker throughout his book refers to the people for whom the story was written as "Eastern Syrians," instead of Assyrians. Evidently, he was influenced by John Joseph's book "The Modern Assyrians of the Middle East: Encounters with Western Christian Mission." It is interesting that, though ancient Assyrians were also known as Syrians, western writers have gone out of their way to deny the association between the two terms.

The religion of Qardagh's parents was Zoroastrian, which indicates that certain segments of Assyrians had converted to that faith. In a chapter titled "The Temple of Ishtar of Arbela at Malkiia," Walker traces the history of the mound where Qardagh built his fortress to the neo-Assyrian period. The "legend of Qardagh" was written during the Persian Sassanian rule of Khosro II (590–628), a time when Christians in Mesopotamia lived in relative peace, but the story was about an event that took place during the persecution years of King Shapur II (309–379).

According to the legend, the young Qardagh was handsome, strong, and a great warrior. When he was twenty-five years old, King Shapur II heard of his fame and his remarkable strength, and summoned him to his palace, he was impressed with his appearance and powerful body; therefore, ordered him to display his skills in the sports arena. Next day at the stadium, at a given time, Qardagh shot five arrows at a target placed on top of a post, all of them landed on the same spot. Later Qardagh was invited by the king to play polo and hunt with him, undoubtedly to assess his other skills. In both cases, Shapur was impressed with his remarkable skills:

"Shapur ordered that Qardagh should be given great gifts, and made him patahsa [protector of border] in Assyria from the Tamara River [the present day Diyala River in today's central Iraq], up to the city of Nisibin. Upon arriving in 'the city of Arbela of the Assyrians' where he would live, he made a great festival for the Pagan gods . . ."

Qardagh began to build a fortress, which included a house and a fire temple for himself on top of a mound known as Malki. According to Parpola during the neo-Assyrian period, the Akkadian name for this spot was Milkia. (Walker t. Joel, 1968, 22-23) The later Sassanian building on top of the Malki mound according to Walker *"stood directly over the ruins of a major Neo-Assyrian temple, the Akitu-shrine of the goddess Ishtar of Arbela, "Lady of Arbela."* (Walker 1968, 249-250)

Cuneiform documents attest to the fact that several aspects of the Neo-Assyrian rituals were conducted at the site. The Akitu-Shrine functioned as the temporary residence for Ishtar during the New Year ceremony. On the eleventh day of the New Year, after gods had determined the human destiny for that year, her statue was escorted back into the city with great celebration. (Walker p. 250, see also footnotes.) When the fortress was being constructed, one night Qardagh saw in a dream that a young knight clad in armor and mounted on a horse stood over him and stabbed him on his side with the tip of a spear, and told him that he would be martyred in front of this fortress on behalf of Christ. When Qardagh inquired who he was and how he could predict such things, the rider replied: *"I am Serguis, the servant of Christ. I have come ahead to let you know what will be."*

One day when Qardagh was going to the Stadium to play polo, Holy Odisho cut off his path and crossed before him. This act greatly angered Qardagh, he instructed his servants to strike him and guard him. Later, in response to a question by Qardagh about where he was from and what was his profession, Odisho informed him:

"As it was told to me by my parents, they were from Hazza, a village in the lands of the Assyrians. But because they were Christians, they were driven out of by impious pagans, and went and settled in Tamanon, a village in the lands of the Kurds."

After a long philosophical discussion between the two about the merits of Christianity and a series of miraculous events that Qardakh witnessed, he converted to Christianity. Soon it was reported to the king that his Marzban had become Christian. After repeated attempts by the king and Qardakh's parents to convince him renounce his Christianity, he did not obey. At the end of the story, Qardakh was stoned to death in front of the fortress he had built. Hazza, which was called Halzu by the ancient Assyrians, survived after the Assyrian defeat and became an important Assyrian town during the Christian era. Given such facts, it is obvious that the author of the legend was well informed about the Assyrian identity of his people and knew well that their homeland was indeed "the land of the Assyrians."

The Legend of Mar Behnam

The Legend of Mar Behnam is associated with the fourth-century Mar Behnam Monastery located in the Nineveh Plain near Nimrud, about thirty-two kilometers southwest of Mosul. The story is about prince Behnam and his sister Sara, who belonged to the family of Sennacherib II, the Governor of Nineveh, some time in the fourth century. As it happened, Mar Behnam and his forty riders in pursuit of a gazelle ascended the Tur-Alphayee ("Mountain of the Thousands" or today's 'Maqloub' Mountain) located a short distance from Nineveh. There they met the Christian hermit, Mattay, who had arrived from the city of Amid/Diyarbakir in Northern Mesopotamia. Mar Mattay, who was a Christian healer, was able to cure Mar Behnam's sister Sara, who was suffered from an incurable disease.

The miraculous healing, inspired Mar Behnam, his troops, and his sister to convert to Christianity. Upon learning of this, Malik Sennacherib II became angry and did everything in his power to persuade them to abandon their newly found religion because he feared of its consequences, but they refused. In a desperate attempt to convince them to relent, he threatened to have them killed if they did not obey. According to the legend, prince Behnam, his sister, and his riders escaped from Nineveh as the King's troop pursued them and caught up with them about six miles northeast of Nimrud, the ancient Assyrian city of Kalkh. During the battle which ensued between the two armies, Mar Behnam and his sister Sara were killed. The tragic and painful incident haunted the king for all his life. As it happened, he too was afflicted with the same disease which Sara had. After trying all manners of unsuccessful cures, his wife convinced him to try the miraculous cure of Mar Mattay, which he reluctantly accepted. After his disease was successfully cured he became Christian and built the Monastery of Mar Behnam in the memory of his son Behnam and daughter Sara, at the site where they died. The edifice stands to this day and is known as the Syrian Orthodox convent of Mar Behnam. According to one account, a plaque in front of this monastery at one time read: *"Prince Mor Behnam and Princes Sara, the children of Sennacherib II, governor of Assyria, with forty horsemen."* Inside the convent, on the eastern side, there is a full-length bas-relief portrait of Sara as well as an engraved representation of Mar Behnam mounted on a horse. The Syrian Orthodox Church observes a holiday on the tenth of December of every year, in remembrance of Mar Behnam and

Sara, children of the Assyrian King Sennacherib II. It is important to note that Sara in the Syriac language means the Moon, which was an important deity of the pagan Assyrians.

SennacheribII is also credited with having built the Mar Mattay monastery on top of the Tur-Alphi Mountain near Nineveh to honor Mar Matatty and his Christian religion. Both monasteries have survived to this day. The Mar Behnam convent contains the tomb of Saint Behnam and an extensive Syriac language library. There are engravings of the Christian icons around the stone doorway of the Mar Behnam Monastery including a Cross that has been rendered to look like the Tree of Life. Dair Mar Mattay, historically has been an important Assyrian monastery in Iraq. According to some accounts, it was built in the fourth century AD. To its left there is a large cave with natural mountain spring water, which some believe it is the water which cured prices Sara and her father from their disease. Sine 484 AD the Mar Mattay Monastery has been in control of the Syrian Orthodox Church and has served as the administrative center of the dioceses of Nineveh and Attur.

During its long history, it became an important learning center but was partially destroyed by the Tamur-lang's army. It was abandoned until 1795 AD, when Basil Ghiwargis II of Mosul renovated it. It is considered sacred by the followers of the Church of the East, the Chaldean Church, and the Syrian Orthodox Church.

The Legend of Ahikar

Syria Manuscript in the University of Cambridge

A fascinating story about an Assyrian scribe called Ahikar written perhaps a hundred years after the fall of Nineveh became popular literature of the ancient world. Evidence indicates that it was translated from the Akkadian into Aramaic, Syriac, and later to Arabic, Armenian, Greek, Slavonic, and Old Turkish. Its various versions are recognizable in the "Arabian Nights, the Koran, writings of Aesop, the Church Fathers, Greek philosophers, and the Old Testament. It was thought to have been originally written in Aramaic, but the discovery of a fifth-century BC Aramaic version on papyrus found on the Island of Elephantine (Philoe) in Egypt proves otherwise. (Cowley A., ed., 1923, 205-209)

Cowley writes, Aramaic is not the original language of the book; and though it was found in a Jewish colony, it *"shows no sign of Jewish origin."* He argues that the Jewish version may have been translated. The original composition of the story is estimated to be about 550–450 B.C. and may have been written in Babylon. The Greek philosopher Democritus, according to Clement of Alexandria, *"borrowed from Babylonian moral sayings written on a pillar [perhaps tablet] and incorporated it with his own compositions, translation of the Akikaros who no doubt is Akikar."*

Comely further notes: *"The debt of the Greeks to Babylon as well as Egypt and even to India in matters of physical science and philosophy is acknowledged."* The names 'Nadan,' and 'Nebusumiskun' mentioned in the story are clearly Assyro-Babylonian. The terms 'Illani' and 'Shamash' are of Assyrian origin and would not have been part of a Persian or Jewish vocabulary. The writer of the story undoubtedly was dedicated to preserving the legacy of the ancient Assyrians. His lavish praise of the Assyrian king in the following segment reveals such bias, when the Egyptian pharaoh asks:

"But now, O Abiqâm! Tell me, thy lord, King Sennacherib, whom is he like? And his nobles, to whom are they like?" And Haiqâr shouted with a loud voice and said: *"Be it far from me to make mention of my lord the king and thou seated on thy throne. But get up on thy feet that I may tell thee whom my lord the king is like and to whom his nobles are like."* Pharaoh was astonished by Ahikars irreverent answer. He stood up from his throne and said: *"Tell me now, that I may perceive whom thy lord the king is like, and his nobles, to whom they are like."* And Ahikar answered:

" *'My lord is the God of heaven, and his nobles are the lightning and the thunder, and when he wills the winds blow and the rain falls. And he commands the thunder, and it lightens, and rains, and he holds the sun, and it gives not its light, and the moon and the stars, and they circle not. And he commands the tempest, and it blows and the rain falls and it tramples on April and destroys its flowers and its houses.' And when Pharaoh heard this speech, he was greatly perplexed and was wroth with a great wrath, and said to him: 'O man! tell me the truth, and let me know who thou really art'." (Ibid)*

If not for the pro Assyrian sentiments of its writer, this story could have been easily written about a Persian or Babylonian king and his scribe, which would have earned the writer greater admiration and popularity among the readers of that nationality.

Hats Worn by the Highland Assyrians

A picture drawn by Layard of the highland Nestorian who worked for him, shows them wearing conical felt hats similar in shape and form to the metallic helmets worn by the ancient Assyrian soldiers, which he believed were their predecessors. The photo of the engraved image of an ancient Assyrian Calvary soldier wearing a metallic helmet was added to the side of the drawing by the author for comparison.

In response to wigram's bringing up this issue, Fiey writes: *"a lot of goodwill is, therefore, needed to compare the ancient helmet to the modern felt cap, which is shorter, flatter, and flared in the shape of a patella."* It is true that the conical shaped hats worn by the highland Assyrians are shorter than the metallic helmets worn by the ancient Assyrian soldier, because felt does not hold shape as perfectly as the metal does, therefore, creating a flared shape ending into a narrow point at the end of the felt hat would not have been easily possible. We also have to consider that the memory of these hats was passed on from one Assyrian generation to another for more than 2,000 years. They did not have factories to produce them to the exact specifications, as were the helmets. The very fact that none of the neighbors of the Assyrians wore such hats indicates that they were uniquely Assyrians. The British officer, Brigadier-Gen. Austin, the Commandant of the Assyrian refugee camp in Baquba after World War I, also likened them to the ancient Assyrian helmets. In commenting about the hats worn by the Tiyaraye Assyrians, he wrote: *"their head-dress consists of conical felt cap as depicted in frescoes of Assyrians of thousands of years ago, and which has survived to this day."* About the national dress worn by the Tiyari men at the Baquba camp, Brigadier-Gen. Austin wrote:

"Fine upstanding fellows they are, . . . their legs encased in long loose baggy trousers of a greyish hue originally, but so patched all over with bits of blue, red, green, and other colors that their pants are veritable patch work. A broad cloth, 'Kammar-band,' or waist band, is folded several times round the trunk of the body, and a short cut-away jacket of amazing colors worn over a thin cotton variegated shirt. The head-dress consists of conical felt cap as depicted in frescoes of Assyrians of thousands of years ago, and which has survived to this day." (Austin H.H., 1920)

1920 photo relatives of Mar Benjamin, the patriarch of the church of the East, including his, sister, Surma, his brothers, and their children are wearing conical and flat-top hats

ܡܘܣܦ ܠܨܘܪܬܐ ܕܡܢ ܠܥܠ ܡܢ ܦܪܨܘܦܐ ܕܦܠܫܝ ܬܘܝܠܝܐ ܀ 5

Photo is from (Yagoo Bar Malik, book, "Atturaye of Tray Plashi Tweelaye," 'Assyrians and the Two World Wars,' Tehran, Iran, 1964, 29

Head Ornament worn by the

Assyrian Women

The silver head ornament traditionally worn by the Christian Assyrian women in this 1920 photo, has striking similarity to a golden crown to the right, which was discovered in 1990 by the Iraqi archaeologists at the Ashurnasirpal's palace (750–700 BC).

The moon emblem on top of the hair jewelry worn by the Christian Assyrian women attests to its pre-Christian Origin. Brigadier-Gen. H. H. Austin, the English officer who was in command of the Baquba Refugee camp in Iraq, from 1918 to 1920, described the ornaments worn by the Assyrian women during weddings as follows: *"circlets of silver sequins [were] falling all around their heads from the head-dresses to which they were attached."* (H. H. Austin Ibid.) Though the Assyrians of the highlands, living in the fastness of the mountains north of Mosul, were poor and isolated from the rest of the world, their men wore coat and pants that were embroidered in different colors with geometric patterns similar to the embroidered tonics of the ancient Assyrian kings, but perhaps not as magnificent. Isabella Bird who in 1890 crossed the Persian border and reached the Hakkari mountain which in those days was the homeland of the independent Assyrian tribes, in her book, *Journeys in Persia and Kurdistan*, published in 1890, describes the articles of closing worn by Tiyari Assyrians as follows;

'There are 115 guests today. Among them are a number of Tiyari men, whose wild looks, combined with the splendor of their dress and arms, are of great interest. Their jackets are one mass of gold embroidery, their shirts, with hanging sleeves, are striped satin; their trousers, of sailor cut, are silk, made from the cocoons of their own silkworms, woven with broad crimson stripes on a white ground, on which is a zigzag pattern; and their handsome jackboots are of crimson leather. With their white or red peaked felt hats

[meaning conical] *and twisted silk* pagris *or head-cloths, their rich girdles, jeweled daggers, and inlaid pistols, they are very imposing.*

About Assyrians of the highland, as to when they arrived in the mountains, Fiey writes:

"Since the dawn of Christianity, there were Christians in the districts of Tiyari, Diz, Baz, Jilu, Thuma in the above highland, and Urmia located in northwest Iran, then he asks, 'is it accurate to call this ancient Assyrian?' Evidently this is not proper Assyria; therefore, a migration from Attur/Assyria to these districts is needed in order to prove the thesis: that all these people are Assyrians who fled from Assyria to these districts." (Yana, George 2008, 71)

Given evidences presented in this book, it is reasonable to believe that they indeed migrated from Assyria to these places, after the fall of Nineveh.

Surnames of The Christian Assyrians

In another attempt to disprove the Assyrian identity of the Christian Assyrians, Fiey in his L'Orient Syrien (Vol. X, 1965) wrote: *"among a list of fifty Christian Assyrian names he had compiled could not find even one that could be traced to the ancient Assyrians."*

He obviously overlooked the fact that the ancient Assyrian names often included references to the pagan deities; therefore, upon becoming Christian, their descendants had to disassociate themselves from their forefathers' religion and give their children biblical names as most other people who became Christians did. The twelfth-century patriarch of the Syrian Orthodox Church, Michael the Great, explains this issue as follows:

"When the invigorating doctrine of the Gospel appeared, these people [Christian Assyrians] adhered to it zealously. Consequently they ignored and scorned the other books where the memories of their ancient kings were written. In an ardent zeal for the religion, they set on fire all the books in which the memories of these kings

were written, because with the names of the kings and their reigns, diabolic stories of their paganism were intermingled. Thus they turned away from these books as from rotten odor. They set the books on fire to prevent the memories from being spread to their children and future generations . . ."

He quotes from the book of Acts of apostles as example: *"The believers brought the books of their fathers, and set them on fire on the feet of the apostles, books that were estimated to be worth of large sums of money."* (Chabot J.B., 1899, 446)

Assyrian Surnames on Facebook

While it is true, ancient Assyrian names that included references to the deities did not exist among the Christian Assyrians, often fragments of the ancient names have survived among them to this day. For example Hammurabi is internationally well-known name, however few in the West know that this name was pronounced in two syllables as Khamu-rabbi in its Akkadian form. The sound of 'KH' is guttural and is common in the Sematic languages, it is pronounced akin to the 'CH' in the German composer name Bach. Dozens of Assyrian families can be found on the Facebook with Khamo or Khammo, as their surname, including; Dani Khamo, who lives in New Zealand, Mary Khamo lives in Tehran, Nadia Khamo, lives in California, Ashour Khammo and so-forth.

Sharbil according to a 2nd century Syriac document known as the Acts of Sharbil was the name of a pagan priest in the city of Edessa/Urhay, who converted to Christianity. Assyrians on the Facebook with the name Sharbil includes: Sharbil Odisho in Germany, Sharbil Btrus in Syria and others.

David Gaunt, on page 363 of his book, published in 2006, titled; "Massacres, Resistance, Protectors: Muslim-Christian Relations in Eastern Anatolia during World War I," describes an interview with an older Assyrian male, who as young man, eye witnessed in 1916 the massacre of the members of the Syrian Orthodox Church, at the village of Ayn Wardo. His name was Danho Keno, Keno also spelled, as Kino is pronounced similar to the second segment of

Sharu-kenu, the Akkadian version of Sargon II, the Assyrian king, who ruled from 722 to 705 BC. Nuri Seyhan Kino, a renowned Assyrian journalist in Sweden, is an example of Assyrians with such surname. Kinu means just in both Akkadian and Syriac languages.

We should bear in mind that the Assyrians on Facebook are a tiny fraction of the total Assyrian population worldwide. Often, they can be identified by a combination of their name, their facial features, the names of their friends, their speaking of the Assyrian language, and their self-identification as such. Fiey had claimed that he could not find one Assyrian name among a list of fifty he had compiled. In response, Odisho Ghiwargis Malko provides dozens of personal names used by the Christian Assyrians in the highlands of Hakkari, before World War I, that can be traced to the ancient Assyrians. It is important to note that since then, such names have survived primarily as surnames, among the Assyrians.

Here are few examples of such names on the Facebook: Sharo is equal to the ancient Assyrian Sharau; which in Akkadian language it means king; Shammo is an abbreviated version of the name of the Assyrian queen Shammu-ramat, whom Greeks called Semiramis; Kandalo was A king of Babylon appointed by Ashurbanipal. Other names popular among the Assyrians of the highlands were Hano, Samano, Belo, and Adamo. These are the names of the ancient Assyrian kings who lived in tents during the Akkadian domination. (www.allaboutturkey.com/asur.htm)

Assyrians on the Facebook, with Samano as their surname, include Jack Samano, Sam Denkha Samano, and others. Assyrians on Facebook with Khano as surname include John Khano, in Australia, Behnam Khano, and Chritine Khano in Lebanon. Assyrians with Kandalo surnames on the Facebook include, George Kandalo and Simon Kendalo. Assyrians with the Adamo surname on the Facebook include Abboud Adamo from Tur-Abdin, Rima Adamo from Aleppo, Syria, and others. Assyrians on Facebook with Bello as surname include, Basim Bello, who is the mayor of the Assyrian town of Tel Keppe, in northern Iraq, and Nisha Bello, who lives in the Assyrian town of Algosh in Iraq.

Hedo, pronounced Haydoo, was a popular boys name among the highland Assyrians of Hakkiari. It is still the surname of some Assyrians. Assyrians on the Facebook with Hedo as their surname includes; Michel Hedo who lives in Dohuk Iraq, Jehan Hedo who lives in Chicago, and Yanoush Hedo who is a student in the university of Mosul. This may sound far-fetched but it shows the antiquity and the complexity of the Christian Assyrians history. The oldest known use of Hedo as personal name belongs to *En-hedu-ana the daughter of Sargon the Great. Her name means "Ornament of heaven"*. She is the first known author in recorded in history to be identified by her personal name.

What is astonishing is that some of these ancient names have survived, among succeeding generations of the Assyrians for as long as 4,000 years. The contemporary Assyrian surnames date back to after World War I, when identity papers were issued in the Middle Eastern countries. In most cases, the names of the grandfather or great grandfather, was registered as the family surname. 'Shalim' is another example of ancient Assyrian names that has survived to this day among the Assyrians; it was the name of the earliest ruler of the independent city-state of Ashur. According to one inscription, Shalim-ahum ruled about 1900 BC. Examples of Shalim found on Facebook include Helen Shalim Mako, Odisho Shalim Toma, Elisha Shalim, and others. Incidentally Ahum meaning brother, in later Akkadian language was written as Ahu.

The name Aho is popular among the Jacobite Assyrians. A search on the Facebook reveals dozens of Assyrians with Aho as their first, middle, or last name, such as Lahdo Aho, Ninous Aho, Aho Suryoyo Cicek, Aho Gharibo, Ilona Aho, and others.

In an ancient Assyrian tablet, "Ashur-Ushalim" is identified as an Assyrian officer of Esarhaddon in Babylon. (Honggeng GUO, JAAS, 2004, 62) A search on the Facebook for Oshalim shows dozens of Christian Assyrians bearing this as their first or last name. Examples include Oshalim Dankha, Sandra Oshalim, and Yousip Oshalim. Mannu is another Christian Assyrian name that dates back to the ancient Assyrians. For example "Mannu-ki-Ashur" was the bodyguard of the eighth-century Sargon (II), according to one cuneiform tablet.

Shaboo is another Christian Assyrian name that has pre-Christian origin. In an inscription by Nenchadrezzar, he writes: *"In A-ibur-shabu, the street of Babylon, I constructed a bridge over the canal, and made its roadway broad."* In this case, Shabu is the name of a street in Babylon. Assyrians on Facebook with Shabo as their surname include; Robert Shabo, Faye Shabo, and Daniel Shabo.

Until recently, there was a tendency among the Assyrians to abbreviate personal names into fewer syllables. For example, the pre-Christian name Esarhaddon is abbreviate as Sarhad, and Sagu is an abbreviation of Sargon. A search on Facebook reveals that Kakko or Kako is the surname of dozens of Assyrian families. It goes back to the ancient Assyrian name "Kakku-Aplo-Usur." Ivon Kakovitch, who in 2002 published a book titled "Mount Semele," a historic novel about the massacre of the Assyrians in Turkey and Iran during World War I, and in Iraq in 1933, often retold a conversation he had with a history professor at UCLA. When Ivan introduced himself as Assyrian, the professor asked: *"How could anyone believe that you are Assyrian with a Russian name?"* What the professor did not know is that Ivan's family surname was Kakku. His grandparents fled to Russia along with thousands of other Assyrians to escape massacre during World War I, and in their adopted country they had to Russianize their names for fear of deportation. Fear of persecution and discrimination often compels minorities to change their names. Long before Iran became an Islamic Republic, Jews living in that country were giving their children Persian names and speaking the Persian language in public to hide their religion and ethnicity. The above evidences shows that as more information about the ancient Assyrians become available, the kinship between the ancient and the contemporary Assyrians becomes more evident. Given such facts, Fiey's premise that Christian Assyrians after 2,600 years of trial and attributions should have been calling their children by names such as Ashur-bani-pal, Sennacherib, or Sin-shar-ishkoon, seems unreasonable. A great majority of the Persians still bear predominantly Islamic names such as Mohammed, Hassan, Husein, Abbas, Akbar, and so-forth, but no one will dare to question their Persian heritage.

Homeland of the Ancient and Christian Assyrians

It is true that due to the passage of time the memories of the Christian Assyrians about the details of their past history had faded, and their learning institutions and books have been destroyed by their persecutors. Most of their population was massacred, and the survivors were mostly driven out of their homeland. Except for few priests, most of the population no longer could read or write the Syriac language, but that did not mean they knew nothing about their past. The excavation of the ancient artifacts certainly increased their knowledge and peaked their interest in their past history. Layard's and Wigram's confirmations of their Assyrian ancestry undoubtedly increased the faint knowledge they already had about the past.

However, their ancient monasteries of Mar Mattay and Mar Behnam, dating back to the fourth century AD had been standing a short distance from Nineveh since the early centuries of Christianity, and they observed a three-day fast, called Baoota d' Ninevaye, or "the wish of the Ninevites," a remarkable tribute to their ancient forefathers, who according to the Old Testament book of Jonah were forgiven and saved from destruction. Mar Ephraim's hymns about the Repentance of Nineveh were recited in their churches every year.

They had lived near Nineveh, for the last 2,500 years. A statement by the twentieth-century British officer Banister Soane who traveled to northern Iraq attests to this fact. He wrote:"

"Next morning early we arose and loaded our animals, and took a course almost due south. First, we re-crossed the historic brook Kauther, passed under the shadow of Nebi Yunis mound [where the ruins of Nineveh were excavated], upon whose sides is a large village, and had before us a great rolling plain, entering which we were upon the ground of ancient Assyria proper. To our left ran a range of low hills, and in their folds were many villages, dull *collections of mud-huts half-buried in the ground. But they contain two races whose history is full of interest. No Mussulmen (Muslim) inhabited this plain; there are but Chaldeans [Assyrians] and Yezidis, those "Devil-Worshippers."* (Soane, 1912, 100)

The villages Soane wrote about in 1912 AD had been inhabited by the Christian Assyrians since the early centuries of Christianity, and even before that by their forefathers. Some of the towns and villages they inhabit are still called by the names the ancient Assyrians gave them. For example, the Assyrian town of Karmales was called Kar-Mullissi,during the ancient Assyrian time. The town of Algush or Elkosh mentioned in the book of Nahum of the Old Testament is still there, together with its predominantly Assyrian population.

Chapter 6

Nineveh After the Fall

General knowledge in the West about what happened to Nineveh after the Assyrian defeat is undoubtedly summarized by the nineteenth-century American Robert W. Roger, in the following statement:

> "the waters of heaven, or from the overflowing river made the soft clay into a covering over the great palaces and their records. The winds bore seeds into the mass, and a carpet of grass covered the mounds, and stunted trees grew out of them. Year by year the mounds bore less and less resemblance to the site of a city, until no trace remained above ground of the magnificence that once had been. In 401 BC a cultivated Greek leading homeward, the fragment of his gallant army of 10,000 men passed by the mounds and never knew that beneath them lay the palaces of the great Assyrian kings."

This perception according to Leick, was due to the fact that ; "for centuries the main source for stories about the city, Nineveh, was doomed to be punished, a city the Hebrew God wanted to see brought low, to have even the memory erased in retaliation for what the Assyrians had done to the Jews." (Leick Gwendolyn, 2001, p. 221).

The dismantling of the Assyrian palaces by the nineteenth-century archaeologists, and shipping their components to the Louver and the British Museums, destroyed the physical structures in the Assyrian palaces of Nineveh, Kalkh, and Dur-Sharukeen which had survived. It further accentuated the impression that all things belonging to the ancient Assyrians had been obliterated. However, a picture drawn by Layard during his excavations in Nimrod (Kalkh) indicates that the walls of the buildings, the sculptured slabs, and the winged bulls guarding the gates were still standing as they had been before 612 BC. *"Layard, an astute observer wrote: some colossal statues which had toppled and even shattered were brought down by convulsion of nature, and not by human hand."* (Brackman Arnold C., 1978, 238)

At one mound alone in Nineveh, excavators cleared clean seventy-one palace halls and nearly two miles of the relief scenes that were carried away. Even the Amherst College of Massachusetts received six reliefs in 1853, which were *"sawed off the face of the alabaster slabs from the palace of Ashur-nasirpal. One of the pieces shows the king holding a bow and libation bowl, flanked by two winged genies who are fertilizing the sacred date palm."* (Kubie Nora Benjamin, 1964, 307)

Even before and after the excavations of the ancient Assyrian cities by Layard, fanatic Muslims who considered the ancient objects the work of the devil destroyed the structures and artifacts when they were found accidentally.

"In 1852 an Armenian Catholic priest reported that a colossal statue had been discovered by men plowing a field at Kouyunjik by

the farmers. *Devout Muslims ordered it to be broken, as they do with everything else that is brought to light."* (Brackman, 1978, 336) James Wellard writes:

"There are a number of reasons for lack of interest in the antiquities of Mesopotamia, the most important one is inaccessibility to the actual sites of the cities where they were located, and the disappointment travelers must feel when visiting the sites but not seeing what they had come to see. The physical remains of Nineveh and Babylon are nothing more than mounds of rubble, left behind by thousands of unskilled workers who with picks and shovels dug for the great treasure hunts of the nineteenth century. By comparison, the lover of ruins has all the imposing or beautiful monuments of Egypt, Greece and Rome to stimulate his imagination and to satisfy visually his historical interest." (Wellard James, 1974, 210).

It is true that cities of Ashur, Nineveh, Kalkhu, and Dur-Sharukeen were ravaged and their inhabitants were partly massacred, some were taken prisoner and others escaped, as was often the case during the ancient wars. The cities of Harran, Arbil, Arapahu which is presently called Kirkuk, Tikrit, Nasibin, and other towns and villages in the region suffered to a lesser extent. There is no reason to believe that inhabitants of these cities after the fall were not Assyrian since they spoke the same language, had the same culture and religion, and were as much Assyrians as those who lived in the cities of Nineveh, Ashur, and Kalkh.

Due to a lack of a centralized authority after the fall, inhabitants of each city preferred to identify themselves by the name of their town because it also described their devotion to its patron deity. For example, Harranians were known by the name of their city up to the medieval times, not because they were not Assyrian, but because of the peculiar nature of the Mesopotamian religion, which mandated that each city have its exclusive patron god. Ashur was the patron god of the city of Ashur; Ishtar was the patron deity of Nineveh and Arbil; Sin, the moon god, was the patron god of Harran. Since Ashuraya (Assyrian) also meant worshiper of the god Ashur, inhabitants of other cities had to be careful not to imply that they were residents of that city, were worshipping Ashur. Even at the present time, clergies of the Chaldean and Syrian Orthodox churches refrain by identifying their people as Assyrians, for fear that may imply that they are members of the Church of the East.

Absence of published information in the Western literature, about what happened to the ancient Assyrians and their cities after the fall, it has contributed to the myth of their demise, which in turn has contributed to the doubt about the identity of the Christian Assyrians. A search for "Nineveh," or "Nineveh after the fall," on the Internet yields non-religious websites writing about how great the ancient city was before the fall, but provide no information after the fall. On the other hand, Jewish and Christian websites compete against each other to declare how wicked Nineveh was, and how it was destroyed as Nahum had prophesized. Archaeological discoveries in recent decades attest to the fact that Nineveh was inhabited after the fall. Historical documents in Syriac language show, that during the Christian era, it was an important Christian Assyrian city, or town. According to Joan Oates:

"*Nineveh, which was considered by them [classical authors], to have been a ruin after **612 BC**, we know to have been the site of a considerable city during both the Seleucid and Parthian periods.*" (Oates, Joan, 1979, p.142) Excavations at the Parthian Nineveh, in 1852, revealed several second-century buildings and burial places, including a palace. Gold masks and funerary items were found in some graves. The general plan of the palace appears to be Neo-Assyrian, while certain features such as the iwān and pitch vaulted brick walls had Parthian features.
http://www.iranologie.com/history/arsacid/chapter5.html

Evidences indicate that Nineveh may have been an important town of the independent state of Adiabene. Roman pottery, coins, and military equipment found in Nineveh indicate that it may have briefly became part of the eastern Roman Empire. Greek records indicate that *"Apollonius of Tyana, the Hellenist, strategos epistates of Nineveh at first century AD had a secretary and acolyte, known as Damis of Nineveh . . ."* Apollonius was said to have seen at Nineveh the statue of a Barbarian type goddess *"with little horns projecting from her temples and just breaking through."* (Burn, Robert, 1962, 109)

Ishtar, the goddess of love, and war, is often pictured with lions, stars, and a horned helmet. The statue he had seen was undoubtedly within the Ishtar temple, which attests to the survival of the Assyrians, and their worship of the ancient religion. (Dalley Stephanie, 1993, 134) An inscription found in the temple of Nabu in Nineveh represents a dedication on behalf of Apollonius. A statue dedicated to the Hermez (Mercury) dated about 200 B.C. is further indication of the Greek's presence in the city. (Oates, David, 1968, 59)

Two significant finds in Sennacherib's palace indicate that it was in use well into the Christian era. The statue of Heracles Epittrapezios, dated about second century AD was found by Rassam in that palace. (Dalley, 1993, 138) A lintel of the doorway, dated back to the Parthian period, was discovered by George Smith on the original floor of the hall in the same building. (Dalley p. 138) Coins were found in either Nimrod or Nineveh. Precious metals were used as raw material for melting and casting ingots. One hoard contained metallic objects such as vase handles, rings, Athenian coins, Alginate, Thracian, and Macedonian coins. (Conway John, 1963, 369-370) According to Tacitus, in the winter of 50 AD, the forces of Carenes crossed the river Tigris, entered Adiabene, and *"captured the city of Ninos, the most ancient capital of Assyria,"* prior to waging war against the Parthian king Gotarzes, on behalf of Meherdates the contender to the throne. (Tacitius Cornelius, 1952, 112)

Beginning in the second century AD, Christian churches, monasteries, and convents dotted the plains of northern Mesopotamia. J. M. Fiey, in his "Assyrie Chretienne," has documented the histories of churches and monasteries located in central Assyria during the Christian era. It is important to note that these edifices belonged to the Syriac-speaking Assyrians, and not Parthians, who spoke the Arsacid Pahlavi and Pahlavanik, a Western Middle Iranian language. Some of these structures built in the fourth century AD have survived the persecutions of the Persians, the invasion of the Arabs, the brutality of the Mongols, and the destruction of the Tatars, as did the descendants of those who built them. A map by Fiey shows dozens of convents and monasteries in the plain of Nineveh that were built in the early centuries of Christianity.

Monasteries owned land, villages, and herds of cattle; as such they functioned as important economic institutions. For example the monastery of Abraham, in Addiabene, owned 689 houses, grain fields, cattle, mills, and vineyards. Dair Mar Michael — located in the Plain of Nineveh. "According to one tradition, was established in mid-fourth century AD by Mar Michael, a student of Mar Ogin. Dair Rabban Hurmiz — built in 640 AD is located thirty-four miles north of Nineveh, about two miles northeast of the Assyrian town of Alqosh. Its construction has been credited to the Ninevite prince who was fascinated with the miraculous healing powers of Saint Rabban Hurmiz. During the time of patriarch Yeshu-yahab II (628-644 AD) Dair Rabban Hurmiz became an academy for religious learning a tradition that continued until Tamerlane attacked it. The existence of Nineveh in the fourth century AD is attested to by documents of the Malabar Christians, as reported by the fifteenth-century Portuguese priests. Accordingly when the Metropolitan of Urhay/Edessa learned in a dream about the plight of the Malabar Christians, he asked the fourth-century Catholics of the East to help them . . . Priests, deacons, and ordinary people were sent to invigorate Christianity in south Indian coastal state of Kerala, among them were residents of Nineveh. Even today, the Khnanayan members of the Syrian Orthodox church trace their roots back to the seventy-two families who traveled from Mesopotamia to India in AD 345 to do missionary work. They brought with them Bible and their Syriac language. Since then until now, the liturgy of this church and its Mass, have been celebrated in the Syriac language.

Wiesehofer writes: *"From the fourth century on, there is a growing number of references to relations between Iran and India, among which the mission of the Eastern Syrians (Assyrians), by sea and by land, is especially striking."* (Wiesehofer Josef, 1969, 196)

The last war between the Persian and Roman Armies was fought in AD 627 at the vicinity of Nineveh. Yeshu-yahab II, who was the Bishop of the city (627–637), fearing being captured by the Romans and held for ransom, fled to his estates in the hill-country beyond the reach of the invading forces and waited there for the storm to blow over. (Young William G. 1974, 87) When Yeshu-yahab II became Patriarch of the Church of the East (628–644) he was sent by the Persian Queen Puran-dokt, (630-631) the daughter of Khosro Parviz, as ambassador to the Byzantine court, to negotiate peace between the two countries. Koriakos, metropolitan of Nisibin, Gabriel from Karkha' D' Bet Suluk (today's Kirkuk), and Paul Metropolitan of Chadib accompanied him. (Malech 1910, 216)

Bishops of Nineveh

The region known as Nineveh was presided over by a long list of bishops from 554 to the late ninth century. Mar Emmeh, the Bishop of Nineveh was elected Patriarch of the Church of the East and served in that position from AD 644 to 647. Ishu-Yahav was the bishop of Nineveh from 627 to 637. Isaac of Nineveh (630–700) served only five months as bishop of that city. A fourteenth-century tablet found in the Assyrian town of Karamles (a village near Mosul), provides a list of thirty five names of clergies who served as bishops in that region. The locations or date of their service is not given, but they are identified as "they were from our country." Fiey asserts that they were bishops of Nineveh. (Yana George, 2008, 45)

Reports of Travelers

When Arab geographer Al Masudi visited Nineveh in 943 AD, he described it as a complex of ruins in the middle of which there are several villages and farms, "It was to these settlements that God sent Jonah" he wrote. (Fagan, Brian, 1971, 18) This undoubtedly echoed the sentiments of the Christian Assyrians. Some of the better known Assyrian villages of Nineveh at that time were Takshur, mentioned by Bar Awraya; Tarra D' Nineveh [Gate of Nineveh]; Ba Gabbari [the Braves], the birth place of Patriarch Ishoo Barnon, located between the walls of Nineveh; and Mosul, mentioned by Yagut in 1220. In addition, Bori was where a beautiful church was built in the seventh century—it was consecrated by Mar Yokhanan Metropolitan of Adiabene; and Gorba was a Jacobite Assyrian village. (Fiey 1959, 488-493)

Though many Europeans visited the Holy Land, during the medieval period, none dared enter Mesopotamia (called Al-Iraq following its invasion by the Arabs). Consequently Western knowledge of Mesopotamia was mostly limited to what they had read in the Old Testament. Rabbi Benjamin, one of the earliest Western travelers to the Northern Mesopotamia, arrived from Tudela, Spain, in 1166 to visit the Jewish community in Mosul. He saw Nineveh during his stay. By then, the Arabs had occupied Mesopotamia for over five hundred years, and in the course of that period they had inevitably altered the political, religious, economic, and social nature of the once predominantly Christian Assyrian region.

Rabbi Benjamin noted in his log that Mosul was connected to *"Nineveh by means of a bridge. Nineveh is in ruins, but amid the ruins are villages and hamlets. The extent of the city may be determined by the walls, which extend forty farsangs."* Some seven centuries following the Rabbi's visit, Layard unearthed the southwestern palace of Sennacherib under the Kuinjik mound. In ruins or not, Assyrians had continued to live in Nineveh. (Fagan Brian M., 1971,17)

The Barber geographer Ibn-Battuta, who traveled to northern Mesopotamia in the fourteenth century, acknowledged the existence of Nineveh and wrote:

"There too is the hill of Nabi Yunus (prophet Jonah, upon whom be peace), and about a mile from it, the spring called by his name. It is said that he commanded his followers to purify themselves in it . . . In its vicinity is a large village, near which is a ruined site said to be the site of the city known as Nineveh, the city of 'Yunus.' The remains of the encircling walls are still visible, and the position of the gates that were in it are clearly seen." (Fagan 1971, Ibid.)

Ibn-Battuta also noted that the Nabi Yunus mosque at Nineveh was once a Christian church before being confiscated by the Arabs, as they had done with other Christian religious centers. This edifice still stands today. According to Wigram it was once the cathedral of the independent patriarch of Nineveh (Fagan, 1971,17) By the eighteenth century, all traces of the early Christian, and ancient Assyrian history in Mesopotamia, were obliterated. Western travelers interested in locating the site of Nineveh had to search for it. Some time between the 1750s and the 1760s, Danish geographer Carsten Niebuhr was led by a native to its location. He wrote:

"I was shown a village on a large hill, which is called Nunia by the Arabs [a corrupted form of Nineveh]. Another hill in this vicinity is called 'Kalla Nunia,' or the castle of Nineveh . . . I also was shown the walls of Nineveh, which I had not noticed in [first] passing through, thinking them a line of hills." (Starr Chester G., 1973, 152)

In 1812 Claudius Rich (the appointed resident of the British Tea Company in Baghdad) reported that across from Mosul, atop of the Nabi Yunus mound, there still stood a village called "Ninouah," a name resembling that of the ancient city. However he was blocked from exploring it by the fanatic Muslim guardians of the "Tomb of Jonah."

Arab's interest in this site resulted from their mistaken belief that the coffin inside the church contained the body of the prophet Jonah. However, the Assyrian writer Bar Saliba, a decade or two before Ibn-Battuta, had identified the person buried in the site as patriarch Hannan Yeshua of the church of the East, who was elected to that office during the caliphate of Abd 'ool-Melek ibn Merwan, c. AD 686. He wrote:

"Hanan-Yeshua resided in the convent of the prophet Jonah, which is situated on the western side of the wall of Nineveh facing the eastern gates of Mosul, and the river Tigris separates the cities. When he died, he was buried here, in a coffin made of ebony . . ." (Badger, 1850, notes, 87 DD)

Following Layard's excavation of the Koyunjik mound of Nineveh, Rassam looked into the possibility of limited exploration under the Nabi Yunus mound, but fanatic guardians of Jonah's mosque frustrated his intentions. About the name of this mound, Rassam wrote:

"The site of ancient Nineveh has never been lost in the memory of the inhabitants of Mosul, because both tradition and history indicate, Koyunjik, and Nabee Yonis, as localities, where the Assyrian monarchs reigned with unlimited power. Nabee Yunus, a mound about half a mile from Koyunjik, contains a mosque dedicated to Jonah, wherein is shown the shrine of the prophet. It was formerly a Chaldean [Assyrian] church . . . Though the natives of the country commonly call the mound "Nabee Yonis" after the prophet Jonah, yet, officially, it is styled "Nenweh." This I learned when I entered into an agreement with the guardians of the mosque to excavate there. They merely mentioned the word "Nenweh" in the document; and when I asked them why they omitted the common name of "Nabee Yunus," they said that, that was the only name they could use officially." (Rassam Hormuzed, 1897, 304)

The fanatic guardians of Jonah's mosque undoubtedly knew better than everyone else that their forefathers had confiscated the area from the Christian Assyrians; therefore, for centuries, they were posted there to discourage Assyrians from reclaiming it. It was not a fluke, nor it was due to the Arabs, that 2,400 years after its famous destruction, a village called Nineveh still existed on top of the ruins of the ancient city. Despite the twists and turns of history, it was the Christian Assyrians, and their pagan forefathers who despite all odds had managed to keep the memories of Nineveh alive. This was only possible because of their devotion to their ancient Assyrian ancestors.

Information attesting to the survival of Assyrians into Christianity to this day, presented in this book, has been compiled from hard-to-find, well-documented historical sources. Deniers of the Christian Assyrian identity and history have not acknowledged these facts, perhaps they had no knowledge of them, or have intentionally ignored them. The few that have mentioned them have often misrepresent their meaning, to imply that they do not mean what they seem to say.

While Jews and Christians around the world have celebrated

the Nahum's proclamation about the destruction of Nineveh, Christian Assyrians have observed a special yearly fast known as Baoota d' Ninevaye (The Wish of the Ninevites), to declare that God did not destroyed Nineveh, in fact he saved it. The other two Christian communities that have observed this fast are the Armenians and the Coptic Church, both of whom were in close contact with the Syrian Orthodox Church and were greatly influenced by it.

Assyrian Fast of Nineveh

The three-days fast known as the "Rogation (asking for God's mercy), of the Ninevites" or "Baoota d' Ninevaye," which begins on Monday of the third week preceding Lent, is based on the Old Testament Story of Jonah who was sent to warn the inhabitants of Nineveh to repent lest God destroys their city. While the rest of world has considered this chapter as an interesting legend, the Christian Assyrians have treated it as an important biblical truth to be incorporated into their religious tradition, perhaps because it is the only Assyrian friendly book in the Old Testament that they could claim as their own.

Mar Ephraim (306–373 AD) who composed twelve homilies about the repentance of Nineveh asserts that the fast was observed as some form of community event at his time. In comparing how his community observed this event with how the ancient Assyrians fasted to please God he writes: "When compared with that repentance,

This of ours is like a dream;
In the presence of that supplication,
This of ours is but a shadow."
(Burgess, 1853, XXX)

Sometime along the way, the fast seems to have been abandoned, but it was reinstituted in the sixth century by the Church of the East during a period of plague that ravaged the land. The Metropolitan of Beth-Garme and Sowrishu, the Bishop of Nineveh, agreed that a fast similar to that of the ancient Ninevites would help to end the period of plague. They shared their idea with the patriarch Ezekiel, and he wrote letters throughout the East urging all to observe a three-day fast that would please God, as did the prayers of the ancient Ninevites, and put an end to the plague. When they had done this, God heard them and banished the plague. Burges writes:

> *"In Edessa, after the church service, Ephraim, accompanied by the musical performance of a choir of young persons he had trained, orated his hymns to deepen the emotions of penitence. The homily would approximately occupy two hours of recitation."*

Some of Mar Ephraim's hymns about the story of Jonah and the salvation of Nineveh were incorporated in Khodra, the liturgy of the Church of the East, by the seventh-century Isho-yahv. Since then, they have been recited in the Church of the East sermons, during the Fast of Ninevites.

The story of Jonah played such a crucial role in the psyche of the Christian Assyrians that their missionaries even took it with them to China. According to Martin Palmer; in 1998 a Pagoda, called Dagin, was discovered in China. It was built by the Nestorian Missionaries in 640 AD, at the Chang-an, Shaanxi Province, it included a church and monastery. Here also was found an artistic work, depicting a nativity scene (the birth of Jesus), side by side with the image of Jonah, sitting beneath the gourd tree, outside Nineveh.

Critics like John Joseph have questioned the national aspect of this fast by stating that Armenians and Egyptian Christians also observe a similar event. Given the considerable influence of the Syrian Orthodox Church on Armenian Christianity, it should not surprise us that they learned to honor this tradition which they call, not the Fast of Ninevite, but the "St. Sarkis Fast." The same can be said about the Copts who had close fraternal ties with the Syrian Orthodox Church of Antioch to an extent that four priests of Assyrian origin served as the Patriarchs of Alexandria, based on cultural and religious exchange. The tenth-century Anba Afrem Ben Zar is credited with having introduced the "Fast of the Ninevite" called "Jonathan's Fast" in the calendar of the Coptic Church. (Dolabani, 1930, 62-64)

In appreciation for Anba's fasting during the "Hercules' Friday," Copts agreed among themselves to honor the "Jonathan's Fast" as a gesture of solidarity with their Assyrian Patriarch. They have continued to observe this event to the present. (Ibid.) Honest observance in this fast had to have been predicated on the belief that Assyrians and Nineveh survived their famous defeat, and had ultimately became Christians. Anything less would have rendered this fast as an obvious farce, which would have been rejected by all.

Badger, who spent few years living among the Eastern Assyrians, wrote that Jonah's mission was common topic in the Syrian (Assyrian) church which was an important part of their liturgical services. Donald Atwater writes that Chaldeans observe the Ninevites Fast *"with special vigor, and the whole of the paslters is recited in the office on each of its days; a Chaldean priest tells me he has known lay people to go the whole of those three days without any food at all."* (Atwater, 1945, 199-209)

One can also argue that if the Ninevites fast was nothing more than ordinary religious practice, then why it was not observed by the Roman Catholic Church and other Christian denominations? Faith in the power of this fast depended on knowledge that it had helped the survival of the ancient Assyrians. In the Old Testament, Jonah has been credited with having saved Nineveh from ruin. God ordered him to travel to Nineveh and warn its inhabitants about their impending destruction unless they ceased their sinful ways. Jonah, who considered Assyrians the enemies of Jews, was unwilling to help them survive. He boarded a ship and hid in its dark hold, but a frightening storm sent by God nearly sank the ship. When the captain and the crew learned that Jonah was responsible for the storm, they threw him into the raging sea, where a whale, according to the God's wish, swallowed him.

Eventually Jonah obeyed the Lord and went to Nineveh, a city so large that it took him three days to walk through. Jonah began walking through the city, and proclaimed "in forty days Nineveh will be destroyed." The people of Nineveh believed God's message. They decided that everyone should fast, and all the people from the great to the least put on sackcloth to show that they had repented, Consequently, God forgave Nineveh and its inhabitants. Unhappy about having helped save Nineveh and its inhabitants from destruction, Jonah sat sulking outside the city walls under the shade of a plant. When God caused the plant to wilt and die, Jonah protested bitterly. God replied: *"This plant grew up in one night and disappeared the next. You did not do anything for it, and you did not make it grow, yet you feel sorry for it! How much more should I have pity on Nineveh."*

Mar Ephraim (306–373 AD) in his homilies about the Repentance of Nineveh chides Jonah for being unhappy about the redemption of Nineveh and its inhabitants, He writes:

"Son of Mattay how has the city of Nineveh
Offended you that you awaited its dying?
But if you are merciful with the faithless,
Why is your anger poured out upon penitent
[of the Ninevites]?
"He [God] sent him [Jonah] to land; he fled to sea.
He sent him to Nineveh; he boarded a ship.
To Nineveh He sent him to awaken the peoples.
He slept on the ship; the peoples awakened him!
On the ship they asked him, 'Who are you and whose?'
In Nineveh they believed him without questioning."

Ephraim Asks:

"Who made known to the Ninevites
These hidden divine mysteries?
That fasting was able to remit
The stern decree of God?
Jonah did not give them this information,
For he feared lest they should be pardoned." (Burges Henry, 1853, 59)

Commenting on Ephraim's ninth homily, where he accuses Jonah of deceiving the Ninevites, Burges points to the differences of perception about Jonah, between the Syriac speaking people of Mesopotamia, and Christians of the West. Burges writes:

"If the Syrian Christians derived all their knowledge about this subject from the Book of Jonah, they would not have been prepared to hear him so gravely charged with lying, and their feeling of reverence would have been shocked by statements of this homily. But, on the other hand, if what Ephraim related were already known to them, no different effect would be produced on them by it than is upon ourselves by the faults which are recorded in the Bible; they would merely think Jonah as worse man than we do." (Burgess Henry, 1853, 116)

There is clearly pro-Assyrian and pro-Nineveh feelings in Ephraim's homilies that pleased the people for whom they were written. Ephraim's homilies continue beyond the story of Jonah to praise the righteousness of the Ninevites after their salvation. One cannot help but feel that he is striking back at the Assyrian bashing so prevalent in the Old Testament. In his sixth hymn, according to Ephraim, Jonah bemoans the moral decay of his own people compared to that of the saved Assyrians.

*"He looked on Ashur and greatly despised
Jerusalem, inflated with arrogance.
Behold! the impure women had become modest.
But the daughters of his people were defiled
He saw the possessed ones in Nineveh
were changed, and had learned the truth;
He saw the prophets in Zion,
were deceivers and full of falsehood."* (Burges, 1853, 83)

Ephraim ends his twelfth Hymn by writing: *"Blessed be he who loves the righteous, who multiplied penitent in Ashur."* Ephraim's belief that the Christians of Mesopotamia were the descendants of the ancient Assyrians is evident in another hymn in which he imagines the Lullaby Virgin Mary may have sang, to the Child Christ, after the Wise Men departed. His pride in his Assyrian identity is evident in his praise of the ancient Assyrians wanting to worship the Christian God. Ephraim's "repentance of Nineveh" hymns are as much patriotic as those of the Jewish writers of the Old Testament who have savaged the Assyrians and the Babylonians for their mistreatment of their people. He was also aware of the history and the origin of the cities where the

Christian Assyrians lived; therefore, there was no reason for him to doubt their ancient heritage. In his commentary on Genesis 10:8-12, he credits Nimrod with having been the founder of Babylonian and the Assyrian cities. He continues in chapter IV to describe how the King of Assyria advised his army and his people to believe in Jonah's message, by these words:

"But now, if we should conquer,
It will be greater than all our triumphs;
And since I have entered into the ranks
In wars and dangers,
I will now take the precedence
In this mighty Battle.
Arm yourselves, then, like me,
And advance, my beloved soldiers!"

Henry Burgess in a footnote writes: "the excellent qualities ascribed by Ephraim to the king of Assyria has no foundation in historical truth." (Burges, 1853, 64 fn) This comment illustrates how people's judgment is usually shaped by their existing biases. Burgess casts a blind eye on the atrocities committed by the biblical personalities, but he is quick to condemn the Assyrian kings. Ephraim, who has read the same Old Testament, refuses to judge the Assyrian kings unkindly. Since his homilies were sang in public, his audiences undoubtedly believed as he did; they could not have accepted or identified with the "Fast of the Nineties" as a suitable religious practice if they were to judge the Assyrian kings as harshly as Burgess did.

"King remained in trouble;
And diligently inspected the city;
He decreed a fast for his camp,
And supplied it with the armor of truth;
He called his regiments to prayer,
For that was their only safety."
(Burgess, 1853, 88)

A statement added to the third volume of the Roman edition of Ephraim's works again demonstrates the contrast between the

Western Christians view about what happened to the ancient Assyrians and that of the Syriac speaking people. Burges writes: "in the Latin version of this homily, from a Greek translation, there is the following addition, of very doubtful genuineness:

"And those who in the first instance repented through the preaching of Jonah were saved; but those who came after them and became worse than their ancestors, altogether perished, as saith the prophet Jeremiah."

Burgess adds: *"there is no such expression or implication in Ephraim's hymns."* It would have been impossible for the people of Mesopotamia to believe that the Ninevites were destroyed by God, since they lived over or Near Nineveh's ruins and they considered themselves descendants of its ancient inhabitants. Others who knew about the existence of Assyrians and Nineveh before and during the Christian centuries could not, in good conscious, claim that they no longer existed. The fourt-century Saint Augustine, who seems to have been one of them, correctly explained the contradiction between the existence of Nineveh during the Christian era versus Nahum's prophecy, stated, *"the city was destroyed but not the people."*

No Jewish or Christian people have treated the story of Jonah as seriously and reverently as Assyrians and their writers have done. It is a fallacy to claim that these people had no emotional investment in believing that they were the descendants of the Ninevites. Ghiwargis Catholicos, (patriarch of the Church of the East 681–684) wrote Hymns, anthems, and a litany for the Fast of the Ninevites, as did Youkhana D' bet Rabban, who wrote poems about this subject.

Patricia Crone and Michael Cook in their book "Hagarism" wrote:

"In order to clear the Assyrian kings off their Biblical disrepute, Christian Assyrians first had to sanctify them. They did it by stating that:

Sardana the son of Sennacherib, thirty second king of Assyria after Belos, and ruler of the third of the inhabited world, [who] submitted to the monotheistic message of Jonah and instituted the Ninevite fast which saved Nineveh from destruction: and the fast having saved the Assyrians from the wrath of God in the past, it was reinstituted by Sabrisho of Karkha de Bet Selokh to save them from a plague a thousand years later. Secondly, the conversion of Izates II of Adiabene to Judaism was reedited as the conversion of Narsai of Assyria to Christianity. In other words, the Assyrians were monotheists before Christ and, Christians after him, and the past therefore led on in the present without a break. Thus the history of Karkha de Bet Selokh began with the Assyrian kings and ends with the Assyrian martyrs: Sargon founded it and the martyrs made it 'a blessed field' for Christianity. Likewise in the seventh century before Christ all the world stood in awe of Sardana, and in the seventh century after Christ the saints took his place as the 'sun of Attur' and the 'glory of Nineveh'." (Cook Corne, 1980, 57-58)

Here we have another example of how people with different biases read the same book but come to different conclusions. When the Western Christians read the Old Testament, because they did not have the same information as the Christian Assyrians did, they wholeheartedly believed that Nineveh and its inhabitants were destroyed, however Christian Assyrians who read the same Old Testament were not willing to do so, because they considered themselves the descendent of the ancient Assyrians. The fact that they lived near Nineveh, or even over its ruins, underscored this belief.

Chapter 7

Survival of the Assyrian Cities

The City of Mosul

Mosul is located across from the ruin of Nineveh, it was probably built on the site of an earlier Assyrian fortress. When Xenophon passed through Assyria in 401 BC, he mentioned the name of Mespila. He wrote that it was near a large undefended fortification. His description indicates that it was the city of Nineveh. Since Mespila was not mentioned in the Assyrian inscriptions, we have to conclude that it was settled after the fall of Nineveh. During the Christian centuries, the city of Mosul often has been mentioned side by side with Nineveh. In January 639 the Arab armies after occupying Southern Mesopotamia branched out toward the north and took possession of the fortresses of Mosul and Nineveh. They made Mosul their Early Islamic garrison city. While the precise configuration of Early Islamic settlement in Mosul is not known, the existence of the early Assyrian churches indicate that the city historically has had a large Assyrian population. As Mosul grew larger, it overtook Nineveh, and in 651, together with Nineveh, was made an ecclesiastic province of the Church of the East. By the eighth century AD it became the capital city of northern Mesopotamia and became a trade center because of its strategic position on the caravan route between India, Persia, and the Mediterranean. Mosul's chief export was cotton, and today's word "muslin" is derived from the name of the city. In later centuries, a number of independent dynasties ruled Mosul. It reached its political zenith under the Zangid dynasty (AD 1127–1222), and the rule of Sultan Badr ad-Din Lu'lu' between 1222–59. The city at that time became famous for its metalworking school and where miniature painting flourished, but the region's prosperity ended during the Mongol's rule.

In the twelfth century, Rabbi Benjamin was one of the earliest western travelers to Mesopotamia. He noted that Mosul was connected to Nineveh by a bridge. Nineveh was in ruins, but there were villages and hamlets in its vicinity. The population of Mosul during the last few decades has been primarily Kurds and Arabs. Before the 2003 U.S. invasion of Iraq, Mosul had a large minority of Christian Assyrians, but since then, because of ongoing terrorism against them, most have abandoned the city.

Historically, Mosul has had a great number of churches, but during the periods of conflict, they were either confiscated by the Muslims, turned into mosques, or were destroyed. Nonetheless, following are some of the ancient Assyrian churches that have survived in Mosul up to the present time.

The Mosque of Prophet Younis, Jonah, located at the left bank of Tigris River on top of the "Nabi Yunis," Jonah's mound, originally was an Assyrian church that was confiscated by the Muslims. According to the archaeologists, its original location was first an ancient Assyrian temple. It became a place for fire worshipers, then a Christian monastery, later a church was built on top of it. Arabs believe that the mosque contains the prophet Jonah's shrine, but according to Assyrian writers, the shrine belongs to an Assyrian Patriarch whose name was Yonan, or Jonah. A winged statue dating back to the ancient Assyrian period was found near the mosque during the period of excavation and restoration.

The Church of Al-Tahira was built as a monastery in 300 AD, but was converted to a church in 1600 AD. It originally belonged to the Church of the East, but in the nineteenth century it was taken over by the Chaldean Church.

The Church of St. Thomas (Mar Toma is one of the oldest churches in Mosul. It is named after St. Thomas the Apostle. It was founded some time before AD 770, its name is mentioned in a correspondence with the Abbasid caliph al-Mahdi.

The Church of St. Peter and Shimon al Safa is known as the Church of two Apostles, i.e, Peter and Paul. It was founded in the ninth century and is considered a very important church due to its archeological value. It lies five meters below the street level.

The Church of Mar Petion dates to before the tenth century and is situated three meters below the street level. It has been destroyed and reconstructed several times.

The Mar Hudeni Church was named after Mar Ahudemmeh (Hudeni) Maphrian of Tikrit who was martyred in AD 575. Mar Hudeni Church as served the Tikriti Assyrian community since the tenth century, when they were driven out that due to persecution and moved to Mosul. It is situated seven meters below the street level. It was first reconstructed in 1970. Next to it, there is a well that some believe has healing power to cure epileptics.

The Monastery of St. George (Mar Ghiwargis) is located to the north of the city and is visited annually during spring by the pilgrims. In 1931 a modern church was built over it, but much of its original plan was destroyed. What remains is a marble doorframe with a Syriac inscription and two niches that date to the thirteenth or fourteenth century. It is important to mention that since the 2003 United States invasion of Iraq, about seventy Assyrian churches in Iraq have been bombed, and most of the Assyrian population of Mosul and Baghdad were terrorized and driven out of their cites. According to an article titled "Muslim Persecution of Christians," published on October tenth 2012, on www.aina.org, Mosul, before the United State invasion of Iraq in 2003 had a population of 75,000 Christians, but now only 25,000 of them remain. The rest were driven out of the city and the country because of terror attacks against the community. Christian homes have been set on fire, their cars are bombed, and they receive threatening letters ordering them to leave Iraq or be kidnapped or killed.

Assyrian Survival in Harran

Harran had been part of Assyria for almost a millennium before the fall of the empire. Its inhabitants spoke the same language and shared a common religion and culture as Assyrians, yet contemporary writers have been reluctant to acknowledge them as Assyrian. As if with the fall of the military and political system, its inhabitants suddenly lost their national and cultural identity and became people of unknown origin. Despite a history spanning several thousand years, the city is mostly remembered as where the Hebrew Patriarch Abraham passed through on his way to Canaan.

Following the defeat of the Assyrian Army at Nineveh in 612 BC, Ashur-Uballit II and his troop escaped westward to Nisibin (Assyrian Nassibini), now within the borders of Turkey, and from there they went to Harran, where he assumed the title "King of Assyria" and made it the new Assyrian capital. With the help of the of the Egyptian army Ashur Uballit was able to defend Harran against the combined Babylonian-Mede attacks, but when the Egyptian army had to return to its homeland in 610 BC, the Babylonians and Medes armies were able to sack Harran in 609 BC, Ashur Uballit II and his troops were driven out of the city. It was plundered of its treasures, and the temple of Sin was partially destroyed. However the collapse of the Assyrian military and political system did not mean the extinction of the Assyrians.

Assyrian survival in Harran is attested to by lady Adda-Gruppi' the mother of Nabunaid, the king of Babylon (555-539). She died in Harran at the ripe age of 104. More than five decades after the fall of Nineveh, in an inscription, she accuses the surviving relatives and the officials of the Assyrian kings of not preforming fumigation to the graves of the monarchs, who had done so much for them, but she served perpetual offerings for them.

"None of their children, none of their families and of their officials to whom, when they had been put in office they had (been) given rich gifts, performed actually as much as a fumigation-offering (to their graves), whereas I brought monthly, without interruption, in my best garments, offering to their souls fat lambs, bread, fine beer, wine, oil, honey and all kinds of garden fruits, and

established as perpetual offerings abundant fumigation (yielding) sweet smells for them." (Prichard, James Ed.,1950, 312)

If the relatives and the officials of the Assyrian kings had survived in Harran, there is reason to believe that the rest of the population was wiped out. Nebunaid who ruled sixty years after the fall of Nineveh refers to Ashurbanipal and Esarhaddon as his "royal forefathers."

Harranians continued to practice an altered form of their ancient religion way into Islam. Their city flourished until mid-thirteenth century, when the Mongols destroyed it. Several natives of Harran, from the family of Bet Qarra, contributed to the Arab civilization, especially in the fields of mathematics and Astronomy.

Harranians refused to convert to Christianity and continued to practice their ancient faith despite pressure from their Christian brethren to convert. Up to the eighth century AD, the Sin temple in Harran contained three ancient documents, in the form of Steles. One of them depicted a person in ancient Assyrian outfit, holding a ringed staff in one hand while raising the other to the three divine symbols of Sin (the moon god), Shamash (the sun god) and Ishtar (the morning star). The cuneiform on one stele provides a new list of the Assyrian kings and describes details of Nabunid's mother's funeral. The other two steles describe Nabunid's attempts to rebuild the temple of Sin in Harran and his disagreement with the priests of Marduk. (Bacon Edward, 1960, 170)

When the Arabs confiscated the temple, a mosque was built on its site. The three steles were buried under the entrances of the mosque so that people would walk over them as an expression of Islam's triumph over paganism. The temple of Sin in Harran originally was founded by Shalmanser II and was rebuilt by Ashurbanipal (668–627 BC), who installed his younger brother as its High Priest. Esarhaddon, on his way to Egypt, paid his tribute at this temple. Its roof was of cedar from Lebanon, its friezes were inlaid with lapis lazuli, and its doors were of silver.

Temples dedicated to the seven planets representing the Assyrian gods existed during the early centuries of Christianity in

Samosata, a short distance north of Harran. The arrangement and the order of the temples, the height of the idols conformed to the position of the planets at ancient times.

The temple of Saturn was hexagonal and black. His statue was made of lead; his day was Saturday. The temple of Jupiter (Bel) was triangular and green. His statue was made of tin; his day was Thursday. The temple of Mars (Nergal) was oblong (or square) and red. His statue was made of iron; his day was Tuesday. The temple of the sun (Shamash) was square and made of gold; his day was Sunday. The temple of Venus (Ishtar) was probably a triangle inside a rectangle. It was blue. Her statue was made of copper, and her day was Friday. The temple of Mercury (Nebu) was probably a triangle in an oblong. It had no allotted color. His statue was made of clay; his day was Wednesday The temple of the Moon (Sin) was probably octagon. Her statue—the moon— was regarded as female and made of silver; her day was Monday.

Although at first glance these temples seem unprecedented, in closer examination they seem to emulate the Assyro-Babylonian Ziggurats. According to Sir Henry Rawlinson the Ziggurat of Bir Nimrod near Babylon consisted of seven stages of brickwork and earthen platforms. Each stage was of a different color and was devoted to one of the seven planets.

"The first stage, which was an exact square, was 272 feet each way, and 26 feet high, and bricks blackened with bitumen; this stage is supposed to have been devoted to the planet Saturn. The second stage was a square of 230 feet, 26 feet high, face, faced with orange-colored brick; supposed to be devoted to Jupiter. The third stage, 188 feet square, and 26 feet high, faced with red bricks, was probably dedicated to Mars. The fourth stage, 146 feet square, and 15 feet high, was probably devoted to the Sun, and according to Sir H. Rawlinson it had been originally plated with gold. The fifth stage is supposed to have been 104 [feet]; the sixth, and the seventh, 20 feet square. These stages were probably devoted to Venus, Mercury, and the moon."

The Ziggurats were often called "House of the Seven Guides" or "House of the Link between Heaven and Earth." As late as the eighth century, the pagans of Harran were examining liver of the sheep to determine the good and the bad omens as they did during the ancient times. (Smith George, 1977, 164–65)

Because most Harranians continued to worship an altered form of the ancient religion, our knowledge about their pagan practices are much greater than from other cities where the population became predominantly Christian. At the full moon nearest to the summer solstice, Harranian women of the Christian era bewailed Tammuz, the Assyrian/Babylonian vegetation deity, whom they believed had died at the time of harvest and was resurrected in the spring. Maimonides, the Jewish writer of the twelfth century AD, wrote that Harranians were still observing the death of Tammuz on the first day of the month, dedicated to his name. (Segal J.B., 1963, 216)

During the imperial Assyrian era, June 20 to July 20 of today's calendar coincided with the month when Tammuz was mourned. The tenth-century Ibn Wahshiya has also attested to the lamination for Tammuz in Baghdad and in Harran during the month dedicated to his name. He writes:

"My own opinion is, that this festival, which they hold in commemoration of Tammuz, is an ancient one, and has maintained itself till now, whilst the story connected with him has been forgotten, owing to the remoteness of his age, so that no one of these Sabians at the present day knows what his story was, nor why they lament over him." (Ibn Wahshaya, 1861, 262)

In ancient Assyria, during the month of Tammuz, people paid their respect to their dead relatives, combining the mourning for a god with lamenting for man. Offering of food and water was made on the grave of the deceased. Sons usually performed the task of purring water to their dead father's grave. According to Segal, *"the full moon of the month nearest the autumn equinox was marked by solemn offering of food and wine and sacrifices of to the dead,"* by the Harranians of the Christian era. Syriac text contend that when Caliph al Mammon passed by Harran on his way to war with the Byzantium, among the well wishers greeting him were Harranians, who wore frock-coats and their hair in long locks, similar to the that of the ancient Assyrians as depicted on their reliefs. The Caliph asked them what the name of their religion was, they could not answer. Later they decided to refer to themselves as "Sabian," a name that is mentioned in the Koran.

Arbil and Adiabene

The origin of Arbil, located north of the River Zab, eighty-seven kilometers Southeast of Mosul, dates back to the Ur III period. The Sumerians called it Orbelum, or Urbilum, and later Akkadians knew it as Arba-Illu. In both cases, it meant "Four Gods." The city was a center for the worship of the Assyrian goddess Ishtar, second only to Ashur. An inscription by Ashur- banipal describes how In the month of Ab (July) while staying in the city of Arbaillu during the festival of the "Great Queen, the goddess Ishtar," he was informed about the invasion of Babylon by the Elamites. After the downfall of the Assyrian Kingdom, the city fell consecutively under the control of the Medes, the Persians, and the Greeks. According to Quintus, Curtius Alexander the Great found princely treasure in Arbela. The dynasty of Seleucus ruled Mesopotamia until 126 BC, when Parthians defeated them and ruled it up to 226 AD. Marcellinus writes that Parthians gave the name Adiabene to central Assyria because it was situated between rivers of upper and lower Zab, which they called Diab and Adiab. Adiabene included Arbil, Nineveh, Gugmamla, and other Assyrian towns and villages. The fact that Adiabene was previously was known as Assyria is specifically attested to by Pliny (His. Nat., V. C. 12).

During Shapur I (240–270 AD), he appointed his son Ardakhshir as the governor of Assyria, and the region's name was changed to Nod-Ardakhshiragan, meaning "Ruled by Ardakhshir."

Segal writes: *"The king of Adiabene (Assyria) at the time of the Abgar the Great was Narseh; he was drowned in the Great Zab by the Parthians for his pro Roman sympathies."* (Segal J. B., 1970, 71) In describing the advent of Christianity in Mesopotamia, Eusebius writes: "When Narses, the king of the Assyrians heard about the teaching and the miracles of Addaeus [Assyrian Addi] the apostle, in Urhay (Edessa), he asked king Abgar to either dispatch the man to his domain or describe his teachings." (Roberts

Alexander, 1869, 28)

Despite the name change imposed by the foreign rulers on Assyria Syriac writers continued to call their homeland Attur, i.e. Assyria, and Arbil (Erbil) become an important center of the Assyrian Christianity. According to Eusebius in his Teaching of Addaeus, people from the east traveled into the Roman territory to learn about Addaeus' teaching, to become disciples to instruct people of their own nation in Assyria. (Roberts Alexander, 1869, 25) Mingana provides the name of nineteen people who served as bishops in Arbil, from 104 to 511 AD. According to Mishkha Zkha, by the mid-second century, Arbil had a Bishop called Abraham (148–163). During the Sassanian era (226–642 AD) Arbil maintained its importance as a center of an administrative province.

The Assyrian city of Nisibin

Nisibin, located some 130 miles northwest of Mosul, was first mentioned in the Assyrian records in 1901 BC. It was captured by the Assyrian king Adad-Nirari II, who incorporated it into the Assyrian Empire. It was classified as an Assyrian province and remained loyal to the Assyrian kings until the end.

In the third century BC Nisibin became the capital of a Seleucid's province called Antiochia Mygdonia. After the Seleucid were driven out of Mesopotamia by the Parthians, Nisibin was ruled by a subsidiary king as part of Adiabene. According to a legend, Addai and Mari, two of the seventy-two disciples of Christ established the church in Nisibin. The first known bishop of the city was Jacob (290–338). By 410 BC, Nisibin was a metropolitan of the Church of the East. During the Shapur II reign, Christians of Nisibin in 338, 346, and 350 AD, fought side by side with the Romans to protect their city from being invaded by the Persians, because they remembered how the Persian kings had persecuted them. During the last siege, the Persian king Shapur II dammed the local river and flooded the town to destroy Nisibin's fortifications; However, the resulting mud, ruin, and chaos obstructed the Persian army and allowed the defenders of the city to ambush the invaders, and drive them out. St. Ephraim who was one of the defenders of the city wrote:

> *"All kinds of storms trouble me, and you have been kinder to the Ark: only waves surrounded it, but ramps and weapons, and waves surround me . . . O Helmsman of the Ark, be my pilot on dry land! You gave the Ark rest on the haven of a mountain, give me rest in the haven of my walls."*
> (http://www.catholic.org/saints/saint.php?saint_id=3)

During a later military incursion into the Persian territory, the Roman emperor Julian was killed. In 363 AD his troops elected general Jovian, as the new Emperor, who negotiated a generous settlement with the Persians to extract his army out of captivity. He granted them the northern Mesopotamia (including the city of Nisibin). Part of the treaty stipulated that the Christian inhabitants of Nisibin should be driven out of the city before transferring it to the Persians. Nisibians objected to the Persian takeover and were willing to fight them without any help from the Romans, but were not allowed. When a Persian officer arrived in the city to raise the standard of his empire on the citadel and to inform the citizens of their impending exile, they were ready to fight back, but they were discouraged by the Romans. Appeals to renegotiate the agreement to allow the citizens of the city to stay were ignored by the Emperor. Anyone who refused to leave was threatened with certain death. The entire city, according to Marcellinus, was full of lamentation.

> *"They mourned the fact that they were being driven out of their homes in which they were born and were brought up. The mother who had lost here children, or the wife her husband, about being torn from the place rendered sacred by their Sahdies [saints and martyrs], clinging to their door-posts, embracing their threshold, and pouring forth floods of tears. Every road out of city was crowded and many were overloaded with as much property as they could carry, most headed toward Edessa."* (Marcellinus Ammianus, 1939, 399)

Among the refugees was Mar Ephraim who among thousands of Nisibians settled in Edessa, some one hundred miles northwest. Many of Ephraim's hymns were written in Edessa. During a year of famine in Edessa, he was entrusted with helping the starving population of the city and the surrounding villages. He organized a suitable shut-off area in the streets, where he made sure that those who were suffering from starvation were provided with beds, food, general care. In later centuries as the Persian persecutions abated, the Assyrian population in what is today known as northern Iraq flourished. Jenkins writes: *"By the seventh century, the Nestorian church alone had six provinces in Mesopotamia, ruling over a substantial hierarchy. Nisibin itself was a metropolitan see with six lesser bishoprics under its control."* (Jenkins, 2008, 61)

Assyrians and Silk Manufacturing

The humiliating peace treaty between Rome and Persia in 363 reduced the trade between the two enemies, but another agreement in 408/9 restored Nisibin as an important trade city between the two empires. Gradually, the Assyrian population in Nisibin increased to an extent that they played an important role in the trade between the Persians and the Romans. According to the Roman historian, Menandaer, another trade treaty between the Byzantine and the Persian empire in 561 AD stipulated that

"Merchants . . . shall not travel by strange roads, but shall only go by way of Nisibin and Daras. If they dare anything contrary to the agreement they shall be hunted down and handed over to the officers of the frontier, together with merchandise they are carrying, whether they are Romans or Atturia (Assyrian)." (Blockley R.C., 1985, 73)

This clause was evidently intended to discourage merchants from avoiding payment of taxes. The Caravans of trade arrived from China at Seleucia-Ctesiphon [called Kohie by the Assyrians]. They brought various products, including raw silk, and returned with Babylonian carpets, which were the forerunners of what was later known as the Persian Carpets. Other products included precious stones from Syria, rouge used by the Chinese to color their eyebrows from Persia, and textiles from Syria and Egypt. Merchandise from Ctesiphon, which had considerable Assyrian population, was taken to various trading centers including Nisibin. (Time-Life Books, 1988, 81)

Silk was a valuable commodity for the Romans, who had built a considerable weaving industry around it. Because the production of the raw silk was kept a secret by the Chinese, Romans had no choice but to buy the raw silk from the Persians who were in control of the trading routes east of Syria. During conflict with Rome, Persians often stopped the trade with Rome or raised their prices to unreasonable levels. Consequently, Romans looked for other possible sources of raw silk to by-pass the Persian control of the silk production but had no success. (Irene Frank M., 198, 156) Historian Procopius writes that Emperor Justinian (527–65) had decided that Romans should not buy silk from the Persians. Soon they were informed about the Nestorian [Assyrian] monks who arrived from India and could help Romans to produce their own raw silk by a process they had learned while they lived in Serinda, a city of Khontan on the border of China and India. (Frank Irene The Silk Road 158-159) Nisibin played an important part in the Silk Road trade before and after it was handed over to the Romans. Luxury goods such as silk, jewelry, spices, perfumes, hides, and wild animals from China, India, Eastern Iran, and Armenia had to pass though Nisibin before going to Rome. In describing trade between the Persians and the Romans, an anonymous writer in 359/60 AD who accused the Persians of being *"skilled in all bad things and wars"* praised the citizens of Nisibin and Edessa by stating:

"There are . . . Nisibin and Edessa, which in every respect have very good men; they are very skillful in trade and also good in hunting. Above all, they are rich and endowed with all goods; for the goods they receive from the Persians they themselves sell to the whole country of the Romans, and what they buy in Roman territory they again trade with the Persians, except ore and iron, for it is not allowed to supply the enemy with ore and iron." (Wiesehofer Josef, 1996, 194)

After concluding a peace treaty with Khosro Anushiravan in 561 AD, Emperor Justinian asked him to arrange a meeting for him with his learned Nestorian subjects to enlighten him about their faith. Khosro sent him Paul the Metropolitan of Nisibin, Mari Bishop of Belad, Bar-Sauma Bishop of Qardou, Isaiah a teacher in Seleucia, Isho-Yahab of Arzoun, who became Catholicos of the Church of the East, and Babai Bishop of Sinjar. [Justinian] honored them all. A debate between Justinian about the theology of the Church of the East was recorded and still exists.

During the Arab rule, Nisibin continued to remain a prosperous city until during the thirteenth century, when the Mongols ravaged it. The massacres of the fifteenth century by Tamure Lang reduced Nisibin, like other Christian towns, to a small village, leaving little that remained of its long history. The only prominent Assyrian structure that still remained in Nisibin, until recently, was the partially damaged ancient two-nave Church known as Mar Yakub used by the Jacobite Assyrians.

Assyrian Survival in Other Places

A Neo-Babylonian tablet reveals that the Babylonian king Neriglisar (559–556 BC) returned the statue of the goddess Anunitum to the Assyrian city of Arrapahu (today's Kirkuk), which was looted during the earlier century. (DalleyStephanie, 1993, 138) This would have been only possible if the city was still inhabited by its surviving population, of the same culture and religion, as before 612 BC.

The fifth-century Greek historian Xenophon attests to the fact that Assyria was a prosperous satrap of the Persian Empire at that time, with an administrative center, perhaps, near Zakho. Georges Roux contends that few Assyrian cities such as Arrapkhu [present Kirkuk] had remained intact. An inscription found in Egypt, written by Arsames, a Persian administrator, corroborates the survival of some Assyrian towns, hereto were considered to have been in ruins. "Nehtihur" a subordinate to the Persian Satrap of Egypt was given a letter authorizing his travelling party to receive rations from the Persian officials along the way. Some of the towns mentioned in the letter were known Assyrian cities including La'ir (Assyrian Lahiru), Arzohin (Assyrian Urzuhina), Arbil (Assyrian Arba'ilu), Ubas (Assyrian Ubase), located twenty kilometers north of Ashur, and Halzu, perhaps Hazza, mentioned in the seventh-century legend of Mar Qardakh. It was also mentioned by Strabo in the first century BC, as one of the four districts in the plains around Nineveh. (Oates David, 1968, 59-60) David Oates writes that this document provides further evidence that the above mentioned

Assyrian cities were well governed administrative centers when Xenophon passed through Assyria, but he expressed no knowledge of their existence. (Oates David Ibid) Evidences presented so far, and others that will be revealed later clearly refutes the idea that the ancient Assyrians were defeated into extinction.

"Recent studies have shown that the level of devastation [in Assyria] was not so total, and that many of the major cities continued at least in a reduced manner." (MacGinnis, 2009, 15)

Chapter 8

Archaeological Discoveries

Until few decades ago, the extinction of the Assyrians during their defeat or thereafter was treated as a forgone conclusion by some, but archaeological discoveries during the last few decades have repudiated such assumptions. Archaeologist David Oates wrote:

"The post-Assyrian period has, moreover, suffered from the neglect of the archaeologists who regarded it, not without reason, as the impoverished descendant of more illustrious forebears, and it has only recently been the subject of serious study." He further contends that: *"The Assyrian population could not have disappeared overnight, and there is in fact evidence from Kalkhu to suggest that some of the inhabitants of the city returned, after its sack in 612 BC, to seek shelter in the ruins."* (Oates David, 1968, 58)

Since then, new archaeological discoveries have provided additional confirmation about Assyrians' survival after their defeat. Five hundred tablets, dated a decade after the fall of Nineveh, found at the Assyrian city of Dur-Katlimmu, on the Habour River in northeast Syria attest to this fact. Dur-Katlimmu was a major Assyrian provincial administrative center. It also housed military garrisons, including a unit of chariotry. The documents show that the city continued to function as it had before the fall. Inscriptions

were written in the Aramaic and Assyrian languages by the same scribes who signed them as before the fall. They were however dated by the reign-years of King Nebuchadnezzar II.
(State Archives of Assyria Bulletin 7/2 (Padua, 1993)

Discovery at Eski Mosul Dam Basin

Explorations, at the Eski Mosul Dam Basin in 1983 by a team of British archaeologist from Edinburgh University unearthed proof of a heavy Assyrian presence about third century BC at Kharabeh Shattani, some forty kilometers to the north-east of Nineveh. The pottery unearthed here was a continuation of prevalent styles in Nimurd at its heyday.

"This impressive discovery, according to Dr. Peztenburg, 'would provide scholars with an incentive to embark on a fresh study of the descendants of the Assyrian empire, whom he believes could in no way have been washed away from the surface of the earth . . . The Assyrians did not suddenly disappear as hitherto has been the general belief. Some of them at least stayed and their metal works, pottery style and building designs found at Kharabeh Shattani confirm this proposition, he emphasized.'" (Barkho L. Y., 1984)

Assyrians in the City of Ashur

Another archive in Ashur after the fall suggests that Assyrian goldsmiths were still working under the Median command. (Parpola Simo, JAAAS, Vol. 12, 1, 16) Archaeological evidences indicate that from 100 BC to 270 AD the city of Ashur was an important administrative center of the Parthian rulers. In addition to the new administrative edifices built to the north of the city, and a palace to the south, a temple dedicated to the Assyrian national god Ashur was built on top his old sanctuary, which indicates that even before the Parthian period Assyrians were living in that city. The Sassanid king Shapur I (241–272 AD) is said to have destroyed the rebuilt city of Ashur. Simo Parpola writes:

"When the Seleucid Empire disintegrated at the end of the second century BC, its Western remnants were annexed to Rome,

while several semi-independent kingdoms of decidedly Assyrian stamp and or identity (Osrhoni, [with its center in Edessa], Adiabene, [with its center in Arbil], Hatra, Ashur) popped up in the East, under Parthian lordship. These kingdoms perpetuated Assyrian cultural and religious traditions but were also receptive to Christianity since it has a central ideology and was felt as intrinsically Assyrian because of Aramaic affinity of Jesus and the deciples." (Parpola, Simo, JAAS, 2004, 20)

Existence of the "Assyrian House of Festival," or Bet Akitu, at post Empire Ashur, and references to the month of Nissan in inscriptions found at the temple of Ashur, indicates that the Assyrian New Year was being celebrated in that city up to the third century AD.

"When the Akitu temple of the high god Ashur was rebuilt in Parthian style, during the first century AD, it still followed the alignment and orientation of Assyrian temple that preceded it." W. Andrae, the original excavator, marveled over this remarkable continuity in cultic architecture. (Dalley, 1998, 151-52) An Aramaic [Syriac] parchments found in the third century Ashur indicates that the Cult of Bel and Nabu, Nergal, and Nanai were still worshiped there. An offering to Nanai written on a big shred of a Pithos reads *"Nany mlk' martan brat bel maralah u bar-Maryn 'lah' ,"* i.e., *"Nanai the Queen, our Lady, daughter of Bel; Lord god, and the son of our Lord god."* (Driverjvers, 1967,46-47) "Bar-Maryn," i.e., Nabu, who was considered the Son of Bell (Ashur in Assyria and Marduk in Babylon). The temple of Nabu was discovered in post-imperial Ashur [and Nineveh]. (Drijvers, 1980, 95) Evidently, Nanai and Bar Maryn, Nabu, were a divine couple during the third century AD in the city of Ashur where the term for god was "Maryan Alaha," i.e., "Our Lord God," the same term is used even today by the Christian Assyrians in reference to God, which attests to the enduring link between the Christian Assyrians and their pre-Christian heritage.

The cult of Nanna, also called, Innana, Ishtar, or Nanai had its origin in the most ancient Mesopotamia. The goddess was known by many titles: lady of ladies, Goddess of goodness, directress of mankind, mistress of the spirits of heaven, possessor of sovereign power, the light of heaven and earth, daughter of the Moon god, ruler of weapons, arbitress of battles, goddess of love. (Rosen field, 1967, 85) Nabu often associated with the planet Mercury was known as the "god that possesses intelligence." His seat of worship was originally in Borsipa, but was worshiped by both Babylonians and Assyrians. There was a shrine for him in Kalkh (Nimrud) and his temple in the city of Nineveh had survived into to the Christian era.

Babylonian economic documents between 625 and 404 BC include over a hundred uniquely Assyrian names. Many of these include references to Ashur, the Assyrian deity, others remain to be identified. (Rosenfield, 1967, Ibid) We need to keep in mind that not all Assyrian names included the name Ashur. Mention of "Distinctively Assyrian names are found in later Aramaic and Greek texts from Ashur, Hatra, Dura-Europus, and Palmyra, up to the beginning of the Sassanian period. [third century AD]" (Rosenfield, 1967, Ibid) Upon conversion to Christianity, the ancient names were abandoned in favor of newly coined Biblical monikers which included the name of Alaha [God] or Eisho [Christ] such as Yav-Alaha: given by God; Odisho: servant of Christ; Sovr-isho: hope of Christ. Such personal names have been used by the Christian Assyrians to date. Roux, in a new book in French titled, "La Mesopotamie," about the astonishing resurrection of Assyria, during the Parthian period. writes:

"Most remarkable is the astonishing resurrection of Assyria. Nineveh, partly rebuilt and repopulated, became an important commercial center, the same as Arba 'ilu (Arbela, Erbil), Kazu (Saidawa), and Nuzi (yorgan Tepe). Ashur, again, became a great city, provided with an agora [An open space section, serving as a meeting ground for various activities], a very beautiful palace and several temples where the ancient gods were honored, including Ashur . . . On the other hand, we know that many Christians lived in upper Mesopotamia." (Roux, La Mesopotamie, 463)

Assyrians at the City of Hatra

Excavations by the Iraqi Department of Antiquities between 1951 and 1955 confirmed the Assyrian presence in Hatra, located fifty-five kilometers northwest of Ashur, where nine temples dedicated to the Assyrian deities where found including "Ashur Bel." The structures in Hatra are built with limestone and gypsum and their architectural style is a mixture of Assyrian, Hellenistic, Parthian and Roman. (Bacon Edward, 1960, p.205)

The date of Hatra's foundation is subject to some debate, but it was originally a small Assyrian settlement that by the first century BC had grown into a fortified religious and trading center. It thrived during the first and the second century BC. Later, it was the capital of semi-autonomous Arab rulers who reigned over several cities along the western Frontier of the Parthian Empire. Judging from the Assyrian temples in Hatra dedicated to Ashur-Bel, Shamash, Nergal, Sin, Nanai (Innana Ishtar), and other deities one has to conclude that a considerable Assyrian community lived in that city.

The standard of Ashur in Hatra was transformed into a three-dimensional statue. The upper part of the Ashur-Bel's head of the statue is broken, but the remaining curled square beard is characteristically similar to that of the Assyrian kings, as shown in their reliefs. The rendition of the Ashur-Bel's disk into a three-dimensional statue has given a new appearance to the deity, but its distinctively ancient elements are preserved. Ashur-Bel is clad in a garment similar to that of a Roman officer, perhaps to emphasis his reputation as a warrior. The Roman influence in clothing and style is also apparent in the image of Shamash at Hatra. The Ashur-Bel's wings, that were part of his ancient insignia, were moved to the back of his statue. Over his

In the left the statue of assurbel in Hatra above is the relief of Shamash.

breastplate is the image of the Sun god, Shamash. By his right and left legs stand two eagles, symbolizing power and conquest; a goddess sits at front by his feet (Bacon Edward, 1960, 205.)

The presence of the Assyrians in the cities of Ashur and Hattra, in the third century AD, and their worship of the ancient Assyrian deities, plus their use of the Akkadian names, attests to the survival of the ancient Assyrians after the fall of Nineveh. Examples of the Ancient Assyrian names in the cities of Ashur and Hatra include: Ashur-da'an, meaning "Ashur is my judge"; this was changed to Ashur-da'yyana in the Aramaic. Ashur-remmani in Aramaic was changed to Ashur-hanani; meaning "Ashur was merciful to me." Khannai, Khanan, Khanania are still being used as Christian Assyrian names. Khnanisho, meaning "Jesus is merciful," is the Christianized version of Ashur-hanani. (Parpola, Simo, JAAS, 2004, Appendix IV.) There were also names such as Natun-Ishtar (gift of Ishtar), Bel-Barakh (Bel-blessed), Nabu-dayan, (Nabu-iddn), Illah-Shamash, (illi-Shamash). The language spoken by these Assyrians is classified as Aramaic. It included words found in Syriac and the Akkadian language. It is also the case with the language Christian Assyrians presently speak. (Ibid)

Who else but Assyrians would have built temples for the Assyrian deities eight hundred years after the fall of Nineveh? Such facts clearly repudiate the claim that because of language change, from Akkadian to Aramaic, those who survived after the Assyrians defeat become Aramized; therefore, they no longer considered themselves Assyrians. The script in Hatra is slightly different from the Aramaic inscriptions of Ashur. Hatra also was attacked by the Sassanian king Shapur I and was destroyed. One tradition asserts that in 241 CE, An-Nadira, the daughter of Hatra's Arab king, delivered the city to the Sassanian king Shapur I, this caused the destruction of the city and the death of her father. Shapur I married her to reward her for helping him to invade the city, but killed her because he feared that she would betray him, as she had done to her father, and her homeland.

It is important to note that structures in Hatra and Ashur have survived because they were built with durable materials, unlike buildings in other regions of Mesopotamia that were built with material that could not survive destruction, erosion, wars, floods, and earthquakes.

144

Chapter 9

Assyrian Towns in the Plain of Nineveh

About Christianity in Iraq, Jenkins wrote:

"Well into the Middle Ages, the Christian strongholds of the Middle East included such currently newsworthy Iraqi cities as Basra, Mosul, and Kirkuk, while Tikrit—hometown of Saddam Hussein—was a thriving Christian center several centuries after the coming of Islam. Nisibin and Jundishapur were legendary centers of learning that kept alive the culture and science of the ancient world, both of the Greco-Romans and of the Persians. In their scholarship, their access to classical learning and science, the Eastern churches in 800 were at a level that Latin Europe would not reach until the thirteenth century." (Jenkins, 2008, 7)

The Nineveh plains, located west of Mosul is part of the Ninawa Governate of Northern Iraq. It consists of three districts: Tel Kepe, Al-Hamdaniya, and Al-Shikhan. The area includes the ancient Assyrian ruins of Nineveh, Nimrud, and Dur-Sharrukin. Several Towns in northern Iraq, in the plain of Nineveh, that have survived to date have been historically populated by the Christian Assyrians. In some cases, the origin of these settlements dates back to the ancient Assyria. Their inhabitants have been known as Nestorians, Chaldeans, or Jacobites in reference to their religious affiliations.

Ancient Assyrian antiquities have been discovered in and near these towns, or in mounds next to them, such as in Bashmoni (Beth Shmoni), tell Mqortaya, tell Karamlis, tell Mar Behnam, and other sites that have been identified as the ancient Assyrian fortresses, or temples. Most have not been excavated, but from time to time, ancient Assyrian items are found near them. An Assyrian statue was found in a well near the Mar Zina church, it is presently displayed in the Mosul's Museum. In 1942 an ancient Assyrian bathroom and several graves were found near the church of Bashmoni. In 1980s excavators found ancient human remains on the grounds of Mar Yonan (Jonah's) Church. The graves are made with bricks in large rectangular shape, similar to that of the ancient Assyrians.

Before the seventh century AD, almost all the towns in the Plain of Nineveh were populated primarily by the Christian Assyrians rather than people of other nationalities. This is evident by the fact that Christianity in Mesopotamia took hold primarily among the Syriac speaking population. It is important to note that both Parthians and Persians who ruled in Mesopotamia spoke their own Indo-European based language. After the Arab conquest of Mesopotamia, due to ongoing invasions, massacres, migrations, and exile, the ethnic demography makeup of Mesopotamia changed. According to the Syriac manuscripts the population of several Christian villages in the Plain of Nineveh such as Ba'jbare, perhaps Beth Gabbare, (Home of the Giants), Beth Gurbaq, Beth Zabaye, and Beth Bore converted to Islam.

By the sixteenth century, Christians of Iraq had primarily survived in the Plain of Nineveh, in the mountains of Hakkari, north of Mosul, South East Turkey, and Urmia, in Northwest Persia. Here are the towns where they have lived since the dawn of Christianity. Historical and archaeological evidences attest to the fact that some of them are still called by the names that ancient Assyrians gave them. It was here that ancient Assyrians lived and ruled; yet some writers continue to deny the Assyrian identity of the Christian Assyrians who have inhabited them.

Town of Alkosh or Elkush

Algosh, or Elkush, is wrongly identified by the Old Testament, as where Nahum lived when Nineveh was destroyed. It is located thirty miles north of Nineveh. Layard, who visited Alkosh in mid-nineteenth century described it as a large Christian village whose inhabitants had converted to Catholicism. In the hills behind the village, he found engravings *"similar to those he saw at Malthaiyah. . . . some having rude ornaments above the entrances, of the doorways, of others, being simply square holes in the rock."* (Layard, Henry, 1852,165)

Other archeological evidences attest to the fact that the name Alkosh dates back to the ancient Assyrian period. Its name, seems to have derived from the Akkadian word "Eil-Koshtu," which means "the god of bow," perhaps in reference to the winged disk of "Ashur." The earliest mention of Alkosh comes from a mural inside Sennacherib's palace about 750 AD, discovered at Kuyunjik behind which is carved, *"This rock was brought from the mountain of Alkosh."* In the ruin of Shayro Meliktha, located about two miles to the west of the city in a temple, where a relief shows King Sennacherib aiming an arrow from his bow. (Qais Sago, 2003, 29)

Some of the districts of Alkosh still bear ancient names such as Sainna Quarter, located at the west of the town. It was undoubtedly named in reference to the ancient Assyrian moon god Sin. Marotha, an Alkosh scholar of three centuries ago, wrote that his ancestors told him people living in Nineveh at ancient times would visit Algosh during the new year to perform religious ceremony in honor of Sin. According to the memoirs of Mar Mikha of Nuhadra (today's Dohouk), when he visited Alkosh in 441 AD he was welcomed by priests of a church built on top of the ruins of a temple (this was the temple of Ishtar). In 640 AD the Christian Assyrian monastery of Rabban Hormozd was constructed a short distance away from Alkosh. It became the residence of various Church of the East Patriarchs. Yoohanna Solana, who became the first Patriarch of the Church of the East in 1553, was formerly the abbot of this monastery. However, he moved to Diyarbakir after he was appointed the Patriarch of the Chaldean Church.

In 1743 Alkosh along with other Assyrian villages in the plain of Nineveh was destroyed by the invading Persian army under the leadership of the Persian king Nader Shah. Most of its inhabitants were killed. According to the church records, the Kurdish Governor of Rowanduz, nicknamed "Mir-koora," whose hatred for Christians and Assyrians is well documented, attacked Alkosh in 1832 and killed over 400 of its inhabitants. According to the church records, he returned on March 15, 1833, to kill another 172 of its men—not counting children and women. In 1840 the brother of Mir-Kora, Rasoul Beg, besieged the town and later set fire to the Rabban Hormozd Monastery and destroyed over 500 of its valuable books. During the last century, partly, because of economic hardship or persecution, most of the inhabitants of the town migrated to other cities of Iraq or out of the country. Before 2003 about 5,000 Assyrians reside in Alkosh.

The Town of Ankawa

Ankawa is located near the city of Arbil. It has a population about 20,000 mostly Assyrians, members of the Chaldean Church. According to the "Salah Addin" university a neo-Assyrian monument was discovered recently near Ankawa at a mound, known as "Tel-Qasra," or the "Castle Hill." The town's original name seems to have been Amka-ava, i.e. established by Amka, in the Syriac language. A yellow tablet found in St. George's Church in Ankaw indicates that it was rebuilt in 816 AD; this means the town had existed before then. According to Bar Hebrious, on Sunday, July 20, 1285, Mongolian troops attacked the Arbil region and the villages around it, including Ankawa.

The Town of Baghdida

Baghdida is located about thirty-two kilometers southeast of the city of Mosul, near the ruins of Kalkh and Nineveh. Historically, it has been inhabited by the Christian Assyrians. Its name dates back to the ancient Assyrian "Bakdidu," meaning "youth's home." In the early Syriac documents, it has been mentioned as "Beth Kdhudhe," with similar meaning. Baghdida was renamed Qaraqosh, a name given to it by the Ottoman Turks when they ruled Iraq. The thirteenth-century Arab geographer Yaqut in his "Mu'ajam al-Buldan)," described it as a village, but as large as a town, situated in Nineveh, east of Mosul, whose majority of people are Christians. During the Saddam's rule, its name was changed to Hamdaniya, after an Arab tribe of Banu Hamdan, which he settled in the region as part of his Arbaization policy.

Assyrians of Baghdida became Christian during the early centuries of Christianity. Its inhabitants, until the seventh century AD were members of the Church of the East, but during the rule of the Persian King Khosro Parviz (579–628) with the help his Christian wife, Shereen, and his Christian physician, Gabriel, the towns of Baghdida and Bartella were taken over by the Syrian Orthodox Church, during the eighteenth century, with the help of the French government, and the intervention of Mohammad Pasha, the Turkish governor, a faction of the Jacobites church joined the Catholic Church.

(www.answers.com/topic/bakhdida) Some residents of Bakhdida trace their origin to the town of Takrit. Due to religious persecutions and high taxation during the eleventh and the twelfth centuries, thousands of Assyrians were forced to abandon that city and migrate to the Plain of Nineveh.

Ba-Nuhadra, The Plain of Nineveh

About the diocese of Ba Nuhadra, Fiey writes: *"In the beginning of the fifth century, Ba Nuhadra (plain of Nineveh) was a prestigious name that made the eyes of the Christians of the "great Oriental Syrians" [Assyrians] glow with pride, because it was a vast fertile province covering all the Plain of Nineveh situated between the Mesopotamian desert and the Kurdish mountains."* (Yana George, 2008, 49)

Ba Nuhadra, or the Plain of Nineveh, is the heart of Assyria, but in recent centuries, the city of Nuhadra has been renamed Dohuk by the Kurds. Here, as in Adiabene, Christianity began among the inhabitants of central Mesopotamia. About five kilometers west of Dohuk there is a mound that is the site of an ancient Assyrian military fortress. It is called Malthaiyah (meaning "elevated" in Assyrian language). When Layard visited Malthaiyah in mid–nineteenth century, he described it as a small Christian village in the valley of Dohuk. He visited the ancient Assyrian monuments that were carved on a rock on top of a hill near the village. He wrote:

"The subjects representing the four bas-reliefs are similar, and appear to be an adoration of the gods by two kings. The first god wears the square horned cap, surmounted by a point, or fleur-de-lys; holds a ring in one hand, and a thong or snake in the other, and stands on two animals, a bull and a kind of gryphon . . . The details in the bas-relief are similar in character to those found in other places in northern Mesopotamia." (Layard, 1852, 163)

He also stated: *"Inhabitants of Malthaiyah are Catholic Chaldeans, their conversion not dating many years."* Assyrian pottery, dating back to the neo-Assyrian era, has been discovered at this mound. Since World War I, a large number of Kurds has migrated to the region. The above historical evidences clearly prove that Layard was much more qualified to declare that Christian Assyrians were *"as much the remains of Nineveh and Assyria, as the rude heaps and ruined palaces."* (Joseph John, 1961, 13)

Village of Baqofa

Baqofa is a small village located fifteen miles north east of Mosul; it was originally an ancient Assyrian town. In 1852 Victor Place excavated one of the two hills surrounding the village and found painted potteries. Other excavations have discovered reliefs with cuneiform text. Baqofa has a church named after the martyr, Mar Ghiwargis.

Town of Bartella

It is difficult to ascertain when Bartilla was founded. It is located thirteen miles east of Mosul. The term "Tilla n Syriac" means mound; therefore, its name means "behind the mound," which indicates that it was established behind a mound covering an ancient Assyrian ruin, which is still there. The new settlement later became the center of Assyrian Christianity.

Random digging, in or near Bartella, has unearthed ancient gold and silver jewelry. Bartilla seems to have existed as a Christian town before the sixth century AD. Its inhabitants were members of the church of the East, but in 610, according to Bishop Marotha of Tikrit, the Syrian Orthodox Church was able to take control of it. Its name was mentioned by Muslim geographer Yaqut (d. 1229) as a town east of Mosul, and part of Nineveh, and that all its inhabitants were Christians. It was also described by Ibn Fadhil Allah al-'Amri (d. 1348) as part of the land and country of Nineveh. Bartilla continued to be the resident of a long list of Syrian Orthodox church Mapheryans including; Gregarious Barsouma, Ghiwargis Matty I, and even Ghiwargis bin al-Ebry (the famous Bar Hebrious" who built the Yohanna bin Najara Monastery, in 1284.

Town of Karmales or Karmalesh

Karmales is built on the remains of a 3,000-year-old settlement between the Assyrian capitals of Ninevah and Nimrud. Historically it has been predominantly inhabited by the Christian Assyrians. It's name dates back to the ancient Assyrian period when it was called "Kar-Mullissi," meaning the city of Mullissi, one of the fifteen gates of Nineveh at the ancient time opened to the road leading to Kar-Mullissi. According to the cuneiform tablets, the son of King Shalmensser III (858–824 BC), known as Ashur-Daneen-Ablo, led a rebellion against his father in twenty-seven cities including Karmales. The city was greatly damaged, to the extent that it had to be abandoned. It was rebuilt by Shalmensser V (726–722 BC) and was expanded by Sargon II (721–705 BC).

Several relief sculptures and cuneiform tablets of Sargon and Shalmanser were found in the hills of Tel Ghani and Tel Barbara. In addition, an ancient temple and a palace were excavated at Tel Ghanim. (http://www.atour.com/education/20040819c.html)

According to Layard, an ancient sculpture and an inscription with entire work of poetry and a platform of brickwork was uncovered near Karmales. An inscription on bricks proved the Assyrian origin of the ruins, which included the name of an Assyrian king. (Layard, 1852, 35-6) Half way between Karmales and Harran, archaeologists have excavated Tilath-pileser's provincial palace that was similar to the one built by Ashur-nasirpal in Nimrud, but smaller. A temple dedicated to Ishtar was also built near the palace. Alexander the Great defeated the Persians in 331 BC near Karmales. (Roux Georges, 1992,309)

The Church of Mar Ghiwargis in Karmales was built in the sixth century. Other religious edifices in the town include the Mar Yonan monastery which dates back to the seventh century. The monastery known as Virgin Mary's daughters in Karmales was built in later centuries. Karmales is also well known for its St. Barbara Church, which it is built on top of an Assyrian temple dedicated to the God Bano. According to a legend, the church was built in remembrance of Barbara the daughter of a Parthian governor of Karmales, who, together with her servant, Yolena, converted to Christianity. No matter how hard her father tried to persuade them to renounce their new religion, they refused; consequently, they were imprisoned and executed by the order of a Zoroastrian priest.

Up to the mid eighteenth-century, inhabitants of the town were primarily members of the Church of the East. Starting at mid-eighteenth century, the Roman Catholic missionaries succeeded in converting the people of Karmales into Catholicism. Since then, they have been called Chaldean, in reference to their denominational affiliation. Presently, some inhabitants of the town belong to the Syrian Orthodox church, and a small minority of Muslims has moved into Karmales during the last century. Since the 2003 invasion of Iraq by the US, inhabitants of Karmales, including the Assyrian living in Mosul and towns in the Plain of

Nineveh, have suffered various terrorist attacks by the Islamists; consequently, there has been an ongoing exodus of Assyrians out of Iraq to the neighboring countries and the West.

The Town of Telkaif

Tel Keepe, or TelKaif in Arabic, is located less than eight miles northeast of Mosul, in northern Iraq. Its name in the Assyrian language means the stone hill. It is located on top of the ancient ruins of Nineveh. Its ancient cemetery and antiquity remains largely unexplored. The first documented mention of Telkaif dates back to the fifth century BC. A vase was found by the Iraqi Department of Antiquities in the vicinity of the Sennacherib's irrigation canals built in the seventh century BC.

It has a population of 5,000 people, most of whom belong to the Chaldean Catholic Church. It may well have been founded perhaps in the eleventh century, during the late Seljuk period. It was first mentioned in the thirteenth century as a Church of the East village in a poem by Ghiwargis Warda, who describes its sack by a raiding band of Mongols in November 1235 when its church of Mar Ya'qob the Recluse was destroyed. The first language of the inhabitants of Tel Isqof is Syriac, but they also speak Arabic, which is taught in the schools.

The ruins of several old churches and monasteries attest to the early Christian population of this town. Presently about 5,000, mostly Chaldean Assyrians live in Telkif. Its low population is due to a constant migration to other regions because of oppression and persecutions by the past governments and the Muslim extremists since the American invasion of Iraq in 2003. Some of its former inhabitants presently live in San Diego, California, and Detroit, Michigan.

Town of Zakho

Zakho, which means "victory" in the Assyrian language, presently has a diocese of the Chaldean church. It corresponds to the early Christianity of the Malthaiyah Diocese; it was a suffragan of the Adiabene or Arbela. It had Nestorian bishops from the fifth to the seventh century.

Due to its strategic location and plenty of job opportunities, Zakho has attracted workers and job seekers from different parts of Iraq and even some as far away as Syria and Turkey. A famous hallmark of Zakho is an ancient stone bridge. Georges Roux cites an old story told by a Khoshaba Zaya, which asserts that it was built by an Assyrian king.

Struggle for Survival in the Plains of Nineveh

Inhabitants of the Assyrian villages in the Plain of Nineveh have suffered unrelenting massacres during their long history. This is the only region in Iraq where Assyrians have managed to survive to this day as a group, in the ancient towns and villages inhabited primarily by them. Documented records of the Assyrian struggle for survival in this region are mostly lost or destroyed during countless attacks, by their Muslim neighbors. The crusaders invasion followed by the Mongol's conquest ushered an era of constant persecutions by the Kurds, Arabs, Mongols, and Turks against them. When the Seljuk governor of Mosul and his army went for an expedition to Damascus in 1171 the Kurds found it opportune to attack the Mar Mattay monastery. (Aprim Fred, @Zindamagazine.com, 1998)

In 1261, according to Bar-Hebrious, the Kurds descended from the mountains and attacked Mosul and its Assyrians villages, killing those who refused to accept Islam. They looted homes and churches, and occupied the monastery of the Nuns (Deir al-Rahibat), killing the nuns and others who had taken refuge there. Only those who managed to escape to the mountains were able to survive. In 1310 the Kurds and Arabs massacred the entire Christian population of Arbil. The Mongols who converted to Islam starting with Kazan's rule became sworn enemies of Christians and massacred them. In AD 1324 the Kurds attacked Baghdida, killed many, and burned four churches. In 1508 the Kurds attacked the Assyrian villages of Nineveh, their inhabitants were killed, children were abducted, and crops were set on fire.

Nader Shah's Destruction in the Plain of Nineveh

During one of the ongoing wars between the Persian and the Ottoman Empires, after occupying Baghdad for a year, the Persian king Nader Shah, sent a small part of his army (8,000 soldiers strong) to occupy the region of Mosul and Nineveh, but the army was defeated. In 1743 in command of 300,000 troops, and 390 canons strong, he headed to northern Iraq. After invading and occupying Kirkuk and Arbil, he moved to punish the Assyrian villages. He bombed Karamles before entering it. Most of the buildings in the village including Churches of Mar Yohanan and Beth Sahda, the "Church of the Forty Martyrs," were destroyed.

According to a 1746 report by the Priest Habash Bin Jomaa, during their four days stay in the plain of Nineveh, Nader Shah's soldiers first attacked the town of Karamles, killing many, kidnapping hundreds of women and children, and plundering the town. From there they moved on to Bartella, where they repeated the same horrors, then they advanced against villages of Tel Keppi and Alkosh they committed same crimes. The surviving inhabitants of the two villages took refuge in the nearby Monastery of Rabban Hormozd, but Nader Shah soldiers descended upon them like a pack of hungry wolves attacking helpless sheep. They committed such horrendous crimes that the priest Habash Bin Jomaa didn't have the heart to describe the atrocities. The villages of Bartella and Bakhdida suffered the same fate. It was estimated that during the Nader Shah's four-day attack against the Assyrian villages, over 4,000 people were killed.

Nader Shah's hatred of Christians and Christianity is evident by his attack against Assyrian monasteries such as Dair Mar Mikhael, Dair Mar Oraham, and Dair Mar Illia, were all partially destroyed, and in most cases their monks were murdered.

In 1828 Bakhdida suffered famine. In the same year, the army of Mosa Pasha, the governor of Amadyia, attacked Alkosh, his army, imprisoned several monks and priests, and caused tremendous damage to the Rabban Hormozd monastery. In 1832 Alkosh and other Assyrian towns were attacked by Mir-Koora, the Kurdish chief of Rawandoz. In Alkosh alone, he killed over 400 people. When he returned in March 1833 he killed another 172 of its inhabitants. In 1840 Mir-Koora's brother Resole Beg attacked Alkosh, besieged it for several months, set fire to Rabban Hormozd monastery, and stole and destroyed over 500 of its valuable books.

Chapter 10

Part 2

From the Fall of Nineveh to Christianity

While the first part of this book was devoted to establishing the link between the ancient and the Christian Assyrians, the second part retraces their history into Christianity and beyond.

Assyrians' Defeat by the Babylonians and Medes

Although for the rest of the world Assyria of the seventh century may have seemed invincible, constant struggle to put down rebellions in Babylon, repetitive campaigns against the kingdom of Urrartu and other provinces of the empire, including the invasion of Egypt had drained the Assyrian manpower and resources. Starting in 635, Civil war in Assyria weakened the empire to the point that it could no longer stand up against a foreign enemy. While the Babylonian sources provide some information about the events that led to the fall of Nineveh, they offer contradictory information about when they happened and in what order. Following is a summery of what led to the fall of Nineveh.

While he was still alive, Ashurbanipal appointed his son Ashur-etel-ilani as successor to the throne, but his twin brother Sin-shar-ishkun did not recognize him. The fight between the two brothers and their supporters forced the old king to withdraw to Harran in 632 BC, to remain there until his death in 627. Ashur-etel-ilani began his rule in Assyria in 633, but his general Sin-shum-lisher rebelled against him, and declared himself counter-king. Later, Sin-shar-ishkun, perhaps in 629, ascended the throne in Babylon.

Since the time of Tiklath-Pileser III and Shalmaneser V (726–727) the Chaldean tribes, who lived among the swamps and lakes along the lower course of the Tigress and Euphrates, were in constant rebellions against the central government, in Babylon. They were often helped by the Elamites, who were eager to dominate Southern Mesopotamia. Though the Chaldean tribes were defeated by Tiklath-Pileser III, they continued to create chaos.

According to Oppenheim, Chaldean tribes refused to pay taxes or render service to the government. If not controlled, they robbed the caravans, attacked and plundered settlements and small cities. When the Assyrian kings attempted to control the region, probably by placing garrisons in key cities and guarding their lines of communication, the Chaldean tribes must have made some kind of agreement with the Babylonian city-dwellers, to disrupt the Assyrian plans. By doing so, despite their anti-urban proclivity, Chaldeans must have been considered champions of the anti-Assyrian movement and the defenders of Babylonian independence. At the same time, there were pro-Assyrian movements in some Babylonian cities by those who wanted peace and security for the sake of their fields, gardens, ships, caravans, and livelihood. Therefore; in large cities such as Nippur the population remained loyal to the Assyrians up to the very end. During the reign of Sennacherib, Babylon was in constant state of revolt, which led to his destruction of the city in 689 BC. Its walls and temples were razed to the ground. To improve relations with Babylonians, his son Esarhaddon rebuilt Babylon to atone for the sins of his father, but that was not enough to ease the ongoing animosities of the Babylonians against the Assyrian rule. In addition, before his death, Esarhaddon appointed his son Ashur-banipal as the ruler of

Assyria and made his brother, Shamash-shums-ukin, the governor of Babylon under the Jurisdiction of his brother. According to a letter sent to Esarhaddon by an Assyrian noble, who was aware of the conflict between the two princes informed their father that "the settlement of the succession in this manner is no kindness to Assyria."

The double monarchy, proved to be a disaster. The Assyrian garrisons in Babylon expressed greater loyalty to Ashur-banipal than his brother, who was the legitimate king in Babylon. Growing friction between the two led to revolt by Shamash-shums-ukin who assembled an anti Assyrian coalition, which included the Phoenicia, Judah, Elam, Egypt, Lydia, the Arabs, and Chaldean tribesmen (Joan Oates Babylon p.123)

After discovering the plot, Ashurbanipal appealed directly to the Babylonians, perhaps to test their loyalty. Since that did not work, instead of taking direct military action against his brother, he besieged the cities of Babylon and Barsipa. According to the Babylonian chronicle the war went on for three years of perpetual clashes. Meanwhile as famine in the city intensified, and Shamash-shum-ukin's allies abandoned him, he committed suicide in 648 BC, in his burning palace. Ashurbanipal undertook various building projects in Babylon. Meanwhile, Assyrian war against Elam, which historically had made it habit to intervene in Babylonian politics, ragged until 639 BC. Babylon enjoyed twenty-one years of peace under the Kandalanu rule. When Kandalu died in 627, Sin-shar-ishkun, a son of Ashurbanipal declared himself King of Babylon, but his primary goal was to take over the throne in Assyria from his brother Ashur-etil-ilani. He succeeded in doing so in 623 BC. While Sin-shar-ishkun was occupied in Assyria, Nebupolassar who formerly was the ruler of sealand, seized the Babylonian throne. However, his rule was disrupted by ongoing struggle with the Assyrian forces that continued to remain in control of Nippur. Babylonian cities were passed from one warring faction to another. By 616 BC Nabopolassar's position had improved to an extent that he marched into the territory previously under the Assyrian control and attacked the ancient Assyrian capital, Ashur, but his forces were repelled. Babylonians took refuge in Tikrit. (Joan Oates Babylon p. 127)

The Babylonian success emboldened the Medes who had become the heirs of the Elamites in Western Iran, and together with a coalition of Scythians and Cimmerians in 614 BC marched against the Assyrian city of Nimrud (kalkh). It was sacked and the walls of Ashur were breached, the city was captured and looted. Nabopolassar hastened to join the attack but arrived late. Near the ruins of the city, he met with the Median king, Cyaxares, and ratified a formal treaty and according to tradition—a marriage was arranged between the Median princess, the daughter of the Median king Cyaxare, with Nebuchadnezzar, Nabopolassar's son to cement the alliance.

In 612, after a year of inconclusive campaigning by the united forces of Medes, Babylonians, Scythians, and Cimmerians, Nineveh fell. The Assyrian king Sin-shar-ishkun is said to have perished in the flames that consumed his palace. The size of Nineveh and its many gates undermined an effective defense against the enemy. Ashur Ubalit II, one of the military officers, along with the surviving Assyrian army fled westward toward to Nisibin, from there they went to Harran, where they held up until 610 BC, until they were driven out of the city by the combined forces of the Medes and the Babylonians.

Persian, Achaemenid Domination of Assyria and Babylon (539–330 BC)

In 550 BC, Cyrus the Persian, captured Ecbatana, the Median capital. Its wealth—consisting of gold, silver, and precious objects—was carried off to Anshan, the center of the Persian kingdom. Consequently, Mada became the first Satrapy of Persia, followed by Assyria, Syria, Armenia, and Cappadocia. On his way to Babylon, Cyrus marched north into Assyria and crossed the Tigris below Arbela. Assyria fell. Nabunaid saved the gods of Ashur and Nineveh behind the walls of Babylon.

To conquer Babylon, Cyrus seems to have previously gained the support and the cooperation of the governor of Gutium in southern Babylon—Gubaru or Gobryas—and perhaps also the help of the priests of Marduk. The defense of Babylon was entrusted to the Nabunaid's son, Belshazzar, who confronted the Persian army at Opis. Cyrus easily defeated Belshazzar, and his army was scattered.

"In the month of Tashirtu, when Cyrus attacked the army of Akkad at Opis on the Tigris, according to an inscription by Cyrus, the inhabitants of Akkad revolted, but he (Nabunaid) massacred the confused inhabitants. On the fourteenth day, Sipar was seized without battle. Nabunaid who was probably present in the city fled. On the sixteenth day, Gobryas, governor of Gutium, and the army of Cyrus entered Babylon without battle. Afterwards Nabunaid was arrested in Babylon. Till the end of the month, the shield carrying Gutians were staying within Esagila to keep it secured. Such precautions indicate perhaps a prior agreement with the priest of Marduk and a payback. On the third day, Cyrus arrived in the city and was received as a liberator by all classes, especially the priests and the nobles. He appointed Gubaru the governor of Babylon.

As one contemporary writer put it: *"It was, in fact, a new master of nations who stood upon the mighty Semite communities that for millenniums had ruled the world. A man of another race, to whom the valley of Tigris and the Euphrates was no longer the center of human power and human civilization, whose ideas of the divine and the human world were formed under other skies, and whose empire stretched far away beyond the boundaries of Assyria in its fairest splendor . . ."*

On the fourth day of Nissan of 538, Cyrus's son, Cambyses, took the hand of Bel in the New Year Festival, and from then on he acted as viceroy with a headquarter in Sipar. In 528, when Cyrus was killed on the battlefield, Cambyses inherited the throne. Babylonians enjoyed a period of relative peace. In 522 BC, during an expedition to Egypt Bardiya, a brother of Cambyses who had been left in charge of Media, Armenia, and Cadusia proclaimed himself king. By July he was recognized all over the empire. According to Darius, upon learning of this, Cambyses committed suicide and the royal spear-bearer who was a member of the royal family from another branch took the throne. Darius also claimed that the new king was a man called Gaumata and not Badriya, according to Darius. Soon after ascension to the throne, Cambyses had killed his own brother to prevent any possibility of usurpation. With the aid of six conspirators, Darius managed to kill Gaumata and took the throne for himself.

Several Satraps (governors of national states) appointed by Cyrus refused to recognize Darius's right to rule. A Babylonian called Nidintu-Bel declared himself Nebuchadnezzar's son, recruited an army, and seized the kingship in Babylon. Darius defeated his forces; he was captured and executed. Shortly after, an Armenian (Urartian) called Arkha, son of Haldita, proclaimed himself son of Nabunaid and declared himself king of Babylon. He too was defeated; together with some nobles and followers he was impaled in Babylon. By the beginning of 520 BC, Darius had defeated all his enemies and was recognized as king throughout most of the Middle East. He put in place an administrative system based mostly on the Assyrian model.

During the kingship of Xerxes, Babylonians made more attempts to free themselves from Persian rule. Two native kings, Bel-Shimanni and Shamash-Eriba, claimed the throne but their rebellion was crushed. In 482, according to some historians, Xerxes retaliated by destroying the city of Borisppa and pillaging Babylon. Xerxes dismantled Babylon's walls; the golden statue of the Marduk was melted down; the priests were arrested and slain; the rebels were tortured and slain.

Because of such revolts, Babylon paid the empire's greatest tribute and was obligated to donate 500 boys to the King to be made eunuchs. The Persian economic practices, which consisted of hording all the gold and precious metals they could collect, resulted in soaring prices beyond all reason. Murder by the members of the royal family was also a problem. In 465 Xerxes was killed by his eighteen year old son Artaxerxes, who also slayed two of his brothers as well as others who stood between him and the throne. Similar court violence continued for 130 years. (Collins, Robert, 1972, 153) In describing why Babylon did not restore a national monarchy, Georges Roux writes that Mesopotamian kings were held responsible by gods for the welfare of their subjects. They were also required to build temples, palaces, fortifications, parks, and gardens. They always made sure that canals were dug and extended. They took care to build dykes and dams, and safeguarded the land rights. These functions were of vital importance for the inhabitants of Mesopotamia. Only a king who resided permanently in the country could be aware of what needed to be done and would be capable of raising the needed funds and the mobilizing necessary labor to take care of such projects on a national scale.

"Without her own rulers, Mesopotamia was to a great extent paralyzed. Sooner or later it could be predicted: buildings left unattended would crumble down, canals would become silted-up and part of the land would revert to desert." (Roux, Georges, 1992, 409) *"The first Persian kings were aware of their duties towards one of their richest and most civilized provinces, carried out some of the royal tasks traditional in Mesopotamia . . . but Xerxes and his successors who engaged in endless wars against Greece, don't seem to have cared for their Babylonian satrapy."* (Ibid)

The Persians monopolized the trade routes with India and the East. At the same time, the Babylonian and Assyrians, who together formed the ninth satrap, were grossly overtaxed. They paid an annual tribute of 1,000 talents of silver and supplied the Persian court with food during four months of the year. Also, they had to contend with the greed of the local governors.

Another issue that undoubtedly prevented the defeated Assyrians and Babylonians from rising to power was the nature of the Mesopotamian religion that assigned a different patron deity to each city. For example, the primary deity worshiped by the inhabitants of Harran was the moon god Sin; the deity worshiped in the city of Ashur was Ashur; the primary deity worshiped in Arbailu was Ishtar. The divisiveness inherent in the Mesopotamian religion is evident by the fact that Babylonians were willing to sacrifice the sovereignty of their nation to rid themselves of king, Nabunaid, who attempted to elevate the worship of Sin above Marduk, the primary patron god of Babylon. Even during the Christian era, theological conflicts between the three major Christian Assyrian denominations has prevented them from uniting under one ethnic identity for their common interest.

Alexander the Great,

the Seleucid Dynasty (331–141 BC)

Alexander and his military, after invading Syria, crossed the Euphrates into Assyria, and on October 1, 331, defeated the army of the last Achaemenids king, Darius III (335–331), at Gaugamela, north of Arbil.

Babylonians greeted the Greeks with hymns, incense, and flowers. The new ruler who planned to make Babylon the capital of his empire began to repair and rebuild the temple of Marduk. He stayed there for a month, then left in pursuit of other conquests. In spring 323 BC, Alexander returned to Babylon. On June 13, 323 BC, at age thirty-two, he died in Babylon. Babylonians had hoped that the young king who avenged the crimes of Xerxes would restore the faded glory of their city, but that was not to be. According to the Babylonian chronicle, the death of Alexander was mourned in Babylon by weeping in the land and plundering in the city and the countryside. After a prolonged war for supremacy between Alexander's generals, Seleucus seized control of the citadel. He began his rule in October 312 at the western provinces, and in March and April 311 in Babylon and the eastern satraps.

Mesopotamia, which had suffered economically during the Persian rule, once again became a member of the economic world. It provided rich agricultural products, renowned carpets, fabric, and perfumes for export. It imported black glazed pottery from Athens and Megara, but by the third century BC was exporting ceramic from Assyria to Anatolia and blue-green glazed pottery to a wider market. To solve Babylon's housing problem, instead of repairing the old city, Seleucus began to build another city some forty miles north of Babylon, which he named Seleucia. (James G, Macqueen, 1964, 230-1) In 275 BC, Antiochus I, the son and successor to Seleucus, forcefully relocated the remaining population of Babylon to Seleucia, only leaving behind the temple priests of Marduk. This act more than anything else contributed to the destruction of the ancient Babylon. According to Strabo, men of Seleucia were called Babylonians and not Seleucians. During the Christian era, some writers often identified southern Mesopotamia as Babylon. Mani, the founder of the Manichean religion, writes that after his return from India to Persia in 241 AD, he traveled to Babylon, meaning Seleucia, and southern Mesopotamia. The Babylonian Talmud, a collection of Jewish religious writings, is called by that name because its authors lived in southern Mesopotamia during the first five centuries of Christianity.

The Parthian Rule (141 BC–224 AD)

The homeland of the Parthians, who were of Persian stock, was in Khorassan and Afghanistan in Eastern Persia. Their empire was called Arsacid (Arshaki) after its first king, Arshak. Their rule consisted of loosely knit kingdoms of warlike barons, each with his personal army, governing a section of the empire. While the ruling class in Mesopotamia was Parthian, the population in Mesopotamia was mostly Assyrian and Babylonian, as the early Christian writers also have attested to.

According to Pliny the Elder (Natural History VI. 112), the Parthian empire consisted of eighteen kingdoms. Seven of them were called lower kingdoms, meaning they were located in Mesopotamia. The center of the lower kingdoms was ancient Babylon, which was directly governed by the Parthian rulers. Beth Garami, in the north, included what is known as today's Kirkuk as its capital. Adiabene with Arbela as its capital was another kingdom. North of it was the province of Beth Nuhadra (Plain of Nineveh), it was governed by a general directly responsible to the Parthian king because it suffered most of the invasions by the Romans. Nisibin was the main city of the desert. The area, it was also known as Beth Arabaye, because it was where Arab caravans passed through. At the end of the Parthian period, the city of Hatra claimed this reputation. In the northwest, there were other principalities such as Sophene, Gordyene, and Zabdicene (near modern Jölemerik in eastern Turkey). To the east of Sophene was Osroene with its capital (modern Urfa), which also included Harran and was dominated by the Romans.

Segal writes that Parthian rulers of Adiabene were called "king of the Assyrians." For example, a contemporary of the Edessan king Abgar O'Kama who ruled Edessa was "Narseh the 'King of the Assyrians' " who was drowned in the river of Zab by the Parthians for his pro-Roman sympathies. (Segal J.B., 1970, 70) The first-century BC Strabo confirms that northern Iraq was known as Assyria at that time. He writes: *"In Aturia is village of Gaugamela, is where (Persian king) Darius was conquered (by Alexander the Great) and lost his empire."* He adds that the village was given that name because Darius kept camels at that estate for travel across the desert. The Macedonians seeing that this was a cheap village said the battle took place near Arbela. (Horace Leonard, 1923, 197) In describing Trajan's 116 AD invasion of Mesopotamia, Roman Historian Dio Cassius wrote:

"And the Romans crossed over and gained possession of the whole of Adiabene. This is a district of Assyria in the vicinity of Ninus [Nineveh] and Arabela and Gaugamela (Goomla) near places where Alexander conquered Darius are also in the same country, accordingly has been called Atyria [Attur] in the language of the barbarians, the double 'S' being changed to 'T'." (Dio Cassinus, 1955, 411)

There has been claims that kings of Adiabene were Jewish. However, Ezad was the only king of that dynasty who converted to Judaism, together with his wife and his mother. It happened with the help of a merchant known as Ananias, in Spasinou Charax, a principality near the Persian Gulf.

Chapter 11
Assyrian Christianity

Though Syriac traditions trace the beginning of Christianity among the Assyrians to the first century AD, there is no substantial evidence to support such a claim. Stewart McCullough writes, it is possible that fifty years of peace initiated by the Roman Emperor Hardian in 117 with the Parthians created an opportunity for Christian missioners from Syria to proceed into Mesopotamia. By the second century there were churches in Mesopotamia, but there is no information about who had built them or when. (McCullough Stewart, 1982, 22) Some Christian historians believe that Christianity arrived in Edessa from Antioch; others contend that it came from the East. This is based on research by Abercius Marcelius who indicated that the Christian faith was first established in Nisibin, or even Adiabene, and from there it reached Edessa. (Ibid.) McCullough writes that Nisibis had a greater Jewish community; therefore, it is more likely than Edessa to have evangelized first. The second-century Marcelious, a bishop of Hierapolis who traveled to Syria and northern Mesopotamia, composed his own epithet, which dates about 192 AD. He writes: *"I saw the land of Syria and all its cities—Nisibin I saw, when I passed over Euphrates, but everywhere I had brethren."* (Ibid. p. 23) According to the chronicle of Edessa in 201, a flood in Edessa destroyed the church of the Christians that was on low ground near river Daisan. Bardaisan (154–222), who was born in Edessa, where the river Daisan passed through the city, was a Christian, and a friend of King Abgar the Great. (Rassam Suha, 2005, 27) According to the Ancient Aramic documents:

> "Judas Thomas, who was the guide and ruler in the church, ministered in Edessa and all the countries round about it and all the regions on the borders of Mesopotamia. The whole of Persia, of the Assyrians, and of the Armenians, and of the Medians, and of the countries round about Babylon, the Huzites and the Gelae, as far as the borders of the Indians, and as far as the land of Gog, and Magog, and moreover all the countries on all sides, received the apostles' ordination to the priesthood from Aggaeus, a maker of silks, the disciple of Addaeus the apostle."
> (Roberts Alexander, vol. 8, 1869, 647)

Abgar O' Kama's Conversion to Christianity

According to a narrative titled, "The Teaching of Addai the Apostle," Addai (Addaeus) arrived in the city of Edessa in the first century AD. Both the Church of the East and the Syrian Orthodox Church consider this as the beginning of their Christianity. Abgar O. Kamma, who according to the legend suffered from an incurable disease after hearing about miracles performed by Jesus, sent a messenger to Jesus in Jerusalem and invited him to come and live in Edessa and cure his leprosy. Though Jesus praised Abgar for believing without seeing, he declined the invitation by saying that he had to finish the mission he had come to fulfill, but he promised that one of his disciples will come to heal him. Bishop Eusebius of Caesarea, who wrote the story about 'Addai the Apostle's arrival in Edessa, in 325 AD noted that he had found the information related to the story at the "archives of Edessa." The letter was well known throughout the East but not in the West. (Segal, 1970, 73-74)

> "Moreover, Narses, the king of the Assyrians, when he heard of those same things which Addaeus the apostle had done, sent a message to Abgar the king: 'Either dispatch to me the man who doeth these signs before thee, that I may see him and hear his word, or send me an account of all that thou hast seen him do in thy own town.' And Abgar wrote to Narses and related to him the whole story

of the deeds of Addaeus from the beginning to the end; and he left nothing, which he did not write to him. And, when Narses heard those things which were written to him, he was astonished and amazed."(Roberts Alexander, 1869, 26)

Segal writes the king of "the Assyrians" who was a contemporary of Abgar O'kama was Narsai and not Ezad as reported by Josephus. Segal, 1970, 70) According to the "Chronicle of Arbil," a history of Christianity in Adiabene, by the sixth-century Assyrian author Mshiha-zkha, a diocese was established in Arbil as early as the beginning of the second century AD.

The Legend of the Wise Men

Various early Assyrian writers have reported that the Wise Men, or the biblical Magi, who followed the shinning star to Bethlehem, were Assyrian/Babylonian astronomers. This is credible because archaeological discoveries reveal that before and during the first century AD, Babylonian astronomers were well known for their extensive knowledge of astronomy. The fifth-century Syriac writer Narsai wrote:

"When the great Assyria realized this [that Christ was born], called upon the Maglite [astronomers], and told them to take gifts and presents to the Great King (Christ). This will rejoice Assyria and would please Pars, Persia." (Odisho Ghiwargis Malco, 2002, 82) The fact that the Syriac language became the liturgical language of Christianity in Mesopotamia, instead of the Parthian or Persian language, provides reasonable credence to such claim. Narsai further writes: *"King Herod (of Israel) felt demeaned by the Assyrian [respect to the Christ by the traveling Maglite] therefore in anger he ordered the killing of the infants."*

Magites or Magians (Greek magoi) denotes the Babylonian priests who practiced astronomy and astrology to predict the gods ordained destiny for each individual. Their gods who resided on the planets included Nabu, Mercury, Shamash (the Sun God), Sin (the Moon god), Bell (Jupiter), Ishtar the Venus. The Magians were also called Chaldeans a name that Greeks gave to the Wise Men and the priests of Babylon as was used in the Old Testament story of

Daniel. Bar-daisan, who lived in the second century AD, describes the Magian as those who are *"governed by the decree of Fate"* and are subject to stars and planets. (Young William G., 1976, 15) *"According to the Bible, Balaam the astrologer came from Mesopotamia, and when the embassy of Balak King of Moab went to call him they brought the fees for divination with them."* (Young William p.3) Star worshiping continued by the pagans during the Christian era, in regions such as Harran. The Persian priests were also called Magians because they had learned similar practices from the priests of Babylon. While Western literature limits the number of the Wise Men to three, the Assyrian account claims that there were twelve Assyrians (Atturaye) astronomers, who followed a bright star from Babylon to Edessa. From there they sent three from among their party to visit Jesus, the infant King. The Western names for the three Wise Men are Malkom, Kasper, and Bagdassar. The etymology of these names attest to their Assyrian origin. Malkoon appears to be a corruption of the Assyrian Malkuna, which means "little king." Bagdhassar seems to be corruption of the biblical Belshazzar, is a variation of the Assyrian Bell-shar-essur, which in Akkadian means: *"Bell appointed a King."* Kasper is KiKhaw-Spar, or the Morning Star. The corruption of these names is understandable, as the Greeks who probably acquired them from other sources passed them on to the West. (Sabro a publication, Dec. 2000, no. 7)

In a homily about the town of Antioch, Addaeus is credited with having brought Christianity to the country of the Assyrians. *"To Simon was allotted Rome, and to John Ephesus; to Thomas India, and to Addaeus, the country of the Assyrians."* [The text actually reads among the Assyrians]. *"And, when they were sent each one of them to the district which had been allotted to him, they devoted themselves to bring the several countries to discipleship."* (Roberts Alexander, 1869, 135)

Chapter 12

Persian Sassanian Domination

(224–629 AD)

The Syriac Chronicle of Arbil indicates that Persians and the Medes had previously tried to defeat the Parthians several times without success. However, after establishing an alliance with the kings of Adiabene and Kirkuk in 224 AD, Ardashir Son of Babak, the founder of the Sassanian dynasty, defeated and killed Arataban, the last Parthian king. According to Tabari, Ardashir advanced from Media through Atropatene (Azarbaiejon), Nodshiragan/Adiabene to Asuristan/Assyria (southern Iraq), probably in 226/227. He conquered Seleucia-Ctesiphon; the capital of the Parthian Empire. He disbanded the local principalities and replaced them with governors and marzbans (protectors of borders), and declared the Persian Pahlavi as the language of the empire, and Zoroastrianism as the state religion, this engendered an inevitable clash with Christianity.

However, between 226–337, during Ardashir's rule, Christianity was left alone to grow and develop a more centralized administration, and its chief bishop continued to reside in the capital cities of Seleucia-Ctesiphon and diocese were established in the principle cities and were administrated by the local bishop, also known as Metropolitan (administrator) of the provinces. Later a uniting head of church was elected by the assembly of the bishops to serve as Patriarch, for the rest of his life. (Young, William G. 1974,17) During the Parthian rule, Christians had been free to practice their religion and speak their language, without restriction. The center authority for the Christian Assyrians living in central and southern Mesopotamia resided in the twin cities of Seleucia-Ctesiphon (pronounced /tees-foon/) near Babylon, twenty miles southeast of Baghdad.

King Shapur I (241-273)

When Ardashir died in 241 AD, his son Shapur, who inherited a well-organized empire, was determent to recapture the rest of territories that previously were part of the Achaemenid's empire. His policy of conquest and confrontation led to continuous wars with the Roman empire, which turned Mesopotamia into a battlefield between the two super powers, as had been the case during the wars between Parthians and the Roman Empire. Ardashir conquered Nisibin and Harran in 233, and threatened Edessa. In the confused fighting of the next ten years, Nisibin and Harran changed hands twice. In 243, emperor Gordian III rolled back the Persian offensive in Resh-Aina, but was killed shortly after. His successor, Philip the Arab, withdrew Roman forces from Mesopotamia, leaving behind garrisons to protect the principal cities.

When Shapur, in 260, laid siege to Edessa, Emperor Valerian crossed the Euphrates to confront the Persians, but the Romans were defeated and Valerian was captured. An inscription by Shapur records the defeat of the Roman army and the capture of their Emperor. Shapur's army advanced to Antioch, captured it and sacked it. Thousands of its inhabitants were slain, and others were carried into captivity.

Bahram II Reigned (277-294)

The fortunes of the Assyrians during the Sassanian dynasty ebbed and flowed depending on the degree of the Persian kings' fanatic dedication to their Zoroastrian religion. The Zoroastrian priests considered people of other religion as threats, and through the power of the throne they persecuted non-Zoroastrians. An inscription by Kirdir, a Zoroastrian priest, describes his success in destroying religions other than Zoroastrian in the empire, during the reign of Bahram II (276-293). His inscription reads as follows:

". . . And the gods 'water,' 'fire,' and domestic animals' attained great satisfaction in the empire, but Ahriman and the idols suffered great blows and great damage. And the [false] doctrines of Ahriman and the idols disappeared from the empire and lost credibility. And the Jews [yahud], Buddhists [shaman], Hindus [braman], Nazarenes [nasra], Christians [kristyan], Baptists [Makdag and Manichaens [zandik] were smashed in the empire, their idols destroyed and the habitations of the idols annihilated and turned into abodes and seats of the gods."
(Wiesehofer Josef, 1996, 122)

Persecutions of Shapur II (310-379)

During the Sassanian dynasty, Zoroastrianism was the state religion, and the Persian kings were considered to be the appointed agents of Ahura Mazda, a divinity exalted by Zoroaster. Wars between Romans and Persians ignited the wrath of the Persian kings and the Zoroastrian priests against their Christian citizens, not only because they refused to worship the Zoroastrian faith but also they shared a common religion with the Romans. Persecutions of the Christians often began in 'Seleucia-Ctesiphon, the capital city, spread to Beth Lapat (Jundi Shapur) located in the present Persian province of Khuzestan—which had a considerable population of Christians—from there, it continued in other cities of Mesopotamia. When Shapur II was defeated during an attempt to capture Nisibin in 338 AD, he was angry not only at the Romans who had defeated him, but also with the Christians of the city who had helped the Romans to stop him from invading it, because of the ongoing persecution of the Christians by the Persians.

A Syriac document known as The Act of the Martyrs describes the forth-century Shapur II's persecutions of the Christian Assyrian as follows. In 339 AD, Shapur II issued an order to his officials to arrest Shimon Bar Sabba, the head of the Christians in Seleucia.

"You shall not release him until he sings this document, and promises to levy and hand over to us a double poll-tax and tribute from all the Nazarene-people living in the territory of our Divine Majesty, and inhabiting our territory. For our Divine majesty has nothing but the troubles of war, and they have nothing but rest and pleasure! They live in our territory, but their sympathies are with Caeser, our enemy." (Young William G, 1974, 24)

Being obstinate, Shimon Bar Sabba refused to sign the letter or collect the taxes, arguing that Christians already paid heavy taxes and were too poor to pay more. His refusal infuriated Shapur and ordered Shimone to be arrested and brought before him. "In the Martyrology of Shimon, Shapur II accuses the bishop of having political motives for disobeying him.

The king said:

"Simone wants to make his followers and his people rebel against my majesty and become salves of the emperor who shares their faith. That is why he will not obey my command."

Then he asked: *"Where is your friendship for me?"*

Simone replied: *"I certainly love you and at all times, I myself and my people pray for your Majesty, as our scriptures command us to do, but the love of my God is better than your friendship. Oh king, any more than that they disobeyed, their churches should be destroyed."* (Wiesehofer Josef, 1996, 202) A period of persecution followed this episode, various Christian "Acts of Martyrs"' have chronicled such events. After Shapur II died his brother Ardashir II succeed him. Like his brother, he was sworn enemy of the Romans and had fought side by side with his brother, against them. During a war in Adiabene and Beth Garmi (Central Assyria) he massacred the Christians.

New School in Edessa

A new school was established in Edessa by Mar Ephraim with the help of other teachers from Nisibin. Ironically, it was labeled the Persian School because its founders had arrived from a city that was under the Persian rule. In the beginning, scripture and theology were the major subjects taught there, but later medicine and philosophy were added to the curriculum. The translation of the Hippocratic and Galenic texts attracted the interest of more students. According to one source, Ephraim added two large hospitals to the school. Segal writes that from the very inception of the Church, Christians were taught to regard the care of the sick as work of prime importance, and Syrian Christians [Assyrians] devoted much of their energies to medicine. (Segal J. B., 1970, 71)

It is known that clinical instructions to the students were given at the hospital adjacent to the school. This seems to be the first instance of such a teaching method in the history of the Medicine. (Whipple, 1967, 13) Before Ephraim's death there was famine in Edessa. While people were dying, those who had hoarded grain did not have any sense of pity. He chastised them by saying their wealth had corrupted them and had driven away compassion from their heart. They said there was no one they could trust to distribute their help honestly. Because Ephraim had a reputation for being virtuous, they trusted their donations to him. He shut off suitable areas in the streets and set up three hundred beds where the sick and the feeble could be taken care of. The ailing inhabitants of the surrounding villages were also brought to where they could be attended to. That year, with the help of the others, many were saved from certain death. However, Ephraim died the year after on June 9, 373, which was a time of plenty. In later centuries, both the Muslims and the Armenians of Urfa revered Ephraim. A spring festival was held near his tomb in the Armenian Church of St. Sargius on the April 28 until recent times.

During the theological conflicts of the fifth century, teachers and students of the Persian School trained in the theology of Theodore of Mopsuestia sided with Nestorius, who contended that Christ had both human and divine properties. The clash between the Dyophysite and Monophysite theologies resulted in turning the majority of the Edessans against Nestorius and his supporters, who contended that Mary was the mother of the human nature of Christ, but not of his Godly nature.

When Cyrus became bishop of Edessa, he convinced the Roman emperor Zino to close the school in 489 and drive out its teachers, students and supporters into the Persian territory. A church was built over the site of the former school and was cynically named "Our Lady of Mary, Mother of God." Consequently, the theological conflict of the fifth century divided the Christians Assyrians into two antagonistic camps: the Church of the East, which had not condemned Nestorius, and the Syrian Orthodox Church, which believed that Christ had only divine qualities. The former was given the derogatory nickname of Nestorian by its detractors, and the latter was labeled Jacobite, in reference to its fifth-century energetic bishop. (Whipple, 1967, 15)

Yazdegerd I (399–420)

In 399 AD, when Yazdegerd I ascended to the Persian throne, the Roman embassy sent bishop Marutha to represent Rome at the new king's ascension to the throne ceremonies. He became instrumental in earning the King's goodwill toward Christians of Mesopotamia who had greatly suffered various persecutions. Perhaps due to Marutha's efforts, Persians and Romans concluded a peace treaty in 410 AD, which resulted in Yazdegerd actively supporting and protecting the Christians from being persecuted by the Persian nobles and the Zoroastrian priests

. Marutha has been credited with prevailing on Yazdegerd to *"summon the first Church of the East Synod to meet in 410."* (William G young 1974, 27) Some forty bishops were invited to participate in the Synod, and instructions were sent by the river post to the local governors to allow them to leave. According to the text and records of the Synod, Yazdegerd put an end to the persecution of the Church. By his order, churches were rebuilt and permission was given to clergies to preach openly. Among the participants in the Synod were "Father Mar Izhaq, Bishop of

Seleucia and Ctesiphon, Catholicos and Archbishop of the East"; the ambassador "Mar Marutha, Bishop, mediator of peace and concord between East and West"; and a group of Western Bishops, including "Bishop Porphyry, Catholicos of Antioch," who had written letter to Marutha for the ear of the Shah." (Young William G., 1974, 28)

Izhaq and Marutha had an audience with the Shah in which he decreed tolerance of the Christians and their recognition as Millet. Izhaq was royally appointed as the head of the Millet. Marutha was a learned man and visited Persia several times. On one occasion, he restored to Yazdegerd his health when his own doctors were unable to do so.

Marutha was also able to obtain Yazdegerd's permission for the Christians of Persia to hold a council similar to the Nicene. Bishops were invited from throughout the Persian Empire and other countries. Some arrived in November 409 and spent the Christmas celebrations in Seleucia, and the council assembled in the great church of the city on February 410 AD. At this synod, bishops of the church of the East came to agreement that the Catholicos, whose seat was at Seleucia-Ctesiphon (Syriac Suluk), located near Babylon, will be the supreme head of all bishops of the East. Previously, the Bishop of Seleucia served as the head of the Eastern Church but was a subordinate to the patriarch of Antioch. Perhaps because of his tolerance of Christians, that the noblemen and the Zoroastrian priests disliked Yazdegerd. Yazdegerd's tolerance of Christianity and his friendship with the Roman emperor ended when some unruly Christians destroyed Zoroastrian temples, which led to another period of persecution.

Bahram V surnamed "Gor" (421–438)

After Yazdegerd I's death his son Bahram V replaced him. During his rule persecution of the Christians intensified, especially against the Persians who had converted to Christianity. Those who renounced their Christianity were forgiven; others who refused suffered cruel tortures. Their limbs and backs were marked with burning iron. Their hands were burned off and were subjected with other forms of frightful tortures. Wealthy Christians were exiled and their property was confiscated, churches were demolished and their stones and bricks were used for building Zoroastrian temples. When some Christians fled to the frontier cities of Arabia and Roman Empire, Bahram ordered they should be returned or he will declare war against the two countries. In the ensuing war between Romans and the Persians, the latter were defeated. A peace treaty between the two countries stipulated that Christian should be allowed to practice their religion without persecution in the Persian empire and the Romans should give the same rights to the Zoroastrians in their territory.

Yazdegerd II (456–485)

After the death of Bahram Gor, in 438, Yazdegerd II succeeded him. In the beginning of his rule, Christians were treated peacefully. But in 445, another persecution of the Christians commenced. Yazdegerd also killed his wife and many prominent men of the empire in 446. Assyrian annals state that Tahmazgerd, the leader of the Zoroastrian religion, and several of his cohorts were ordered to bribe Christians to become Zoroastrian, but that they should be tortured if they refused.

On July 15, 446 AD, the high priest and his lieutenants arrived in the city of Nisibin. They imprisoned prominent Christians and held them in a given area. Soldiers were sent to other cities to bring more prisoners so that all could be transferred to Seleucia for trial. Among the prisoners were women, children, bishops, and other religious personalities.

Their horses and cattle were confiscated also. It was estimated that 133,000 men, women, and children were taken to Seleucia in addition to 20,000 inhabitants of that city who were previously arrested. Again, prisoners were informed that if they renounced Christianity and worshiped the sun, the fire, the water, and the King, they would be free to go; but if not, they would be tortured. Sixteen elephants were brought to trample to death anyone who refused. A letter sent by the King that was read also promised that anyone who renounced Christianity would be rewarded with riches and be honored, but those who refused would die. (Malech, 1910, 162-

65)

Theological Disputes:

Why Church of the East is not Nestorian?

Regardless of what Christian Assyrian historical identity may be, the idea that the proper name for them is Nestorian is not only incorrect, but also it can be described as simple minded. It implies that Assyrians as a people did not exist before the Church of the East, and its followers did not exist before the nickname Nestorian was imposed on them in the mid-fifth century AD. Nestorius was born in Germania, a city of eastern Cilicia. He was installed as patriarch of Constantinople by the Eastern Roman Emperor Theodosius II in 428, —three hundred or more years after the establishment of the Church in Mesopotamia, which he did not visit before or after his ordination. The Church of the East was wrongly labeled Nestorian because a number of the students and teachers of the so-called Persian School in Edessa/Urhay who supported Nestorius were driven out of that city and took refuge in the Persian territory.

Careful analysis by neutral Christian scholars during the last two hundred years have proven that neither Nestorius nor the Church of the East were as Nestorian as they have been accused of being. But such facts have gone un-noticed by writers who have insisted to define the Church of the East and the Assyrians as Nestorians.

During the first four centuries of Christianity, because there was no common consensus about the nature of Christ, his divinity, and humanity, religious leaders presented conflicting ideologies about this issue. In response to the Arian heresy, which claimed that *"since Christ was created by God, he could not have had the qualities which his father possessed,"* the council of Nicaea was convened in 321 AD. Arian and his ideology were condemned, in AD 381; the Nicene Creed became the official faith of the Roman Church and its affiliates, including the Assyrian Church in northern and southern Mesopotamia. However, the Nicene Creed's total emphasis on the deity of Christ for many was inadequate, because it ignored his humanity, which meant without a human intellect Christ's sacrifice, as man for man, would have been defective. (Vine, Aubrey R., 1937, 23) When Nestorius, a bishop of Constantinople, preached that Mary could not be considered the mother of God, his preaching was condemned. He was banished to the Oasis in Egypt.

"The usual view of Nestorius teaching was that Christ's body was conceived miraculously by the Holy Spirit in the Blessed Virgin Mary, but that he was born a man; the Holy Spirit afterwards descended on him, and then the Godhead entered into him. Such is the account given by St. Augustine." (Whipple, 1967, 14)

Christian scholars who have detailed knowledge of the Church of the East contend that neither Nestorius, nor the Church of the East, should be accused of heresy. George Percy Badger, who lived among the Assyrian of the Church of the East, the Chaldean Church, was well informed about the Syrian Orthodox Church, and was a scholar of the Syriac language, in a paper titled "Christians of Assyria," published in 1869, writes:

"But the question which more immediately concerns us is whether the so-called Nestorians of the present day hold the heresy attributed to Nestorius? My own solemn conviction, after careful study of their standard theology, is that they do not." He quotes Gibbon and Assemani who did not *'discern the guilt and error of the Nestorians."* (Gibbon, chpt. 47, note)

He further quotes Richard Field, who stated: *"But they that are now named Nestorians acknowledge that Christ was perfect God and perfect man from the first moment of His conception, and that Mary was rightly be said to be Mother of the Son of God, or of the Eternal Word, but think, it not fit to call her the Mother of God, lest they might be thought to imagine that she conceived and bare the Divine nature of the three Persons—the name of God containing Father, Son, and Holy Ghost."* (Field then goes on to say that the Greek Theotokos that rendered into "Mother of God" is much stronger than the Greek title, or the Latin equivalent "Depard" implys that the Blessed Virgin was as much the parent of the Divinity as of humanity of Christ." Badger adds: *Therein, also, I fully concur with the profound divine . . .* " (Badger, Christians of Assyria, 1869, 3-4)

The last outpost of the so-called Nestorians in the Byzantine Empire was the Persian School, established by the Assyrians of Nisibin who were driven out of Edessa in 364 AD, when their school was closed. Barsoma a former student of the Persian School who arrived in Nisibin long before others and was elected as Bishop of the city, became a primary force in advocating the so-called Nestorian creed within the Church of the East. In 484 he called a synod in Beth Lapat (Jundi Shapur) that was Nestorian in character. But shortly after, King Peroz died, and the new king, Balash (484–488), appointed Acacius (485–496) as the patriarch of the Church of the East. At a Synod held in Beth Adri in 485, all that had been decided at the Beth Lapat Synod was declared null and void. (Vine Aubrey R., 1937, 51)

When, Barsoma as the Metropolitan of Nisibin, and Acae, the patriarch of the Church of the East, were sent as ambassadors of King Peroz to the Emperor Zino. They were both cordially received. At the emperor's request, Barsoma drew up a statement explaining the doctrine of his church that described the divinity and the humanity of the Blessed Lord, and was lauded by the Greeks. (Badger, 1869, 4)

"Nearly a century later, about 581 AD, Hurmoz, son of Khosro Anushirwan dispatched the patriarch Mar Yeshaua-yau to the Emperor Maurice on a similar errand; and about AD 628, another Mar Yeshaua-yau along with several Metropolitans and bishops were sent to the Emperor Heraclius. In both cases, the visitors were also requested to draw up a formal declaration of their creed. It was regarded as Orthodox, and they were invited to celebrate the Holy Eucharist, the Greeks communicating with them, and they subsequently communicating at the celebration by the Greeks." (Badger, 1869, Ibid.)

The AD 628 creed drawn up by Patriarch Yeshaua-yau of Jedil that Badger considered non-Nestorian is also published in his

"Christians of Assyria" pamphlet. (Ibid. 15)

The seventh-century patriarch Ghiwargis I, (661–681) in a letter to a pastor and Chorepiscopus in Persia, explains why his church is wrongly defined as Nestorian. Badger further adds that the cessation of brotherly interaction with the Greeks, probably had more to do with the invasion of the Middle East by the Muslim Arabs. In a letter to Mina, Pastor and Chorepiscoups in the Persian Empire, the Church of the East, Patriarch Mar Ghiwargis I (661–680) rejected the accusation that his church was Nestorian, he wrote:

"Thou, our beloved brother, must know that this letter is not from the teachings of Teodorus, or Nestorius—these two good men have been held in contempt and scorned by foolish persons who lack knowledge and understanding—but the words of this letter are the words of Jesus Christ, our Lord. He has given them to his apostles by the Holy Spirit, and in brotherly love, we give it to thee." (Malek, 1910, 235)

After describing the divine and human nature of Christ, he contends that *"the writings of Ignatius, the first patriarch of Antioch, Antonius, the first bishop of Alexandria, Ambrosias, bishop of Milan, and many others have born witness to the apostolic origin of the true faith, the two natures of Christ."* (Ibid)

Badger also wrote:

"The existing members of their church, (Church Of the East), *very seldom call themselves Nestorian,"* except out of bravado or to distinguish themselves from the members of other Christian communities, preferring the National designation of Suraye (Syrians) or comprehensive title of Meshikhayi (Christian)." (Badger Ibid, 15)

The Second Assyrian School of Nisibin

The first School of Nisibin was established by bishop Mar Jacob in 325 after his return from the council of Nicaea. One of its first teachers was Mar Ephraim. When the Christian citizens of Nisibin were exiled, the school in that city was dissolved. After arriving in Edessa, its teachers established another school, known as the School of Persian, to differentiate it from the existing school in that city. *"The brilliance of its teachers brought the School more than local fame."* The first principal of the school was Qiyore, who was later replaced by Narsai and the staff was increased. The initial Curriculum included recitation, pronunciation, grammar, homily, and writing.

Studies were based on the St. Ephraim's commentaries and the works of Theodore of Mospsuestia. Later, the Greek's philosophy works were translated into Syriac, and history, rhetoric, and some fields of natural sciences were added to the curriculum. (Segal, 1970, 150) Bar-Soma, a student of the school in Edessa, upon arriving in Nisibin in 489 established a new school. In many ways, the second School of Nisibin was a continuation of the school in Edessa. When Mar Narsai arrived in Nisibin he became its first director. According to the historian Barhad Bashabba, Narsai had served as the director of the Persian School at Edessa for twenty years, and was employed as director of the second school of Nisibin for forty-five years. When he died in AD 509, Elisha held this office for seven years. At one time, the school in Nisibin had eight hundred students. They came from the central and southern Mesopotamia. Students lived in the dormitories and were not allowed to wander away form the school. There is evidence that they studied medicine also, but the medical school was independent from the rest of the school. Jenkins writes:

"The primary home of the Syriac scholarship was in Nisibin, which by the sixth century had developed into what can be described as a Christian university, a worthy successor to the academies of the ancient Greece. The fame of the school in Nisibin had spread around the world to an extent that it became a model for the pioneering Latin Christian scholar Cassiodorus in Italy. Much of the ancient world's learning was kept alive in Nisibin and was translated first

in the Syriac language, then was made available in Arabic to educate the succeeding generations of Muslim scholars, and via Arabic was transferred to the Europeans. In 1026 in a debate between a Muslim vizier and Nestorian bishop Elijah, the latter argued about the superiority of the Syriac Language over the Arabic language by stating that Arabs had learned most of their science from Syriac sources, while the reverse had seldom occurred." (Jenkins, 2008, 77)

As an example, Jenkins mentions *"the holy bishop Severus of Nisibin, who is known as Seboukt of Nisibin and headed the Jacobite monastery of Ghen-Nishrin, meaning "Eagles' Nest," on the Euphrates. In the mid-seventh century he wrote extensively on cosmography, on the causes of eclipses, and on geometry and arithmetic. Plus, he offered a classic account of the astrolabe. He also wrote commentaries on Aristotle's logic and translated the Analytics.* (Jenkins, 2008, 78)

The downfall of the Nisibin School is attributed partly to its being closed for two years from 540 to 541 by the order of the Persian king, Khosro Anushirwan, who began a new persecution of Christians because of his conflict with the Catholicos, Mar Aba, who was exiled to Azerbaijan. (McCullough Stewart, 1982, 155) The school was reopened in 542, but it was never as it had been. Its students were dispersed; some went to the school at Seleucia.

Khenana of Adiabene, who became a new director of school in c. 570–71, was a great instructor, but very controversial, because he injected theological disputations within the school. His theological leaning was considered identical to that of the Monophysites, a matter that was of concern to the leaders of the Church of the East. Consequently, the dissidents founded another school, near Nisibin. Khenana was repudiated by the Church of the East, but was supported by the Persian king, due to the efforts of his Monophysite physician Gabriel, and strangely, by the Patriarch Mar Aba. (McCullough, 1982,156) Because Khenana's opponents could not oust him, some three hundred students and teachers abandoned the school, he was left with few teachers and students. The school continued to function for a few more years, but as a teaching center and scholarly institution; its heydays were over.

The Rule of Khosro Anushirwan
(540-552)

Assyrian historians have praised Khosro Anushirwan for his tolerance and kind treatment of their people. The change in his attitude toward Assyrians, compared to other Persian kings, was partly because of the Persia's improved relations with Rome and also according to Assyrian sources it was due to the heroic efforts by the Assyrians who rescued the Persian army under Prince Anushirwan's command from disaster, when it was stranded without water in the desert of central Mesopotamia near Nineveh, as it was on its way to stop the White Huns before they could cross the Persian frontier. White Huns, also known as the Ephthalites by the Byzantine historians, by the fifth century had expanded westward toward the Sassanian territory. In 484 the Hephthalite chief Akhshunwar defeated the Sassanian army of King Peroz (459–484) and killed the king. The Huns took over the cities of Merv and Herrat that were previously ruled by the Sassanians.

Rescuing the Persian Troops

Assyrian writer Jacob of Edessa (640-708) of the Syrian Orthodox Church, in his chronicle completed in AD 692, documented an event that took place in 506 AD, when the *"White Huns with great number of fighters arrived in northern Mesopotamia, which was within the Roman territory, and killed thousands indiscriminately in Amadiya."* This chapter was published in Syriac by Arsanos Benjamin, in 1953, pages 15-40.

"The Persian king Govad suspected that after the Huns were done in northern Mesopotamia they would descend into the central and southern Mesopotamia, and from there it would have been easy for them to follow along the shores of the Euphrates River to attack the Persian capital cities of Seleucia-Ctesiphon. He hastily assembled a large army to confront the Huns before they could arrive within the Persian territory. He made peace with the Emperor Anastasias and informed him of his plan. The Persian army gathered at Beth Aramaye in southern Mesopotamia under the command of Prince Khosro Anushirawan and headed toward the northern frontier. They were in a rush to get to the northern border before the Huns crossed it. They chose to travel in a straight line, in the desert, far away from the shores of the Euphrates, so that they could arrive faster to their destination, and the Huns would not have been tipped-up about their location. Since they had no access to water, they loaded hundreds of elephants and camels loaded with war supplies and sheepskin containers filled with water and headed for the northern border.

The first two days of the journey went well. When they stopped to rest and to feed the troops and the animals, they downloaded the sheepskin containers to have easier access to the water for drinking and giving to the animals. The third day of their travel was much hotter than the first two. The thirsty elephants, during the rest-stop became uncontrollable. They stampeded toward the sheepskins crushed them under their feet, to drink and cool their bodies by rolling over the wet sand. By the time they were brought under control, not much water was left for the rest of the journey. The troops could not afford to waste much more time, and they continued on their way in hope of getting water and other supplies in the villages further north. However, before getting there, the extreme heat and thirst had taken their toll.

As it is often the case when traveling in the desert without water under unrelenting sun, the thirsty travelers become dehydrated and experienced what is known as a mirage. The tired fighters strained their eyes to find water. And in the distance they saw visions of a lake full of clear water, surrounded by trees. But after stumbling toward it, the vision faded, and all around them was nothing but dry, hot sand. Such visions intensified even more their mental anguish. Most of the troops were no longer able to continue on their way; they were either chasing the illusions of the oasis in every direction or had fallen on the ground unable to stand up. The survival of the Persian Empire and its people depended on these troops; without them the country would have been overrun by the enemy at no time.

As some were pondering such a tragic possibility from far away, they saw a small group of riders coming toward their position, but stopped to take a good look, then they turned around and disappeared in a distance. Fearing that they were the forward scouts of the Huns, the officers haplessly tried to mobilize their troops to get them organized, to stand up and fight, but the animals and the disoriented troops, suffering from nightmarish visions, had scattered in every direction in search of life saving water. They were in no shape for battle. As it turned out, the riders were not Huns, but were Assyrian scouts searching to find out if the Huns had crossed the border or had arrived near the Assyrian region to inform their leader Uballit, the governor of Nineveh, about the movement of the enemy. [It is interesting that about a thousand years after the fall of Assyria Uballit is cited as the name of the governor of Nineveh. Ashur-Uballit II was the name of the last Assyrian king, who ruled between 611–609 BC, in Harran, after the fall of Nineveh. Furthermore, it was not until the nineteenth century AD that his name was deciphered in the Babylonian Chronicle.

When the night fell, Persians had a chance to rest, but their situation had not improved much in the morning because their dehydration had worsened. Meanwhile, at dawn, Assyrians in the villages near Nineveh were awakened to the sound of drums, informing them that something unusual was about to happen. Later they were instructed to deliver as many containers of water to the ailing Persian troops as it was possible, to save them from certain death. Thousands of people were mobilized for this task. Enough water was delivered to the parched Persian troops to restore them back to health. Meanwhile, church bells rang across the plain, and bands of drum beaters and pipe players were told to play continuously to make the Huns to believe that a large army was approaching to defeat them. As it turned out, the Huns, for whatever reasons, did not bother to enter into the Persian territory.

In 557, when Khosro Anushirwan became king, he allied himself with steppe people from inner Asia and married a daughter of their chief, Sinjibu, who was the leader of the boldest and strongest of all the tribes and had the largest number of troops. The white Huns were mercilessly attacked from both sides and were defeated, and their king was killed. By 565, only small numbers of them had survived; they fell to the Arab invaders in the seventh century. In his res-gestae, (statement made by the emperor),

Khosro Anushirwan brags about his tolerance of other religions, He writes:

"We have never rejected anybody because of their different religion or origin. We have not jealously kept away from them what we affirm. And at the same time, we have not disdained to learn what they stand for. For it is a fact that to have knowledge of the truth and of sciences and to study them is the highest thing with which a king can adorn himself . . . "
www.cultureofiran.com/medicine_in_iran_01.html

He had a Christian wife who despite pressure by the king and his family refused to renounce her religion. According to the Persian writer, Firdausi, the king's friends and relatives shunned her and her son, Prince Anushzad. Consequently, he grew up as Christian. In his teens, Anushzad was separated from his mother and sent to a far away region to be educated about the Zoroastrian religion, in hope that he would choose his father's faith. But the young man fled to Rome and lived there for many years before returning home.

He was exiled to Bet Lapat (Jundi Shapur), where he lived in disgrace and was constantly under strict observation. When his father became dangerously ill, Anushzad found the means to marshal an army of dissatisfied Persians and Christians to confront his brothers at Seleucia in quest for the throne. His troops were defeated, and he was killed in the battle. His corpse was taken to Bet Lapat, so that he could be buried according to the Christian rites, as his mother had requested. (Malech, 1910, 188)

When Anushirwan's health improved, Zoroastrian monks demanded that Mar Ava, the Patriarch of the Church of the East, who was a Zoroastrian before converting to Christianity should be executed because they claimed, *"if he was not part of the conspiracy he would have prevented this tragedy."* They put him in heavy chains and took him to the king's palace together with an executioner. (Nafissi Saeid, 1964, 238)

Rather than confronting Mar Ava personally, Anushirwan sent loyal officers to deliver his order, which was:

"You have plotted against the King and have incited the Christians to rise up in many cities, against the Mobidan (Zoroastrian monks) and the judges. Christians have attacked them and have destroyed their property, and now they have revolted, and you are appointing priests and sending them to provinces without consulting with us, therefore I command that your eyes to be gouged, and be thrown into a pit until you die." (Nafissi, ibid.)

It is not clear to what extent this report is accurate because by the end it states that Khosro did not carry out this threat, instead he asked that Mar Ava instruct his priests to refrain from helping Anushzad, which indicates that it may have happened before the boy died. It has been also reported that Mar Ava wrote to the religious leaders in Bet Lapat asking them to maintain the peace. (Nafissi, ibid., 239) Mar Ava, was constantly harassed and threatened to death by the Zoroastrian monks. They succeeded in having him imprisoned for a total of nine years. He died in 552 AD. (Ibid., 240) Elaborate public funerals were held for him in various cities. There were indications that Mobidan had planned to steal his corpse to desecrate it, but widespread anger against such plot changed their mind. (Ibid.)

The Age of Enlightenment

Assyrians and the Jundi Shapur Academy

The city of Bet Lapat in southwest Persia, according to Mashikha-Zkha, was one of the twenty bishoprics of the Church of the East in 225 AD. (Young G William, 1974, 38)

After defeating the Roman army of the Emperor Valerian near Carrhae and invading Edessa/Urhay in 271 AD, the Sassanian king Shapur I rebuilt Bet Lapat and changed its name to Gondi Shapur, It was called Jundi Shapur by the Arabs in the later centuries. Shapur I is credited with having founded the Jundi Shapur Academy by ordering a collection of Greek works of philosophy and medicine to be translated into Pahlavi and to be available at the

Academy's library. He had married a Christian princess, the daughter of the Roman Emperor. She brought with her artisans to build and decorate her residence, and her personal physicians followed her to care for her in case of illness. The Persian king Govad, who was eager to distance the Christians of his empire from the Roman Church, welcomed the exiled Assyrian students and teachers of the school of Edessa. He was on good terms with the Assyrians who had saved his army from total disintegration, when stranded in the desert in central Mesopotamia during a war with the White Huns. Some of the exiled went to Nisibin to join a new school that was being established in that city; the rest were offered assylum in the city of Jundi- Shapur in southern Iran, in the province of Khuzestan, which already had a considerable Christian population. Arrival of the teachers and students from the school of Edessa transferred the Jundi-Shapur Academy into a world-class learning center. Whipple writes:

"The medical teachers and students brought with them their Syriac translations of Hippocratic and Galenic medical texts as well as their translations of Plato and Aristotle. In Jundi-Shapur they rebuilt their medical school and hospital. This center became the most important and influential link between Greek and Arab medicine." (Whipple Allen O, 1967 p.16)

Jundi-Shapur soon became a significant cultural and educational hub with a famous library and university. It also was the center of silk production in Iran with Assyrians being involved in every aspect of the production, management, and marketing. Greek philosophers and teachers arrived in Jundi-Shapur after the closing of the Plato's Academy at Athens. They brought with them works of Euclid's mathematics, the philosophy of Aristotle, Plato, Ptolemy and others. They wrote, taught, translated and held discussions with Nestorian scholars and with the king. Indian scholars who were brought to the school taught Sanskrit moral and ethical teaching as well as Indian astronomy and mathematics that included the use of Hindi numerals, which were later passed on to the Arabs and ended up in Europe to kindle the Renaissance.

"Students were initially taught in Greek or Syriac, but in the sixth century AD, Pahlavi language was added to the educational

curriculum, especially for the teaching of pharmacology." (Soylemez 2005: 22: 1)

According to the Egyptian historian Ibn-Qefti, (568–648 AH, 29): *"In the twelfth year of Anushirwan's rule, the physicians of Jundi-Shapur convened by the order of the king to discuss various scientific subjects. The therapeutic approaches of the Jondishapur physicians were considered more advanced than the Greek and Indian methods, because of the development of a new system of diagnosis and treatment that was developed there. The physicians were required to pass special examinations and obtain a license in order to practice medicine."* (Whipple, 1967, 18)

Before the rise of Islam, the Academy had brought together the collective knowledge of the Greeks, Romans, Jewish, Assyrian, Persian, and Hindu scholars. The high standard of medical teaching at the Jundi- Shapur School and hospital continued until the eighth century when many of its well-known physicians were called to Baghdad by the Caliph al-Mansur. After surrendering to the Muslim military leaders in 636 AD, the Academy was left undisturbed; however, after the establishment of the House Of Wisdom at Baghdad, the importance of Jundi-Shapur was overshadowed, and it gradually disappeared. However, its influence continued until the eleventh century because the first generation of scholars who arrived in Baghdad were graduates of the Jundi Shapur Academy.

Translations Into the Pahlavi Language

During the rule of King Govad and his son Anushirwan many books were written or translated by the Assyrian scholars into the Pahlavi language.

1. Metropolitan Eisha Bar Khozaey translated "The Christian Faith" for the Sassanian king Govad (488-531 AD)
2. Catholicos Acacius [Aqiq] translated "The Religion of Christ" into Pahlavi for king Govad.
3. Paulus, a Christian scholar of philosophy from Nisibin who

later converted to Zoroastrianism, wrote a books in the Pahlavi language titled "History of Philosophers and their Works," by Porphyry, in four essays, from Thales to Plato..

4. "The Logic of Aristotle," a selection in Syriac based on anthology of Sarguis of Reish-Ayna was translated into Pahlavi and dedicated to Khosro Anushirwan (531-579) by Paulus of Nisibin.

5. "The Philosophy of Aristotle" (concise), originally translated into Syriac by Nicholas of Damascus, was rendered into Pahlavi for Khosro Anushirwan.

6. Beloos of Basra has been credited with writing and translating into Pahlavi "The Book of Logic", for Khosro Anushirwan. He also wrote a book in Latin titled "Instituta Rularia Divinae Legis."

One of the earliest translators of the Greek works into Syriac was Sarguis of Ras-al-Ayna (Reish-Ayna). He was born about 536, studied in Alexandria where he mastered the Greek language, and became a celebrated physician. His translations into the Syriac included various works of medicine, philosophy, astronomy, and theology.

Mana, an Assyrian scholar of the fifth century from Nisibin and a priest of a church in Beth Ardashir, published several books about the Greek's philosophy and science. His scholarship seems to have transformed that city for centuries to come into an important learning center. Yagout, in his "Mojaem al-Baledan," wrote, in the thirteenth century, a group of scholars in 'Bet Ardashir' were still writing books about medicine, astronomy, and other sciences.

The Rule of Khosro Parviz (592–627)

After Anushirwan's death, Hormozd IV ruled until 590 AD. His death temporarily put an end to war with Constantinople. His son, Khosro II, had trouble claiming the throne because one of Persia's generals, Vahran Chobin, refused to acknowledge Khosro's right to govern. A civil war ensued, which led to Khosro taking refuge in Roman Circesium. From Circesium, he wrote to Emperor Maurice (583-602) asking for his help. Despite disapproval of the senate, Mauris assisted Khosro. According to Michael the Great, (Cabot Chr. de Michael, 2, X, xxiii, 371-72), Khosro went to Edessa and waited for forces to be sent by Mauris. With additional help from Persian Armenians, Khosro invaded his own country. After capturing Ctesiphon, he became the legitimate ruler. A peace treaty was signed with Maurice. However, in 602 during a revolution, Maurice was dethroned. He and his five sons were killed. Phocas was proclaimed king. When Khosro heard about this, he was enraged and decided to avenge his death by attacking Syria. (Cabot Chr de Michael, 2, X. xxv, 377)

War Against Syria

As one Persian army occupied Anatolia, the other conquered Syria. At Antioch, the Jacobite and the Nestorian Patriarchs held a joint council to discuss common action against the Orthodox. Phocas sent an army to punish them by killing thousands of their followers. (Runciman Steven, 1996, p. 9) Persian wars against Romans continued for twelve years. The inability of Phocas to stop the Persians as well as other issues led to his being dethroned. Heraclius, who was of Armenian descent, was appointed as emperor.

Antioch fell in 611; Damascus fell in 613. Persian general Sharbaraz entered Palestine in 614. His army pillaged the countryside and burned churches along the way. On April 15, it laid siege to Jerusalem. Patriarch Zacharia was willing to surrender, but Christian inhabitants refused to comply. On May 5, with the help of the Jews within the walls, Persians entered the city. Churches and houses were torched, and Christians were massacred, partly by the Persian soldiers and even more by the Jews. More than 60,000 were killed, and 35,000 were sold in slavery. The sacred relics of the city were sent to Persia. (Runciman Ibid p.10)

The part played by the Jews in the destruction and the killing of Christians in Jerusalem was never forgotten or forgiven. The fall of Jerusalem was a shock to Christendom. Khosro II, like Anushirwan, had a Christian wife, whose name was Sherin. She was renowned for her beauty, wit, and singing. At first, she was a member of the Church of the East. She was unable to bear children, but the court physician Jibrail (Gabriel) of Shingar, a member of the Syrian Orthodox Church, gave her a treatment that helped her to have a son, named Mardanshah. (Young, 1974, 74-5) Therefore, she joined the Jacobite Church and together with the doctor worked against her former Church. The love affair of Khosro and Sherin is legendary in the Persian literature. She was the only one who remained by his side to the end. Her son Mardanshah was killed by Khosro's son, Govad II, who killed sixteen of his brothers after Khosro's defeat.

Defeat of Persia near Nineveh

It was not until 622 that Heraclius could take the offensive against the Persians and drive them out of most of the Roman lands. The last battle took place in December 627 near Nineveh. Before the war, the Persian General Razates, who had been ordered by Khosro to either win or die, challenged Heraclius to hand-to-hand combat. Heraclius succeeded in defeating and killing him. Nightfall ended the war, which resulted in overwhelming victory for Romans. Khosro Parviz abandoned the battlefield and fled south. Heraclius marched southward on the eastern bank of the Tigris and spent the Christmas in the "Paradise" of Yesdem south of the great Zab before advancing. Xenophon described this park as being populated by ostriches, gazelles, and wild asses. The first Roman destination was Dastagherd, where Khosro had built a palace near the river Arba, some seventy miles north of Ctesiphon. Its inhabitants were treated well, but the building with its entire splendor was burned to the ground.

Khosro, along with his wife, Sherin, fled to Ctesiphon but did not dare enter the city because his astrologer had warned him that if he stepped inside, his doom was certain. He rejected the peace offer sent to him by Heraclius and continued his escape while ordering the old men, women, and children to defend the city. He was eventually caught and imprisoned by his son Govad II Sheriva, who took delight in killing his sixteen brothers as his father watched. (Bury, 1899, 249-252) Sheriva made peace with Heraclius and brought to an end the last war between the two empires. Assyrians were given additional freedom because of request by Heraclius that Christians should be treated well. The Church of the East, long prohibited from electing a patriarch, chose Ishu-yahav II (628-644), the former bishop of Nineveh, as its new leader.

Bloodletting and disarray followed the utter defeat of the Persians by the Romans. after a short reign Govad II Shervia died in Dastegerd in 630 AD. During the following thirteen years, three kings and two queens ruled the Persian throne, each was killed after the other. Special mention is made in the Assyrians' history of Queen Purandokt who sent the Patriarch of the Church of the East, Mar Ishu-yahav, together with Goryagus, Metropolitan of Nisibin, and Gabriel Metropolitan of Kerka d' bet Suleuk (Kirkuk) along with Shahduma, the messenger, to the Byzantine court. (Malech George, 1910, 216-217)

Chapter 13
Arab Conquest of Mesopotamia

Four hundred years of warfare, between Romans and the Persians had exhausted both empires. The last war between the two, which took place in 627 AD, resulted in humiliating defeat of the Persians. The murder of king Khosro Parviz and the resulting turmoil in the country had undermined Persia's military capabilities. Consequently, after defeat of the Roman's in Syria by the Arabs in 635 AD, they easily vanquished the Persians at Kadisiyah. Victory of the Muslim was also made possible with the help of the Arab tribes in Syria and Southern Mesopotamia, who joined their Arab brethren against Romans and the Persians. The Syriac-speaking Christians who had suffered greatly by the continuous wars between the Romans and the Persians and had been oppressed and were over taxed for centuries were in no position to fight against the new invaders. The city of Ctesiphon fell to the Arabs in 637 AD. The wealth accumulated in the city was so great that each Arab soldier received 12,000 silver coins, and gold was as plenty as silver. Items among the fabulous wealth included:

"a life-size silver camel with rider of gold and a golden horse with trappings of gold, emeralds for teeth. And its neck set with rubies. . . . There was also a royal banquet carpet, measuring 105 by 90 feet, portraying landscape within a gold background, divided by various paths of silver; meadows made of emeralds; cascading streams of pearls; trees, flowers, and fruits studded with diamonds,

rubies, and other precious stones. It was cut into pieces and divided." (Nettleton Fisher Sydney, 1969, 48-9)

The second defeat of the Persians in Nekhavend gave the Arabs control of Persia. The last king of the Sassanian was Yazdegred III, who came to power after killing the previous king Hormezd V. By 642, the Arabs had complete control of Persia, and Yazdegerd remained as a shadow king, encamping from one place to another. In 651–52, he was killed for his jewelry while hiding in a flourmill in Khorassan. A Christian priest buried his body, which had been thrown out in a field.

By then the Arabs had invaded the Eastern frontiers of the Exus and the Afghan. Meanwhile, in 639, a Muslim general invaded Egypt with only 4,000 men. Inhabitants of the conquered lands continued to work and live as they had for centuries. Since the Christians were promised a greater freedom of faith, Arabs had little problem in obtaining cooperation from the local people. And since the new rulers had acquired great wealth and received additional taxes from their subjects, there was no reason for them to change the statue quo. Because of repeated persecutions, expulsions, and conversions to Islam over many centuries, the Christian Assyrian population in its historical homeland—including today's Iraq, southeast Turkey, and northwest Iran—has been reduced into insignificance and replaced by Muslim Arabs, Kurds, Turks, and Persians.

By looking at Iraq and southeast Turkey today, it is hard to imagine that they once had a considerable Christian Assyrian population. The Muslim population in these regions that have historically treated Christian Assyrians as uninvited foreigners in their own homeland. During World War I, the Assyrian population—including members of the Church of the East, the Syrian Orthodox Church, and the Chaldean Church—was massacred in Turkey and northwest Iran in what is often called the Armenian Massacre. Most people in the West seem to be unaware of the fact that there are non-Muslim minorities in Iraq and other countries of the Middle East who have lived there since before the seventh-century Arab conquest of the region. Assyrians in the West are often confronted with the question, "When did you become

Christian?" The assumption being that they were Muslim and converted to Christianity in recent centuries, with the help of the Western missionaries. In fact, Assyrians are known as one of the oldest Christian people in the world. They still speak a language related to the Aramaic that was spoken by Christ.

The Oldest Church in Karbala

Christian Assyrian history in Iraq, Turkey, and Iran remains buried under a layer of Islamic culture superimposed over it, but is easily revealed with a little digging. For example, the city of Karbala, located 140 kilometers south of Baghdad, is considered by the Shi'a Muslims as the holiest place in the world. In a battle on October 10, 680 AD, Imam Hussein ibn Ali, grandson of Mohammed, who was pretender to the Caliphate, was killed along with seventy-one of his followers and members of his family. They were buried in Karbala. An article dated January 2005 that was published in the Al-Ahram weekly, a leading English-language newspaper in Egypt, titled "Buried in a Muslim Stronghold is the Oldest Church in Iraq." Nermin Al-Mufti visits the ruins of a church that was discovered in 1970s, about twelve miles from Karbala, where a crypt was found bearing Syriac text. The Arabs call this Church Gasser.

Another article titled "Karbala throughout History" on a Shia Islamic website asserts that *"The origin of the word 'Karbala' is Assyrian, and it is composed of two syllables: 'karb,' meaning 'near,' and 'alah,' which is derived from 'Iyle,' an Aramaic word standing for 'God.' Hence, the term 'Karbala' signifies 'near God'."* Based on the name of the city, we come to the conclusion that Assyrians had inhabited this region before the Arab Conquest. This is also supported by the fact that a nearby village called Ninawa, like the capital of ancient Assyria in northern Iraq was mentioned in the elegies of Al-Hussein, side by side with Karbala, along with two other names, "At-Taft" and "Al-Ghadiriyyah."

The existence of a village called Nineveh in southern Iraq indicates that Christians who lived in that region were aware of their Assyrian identity. This should not surprise us because Southern Iraq was a Persian Province known as Asorestan during the Sassanian dynasty. In describing the history of the Church of the East, Nermin Al-Mufti wrote:

"The origins of the Church of the East date back to the decades immediately following the death of Jesus Christ. While several of Christ's apostles preached in Mesopotamia, including St. Thomas from 35–37 AD and St. Peter in 54 AD, the Church of the East, of which the Chaldean Church is a daughter, credits its formal establishment to St. Thaddeus, who preached in Mesopotamia from 37 to 65 AD. After the martyrdom of St. Thaddeus his disciples continued the missionary work."

The Oldest Christian Cemetery in Najaf, Iraq

Najaf in southern Iraq is widely considered to be the third holiest city of Shia's Islam and the center of Shia political power in Iraq. Recent archaeologist discoveries indicate that before the seventh-century invasion of Mesopotamia by the Arabs, Najaf, like Karbala, was the city of Christian churches and monasteries. According to an article published in ankawa.com, on March 9, 2012:

"The remains of 33 churches and monasteries are still standing and scattered in the area of Al-Najaf. They represent physical history of the city churches, and their bells that were instrumental in spreading Christianity to the world." According to researcher Selma Hussein: *"The well-known Christians in Najaf in that time were scientists, doctors, and logicians, such as Mar-Athelia, Saint Hanna Neshoa, Saint Youhanna (Hochagh), and Shimon bin Jabir."*

In another article dated February 13, 2013, Ankawa.com reported about the discovery of the largest cemetery in Najaf Iraq. According to the director of the excavation in Najaf, the findings confirm that Najaf had the largest Christian cemetery in Iraq. The area of the cemetery was approximately 1,116 acres. He said the graves of Christians were represented by sign of the cross on their gravestones. In the graves were found glass bottles used to store perfumes of different kinds. The oldest of the graves dated back to the Sassanid period, almost two thousand years ago. Some graves also included Christian relics such as crosses and gifts buried with the dead. Also, items such as clothing, jewelry, that the deceased would have needed at the underworld. Graves at a lower level, dated back to the Babylonian period, included clay tablets.

The Founding of Baghdad

In 750 AD, with the help from non-Arab Muslims of Iran, Abu al-Abbas succeeded in overthrowing the Umayyad dynasty. After this, he establish his own line of Caliphates, and moved the center of Islam from Syria to Mesopotamia. The first 'Abbasid Caliph lived at al-Anbar, on the Euphrates. The second Caliph, Abu Ja'far Al-Mansur's (754–75), who succeeded his father, founded the city of Baghdad as the center of the empire. In describing how the site for the city was chosen Al-Tabari writes:

"He came to the area of the bridge and crossed at the present site of Qasr al-Salam. He then prayed the afternoon prayer. It was in summer, and at the site of the place there was then a priest's church. He spent the night there, and awoke next morning having passed the sweetest and gentlest night on earth. He prayed, and everything he saw pleased him. Then he said, 'this is the site on which I shall build. Things can arrive here by way of the Euphrates, Tigris and a network of [existing] canals. . . ."
(Hourani Albert, 1992, 33)

It was here where he decided to build the capital city of his empire, where there was a town of considerable antiquity, known as Bag-Da-Du in the Babylonian times, which explains why the new city was called Baghdad. The city was built among orchards and fields surrounded by Christian churches and villages. a section of the city was allotted to the Christians, it was called "Qal'at an-Nasara (Christian quarter). In later centuries, Christians dispersed beyond the confine of this neighborhood, mostly towards the western side. During the Abbasid rule, at one time, there were fourteen monasteries and as many as eighteen churches in the

Baghdad.

Mesopotamia During the Arab Rule (639-258)

At first the Arab troops were set in camps near the desert, but later camp cities were established in Basra and Kurah, in central Mesopotamia. Non-Muslims were forbidden from bearing arms, and were subject to their own laws. The land and taxes belonged to the Muslim community. The income of the state came from different sources: Kamus, or one fifth, of the booty, as directed by Mohammed; Jiza, or poll tax levied on non-Muslims; and land tax levied on the non-Arab cultivators. The total was so large that Arabs no longer had to pay Zakha, and since the proceeds belonged to the Umma (Arab Nation) anything above what was needed for defraying the expenses of war, administration, and public welfare was distributed among them.

The taxation policy in reality served to transfer wealth from the non-Arabs to the people of Arab ancestry. In addition, for being exempt from paying Zakhah, all Arabs received an annual stipend, depending on the length of their faith in Islam, service to the prophet, and tribal position. Relatives of the prophet received as much as 12,000 dirhams (about $3,000) annually. Since Islam in the beginning was equated with being Arab, soon non-Arabs professed Islam to escape the grinding taxation and social degradation and to receive the stipend and be entitled to power and prestige. While the top level of the society was reserved for the Arabs, the second level consisted of the Christians, Jews, and Zoroastrians. The work of cultivation, trade, and local administration of various districts was left to the non-Muslim inhabitants, who were called "ra'iya," or herd laboring for the benefit of Islam. The local bishop was put in charge of the affairs in the Christian territories.

While the Greek, Roman, Persian, and Islamic contributions to human civilization are often acknowledged, those of the Syriac-speaking Assyrians is seldom mentioned. Between the dawn of Christianity and the tenth century AD, the Syriac speaking population played an important role in the advancement of the human civilization, but it seldom has been given proper credit, because at later centuries it was overshadowed by the Arab culture, which matured into prominence due to its military power and newfound financial clout.

Long before the conquest of the Middle East by the Arabs, at the seventh century AD, the Syriac speaking civilization had become a repository of the existing knowledge. The Greek's books of medicine, philosophy, and other sciences, which no longer were appreciated in the West, were translated into the Syriac language. Teachers and graduates of the Assyrian schools of Edessa, Nisibin, Harran, and Jundi-Shapur had already opened the treasures of the science and philosophy to the Persians, as they did later for the Arabs.

Chapter 14

Assyrian Contributions to the Arab and the Islamic Civilization

According to Philip Hitti, between the fifth and the tenth century AD, Assyrian scholars helped the advancement of science, medicine, philosophy, and mathematics.

"The Syrian Nestorians who translated first into Syriac and then from Syriac into Arabic, thus became the strongest link between Hellenism and Islam, and consequently the earliest purveyors of Greek culture to the world at large Before Hellenism could find access to the Arab mind it had to pass through a Syriac version." (Hitti Philip, 1970)

Redirecting the energy and creativity of these Assyrians to educate the Arabs, coupled with ongoing persecution of the community, gradually resulted in the decline of the Syriac-speaking civilization. Although Arabs had brought with them an intellectual curiosity and eagerness to learn, they had no knowledge of art, science, or philosophy. Even their literature was at a primitive stage. It was enriched greatly because of the extensive translation from Syriac or Greek languages. Furthermore Aba Al Aswad Al-Du'ali (688 AD), who is considered the father of Arabic grammar, contacted the Syriac scholars in Koufa, and asked their help in creating Arabic grammar. He followed the same order of organization, classification, and rules of the Syriac language. He also borrowed the Syriac dot system that helped to facilitate the correct pronunciation of the written word. This system was invented by Mar Yacub of Urhoy/Edessa; it is still being used in the Arabic writing. Arrival of the Assyrian scholar's in Baghdad sparked great interest in knowledge and science from the seventh through the ninth century. Scientific centers such as schools, clinics, drugstores, universities, and observatories were established and expanded into more specialized institutions. The later Arab and Persian writers such as Ibn-Sin acquired their knowledge from books that were translated into Arabic via the Syriac translations. Arab Philosopher Al-Kindy confirmed the above facts when he wrote:

"They ([As]Syrians) were to us a way and means to a lot of knowledge. Without them, these pioneer authentic works would not have been made available to us." Another Arab scholar writes: *"We can say that it was the [As]Syrians who first taught Muslims philosophy, it is them who translated to us, secondly; therefore, Muslems were influenced by the philosophy of the As]Syrians.* "http://f16.parsimony.net/forum28457/messages/1564.htm

Harith Ibn-Kaladah was the earliest Arab doctor educated in the medical school and hospital of Jundi-Shapur. He returned to Arabia where he practiced medicine. Among his patients were the Prophet and the three early Caliphs; most of the hygienic rules mentioned in the Koran were undoubtedly influenced by Ibn-Kaladah.

Whipple writes, the kind treatment of Nestorians (Assyrians) by the Muslims when Jundi-Shapur was invaded by the Arabs has been attributed, by him, to three reasons: (1) their excellent teaching and work at the medical school, and because the hospital was known to the Prophet and his early Caliphs, who were treated by the Arab doctors such as Ibn-Kaladah, and Ibn-Uthal, who studied there; (2) *"Arabs had no knowledge of the medical science, and looked upon the Jundi-Shapur institution with wonder and admiration.";* (3) the Byzantine Catholics had excommunicated Nestorians because they did not believe that Virgin Mary could be considered the Mother of God, although they acknowledged that Jesus is her son. (Whipple PP. 21-22) Arabs eagerly sought to learn the Hippocratic and Galenic medicine from the Nestorian (Assyrian) scholars in Jundi-Shapur, who kindled their interest in science and medicine.

The Most influential Assyrian Scholars

When the physicians of Al-Mansur, were unable to cure his gastric disorder, he summoned the Nestorian [Assyrian] physician Ghiwargis, son of Gabriel Bakht-Eisho, the head of the academy and hospital at Jundi-Shapur. This was the first contact between the Caliphs at Baghdad and the Assyrian scholars, it played an important part in educating the Arabs.

Ghiwargis, who was called Jirjis by the Arabs, remained in Baghdad as court physician until he reached advanced age. Then he asked the Caliph to allow him to return to Jundi-Shapur because he wished to be buried among his friends and relatives. Before letting him go, Caliph advised him to stay in Baghdad and convert to Islam, so that he could enter paradise. The doctor answered: *"I prefer to be where my ancestors are, be it in paradise or in flames."* He was granted the consent to leave Baghdad and was given 10,000 dinars as a token of gratitude. Two of his students who had come with him to Baghdad remained in the capital to take care of Caliph's health.

In 785 AD, Jibrail (Gabriel) Bakht-Eisho II, son of Jirjis, was invited by al-Hadi to succeed his father as the head of the academy and hospital in Baghdad, but at court he was opposed by Abu Quraysh, the Queen's physician; therefore, he was sent back to Jundi-Shapur. However, under Harun Al-Rashid, he was again summoned to the court to treat the Caliph for severe headaches. He remained there until his death in (828–9). The Abbasid Dynasty was closer to pre-Islamic Persian culture and was influenced by the

Sassanian practice of translating and creating libraries. During Bakht-Eisho II's stay in Baghdad, there was a push by Vizier Barmakid Yahya to educate the Arabs about the available scientific knowledge of the Greeks that was already well known amongst the Syriac-speaking Christians. He had been well aware of this since the time he lived in Marv and had enthusiastically supported the Nestorian scholars at Jundi-Shapur. (Abdolla, Michael, 2002, 8, fn. 10)

From then on, Baghdad became a center for scholars and men of knowledge during the Abbasid period. Later, new converts to Islam, known as Mawali, continued to promote Greek and Assyrian intellectual traditions among the Arabs. It is important to note that the Assyrian scholars are primarily known by their Arabized names, because that is how they were introduced to the West. The term 'Ibn' in the middle of their name means son of, in Arabic. The Assyrian term for, son of, is 'Bar', such as Yuhanna Bar Masawayah.

Translation of the Scientific Texts into Arabic

During the Haroun Al-Rashid rule, through the efforts of Jibra'il Bakht-Eishu II, major translations of the scientific text from Syriac into Arabic began. He later suggested to Caliph al-Mamun the establishment of an academy, which was called Bait al-Hikmah, (House of Wisdom), which was primarily concerned with collecting and translating all the known knowledge at that time into the Arabic language. It was founded by Al-Mamun in 830 AD, and its first director was Yuhanna ibn Masawayh, a noted Assyrian physician and scholar.

Bakht-Eisho ibn Jirjis (Ghiwargis) was one of the highest paying court doctors. His wages from Caliph, Haroun al-Rashid, each month, was 10,000 dinars. He received a gift of 300,000 dirhams annually from the Caliph for his various medical services. He received 40,000 dirhams annually for medical services to the Caliph's family, plus 250,000 dirhams from Harmakian, and 50,000 dirhams from medical services to the public. His annual earnings were approximately four million dirhams. (Whipple, 1967, 389) Jirjis, the Caliph Wasseg's physician, with the permission of the ruler, returned to his hometown. But when the Caliph became sick, the doctor went to Sammera to cure him. Before his arrival, Wasseg died. When Motawakkil succeeded Wasseg, the overspending Caliph had exhausted the treasury and was ready to sell government properties to pay for a castle he was building. Bakht-Eisho offered to give him a loan. Caliph decided to help himself to the doctor's wealth. He let go Bakht-Eisho from his position and confiscated his fortune. However, Bakht-Eisho III was still well to do even after such financial loss..

In addition to performing medical services, the Bakht-Eisho doctors are well known for their contributions to medical science and their direct and indirect translation of medical books into Arabic from the Greek language. They were called Hakims, i.e., doctors, philosophers, and meta- physicians. From time to time, they succeeded in using their influence with the Caliphs to stop planned persecution of the Christians. They served the subsequent Abbasid Caliphs for almost three hundred years, from 765 to 1058. The last known doctor of Bakht-Eishu family was Abu Sa'id Ubaid Allah (940–1058). One of the reasons cited for the disappearance of the Bakht-Eisho family name from history is the conversion of its final doctors to Islam. (Abdalla Michael, 2002, 5-28)

Despite Assyrians contributions to the Arab civilization, the Caliphs after returning from their pilgrimage to Mecca or suffering military defeat turned aggressive towards Christians, Jews, and their Muslim opposition. After being defeated by the Byzantines in 806, upon returning to Iraq, Caliph Harun al-Rashid adopted a hostile policy towards Christians, especially the Jacobite who inhabited the region near the Byzantine border. On his visit to Raqqa, in 807 AD, he gave orders to destroy churches, and issued a decree that Christians and Jews should not wear a blue belt and Jews wear a yellow belt. Only Muslims could wear Green. Non-Muslim could not ride horses, but were allowed to use donkeys instead. When the Caliph returned to Baghdad, doctor Gabriel visited him wearing the clothes prescribed for Christians. His outfit embarrassed the Caliph and commanded him to change it immediately, but the doctor refused, and said: *"I am one of the ahl-addimia (dhimmis) and it would be improper for me to wear clothes different of these that they wear, by the Caliph's will.'* This thoughtful, calm and intelligent response moved the Caliph revoke his order."(Abdalla Michael, 2002, 5-16)

Yuhanna ibn-Maswayh

Yuhanna, son of Masawayh (d. 857), was a graduate of the school of Jundi-Shapur and an associate of the Bakhtishu family. His father had come to Baghdad after many years of service at the Jundi-Shapur's hospital. Yuhanna became the personal physician of Harun al-Rashid in Khorasan before he became Caliph. Later Yuhanna was put in charge of translating the Greek manuscripts that were obtained through conquest or treaty. In his capacity as court physician, Yuhanna served four Caliphs, and his reputation as a clinician and a teacher exceeded that of all others in Baghdad.

When the first Arab University was founded by Al-Mamun in 830 AD, it was headed by Yuhanna ibn Masawayh. His students had the reputation of being well versed in logic and the writings of Galen. The most famous of them was Hunayn ibn-Ishahq. (Whipple, 1967, p.25)

Yuhanna, also known as Mesue to the Latin reader, was concerned with both practical and theoretical aspects of medicine. He has been credited with having written nearly fifty works. He conducted an assembly in Baghdad on a regular basis known as "Majlis," which was a combination of lecture room and consulting hour where he saw patients, lectured his students, and discussed scientific topics for the benefit of the general public. People of all classes, including theologians, philosophers, and doctors often crowded his assembly. He maintained a small menagerie, which included an ape—which he had intended to dissect, but was given another one by the Caliph Al Muata'sim instead. The result was a book of anatomy, the first in Islam of its kind. (Dunlop D. M. 1971, 220) The list of his writings includes several works on ophthalmology, two on "migraine and dazzlement," work on poisons and their antidotes, and a book on elephantiasis; the earliest one on the subject in Islam. His book of "Medical Maxims 'al-Nawadir at-

Tibbiyya" was twice translated into Latin. It included maxims about dieterics, pathology, diagnosis, and therapeutics. He translated various Greek medical works into Syriac. He dissected Apes supplied to him by the caliph al-Mu'tasim c. 836. A number of anatomical and medical writings are credited to him, the most popular was the "Disorder of the Eye" ("Daghal al-ain"), it is the earliest Systematic treatise on ophthalmology which survived in Arabic, and the Aphorisms, the Latin translation of which was very popular in the Middle Ages. When Yuhanna died, a poet commented on the irony of his death:

"Verily the physician, with his physic and his drugs,
Cannot avert a summons that hath come.
What ails the physician that he dies of the disease?
Which he used to cure in the days gone by?
There died alike he who administered the drug,
and he who took it."

Hunayn ibn Ishaq

Hunayn known in Latin as, Johnanitius (809-873), is considered as one of the greatest translators because of his accuracy and productivity. His biography exists in the form of letters he wrote to Ali ibn-Yahya in 875. He was born of Nestorian parents in southern Mesopotamia near Babylon, in the city of "Hira," which means "free" in the Syriac language. Though he was ethnically Arab, he was Christian snd a product of the Assyrian culture.

His father was a druggist. As young man Hunayn was a student of Yuhanna ibn Maswayh and served as his drug dispenser, but he irritated his teacher, therefore, he was forced to drop out. He traveled to Asia minor where he studied the Greek language, then returned to Mesopotamia and worked in Basra where he studied Arabic grammar. From there he went to Jundishapur. A friend of his, Yusuf, a physician, saw him with his long hair and heard him reciting "Homer", as he was walking. He told Yusuf he did not intend to resume his medical studies until he had mastered the Greek language.

After the completion of his medical studies, Hunayn went to Baghdad. The sons of ibn-Maswayh introduced him to Jibra'il Bakhtishu, who in turn informed Caliph Al-Ma'mun about his translation capabilities. Because of Hunayn's knowledge of Greek and his excellent scholarship, he was appointed by Al-Ma'mun as the administrator of the "House of Wisdom" and was authorized to initiate and supervise translations of the scientific, medical, and philosophical manuscripts from the Greek and the Syriac into Arabic. *"Hunayn trained a group of pupils who became competent translators into both Syriac and Arabic."* Among them was his nephew, Hubaysh, who was proficient in Arabic, and Hunayn's son Ishaq who was competent in Syriac. (Whipple, 1967, 26)

"From that time on, his work progressed steadily until the Arab students had access to the Arabic translations of a great part of works by Hippocrates, Galen, Paul of Aegina, Ptolemy, Euclid, Aristotle, and Plato." (Ibid)

In 855 AD, Hunayn succeeded Yuhanna ibn Masawayh as director of the House of Wisdom. Here Muslim scholars such as Khwarizmi, Al-Kindi, and Al-Hajjaj—the first translators of Euclid's Elements—worked together with Hunayn, and later with Thabit ibn Qurra, an Assyrian scholar from Harran. Jibra'il is also credited with suggesting to Al-Rashid to send emissaries into the cities of Asia Minor to collect Greek manuscripts to be translated into Syriac and Arabic. No less than one hundred works of the Greek philosophers were translated into Arabic at a time when Europe was ignorant of Greek thoughts and science. (Whipple, 1967, 24)

Hunayn Master Translator

Hunayn, soon was famous and participated in the scholarly meetings where physicians and philosophers discussed challenging problems in the presence of Caliph Al-Wathiq.

"According to Ibn-abi-Usahbi'ah, Hunayn was the author of

more than one hundred original works, but few of these are extant" (Whipple, 1967, 27). His popular medical manual, Masail (or Isagogue), "was translated into Latin and was part of the Articella—a required reading in the West." (Javiddon Mohesen 1352, 164-65) "Altogether Hunayn translated into Syriac twenty books of Galen, two for Bakhtisho, Jibra'il's son, two for Salmawaih ibn Bunan, one for Jibra'il, and one for Ibn Masawayh, and also revised the sixteen translations made by Sergius of Rishayna. He translated fourteen treatises into Arabic, three for Muhammad, one for Ahmad, sons of Musa. He and his assistants produced versions both in Syriac and Arabic, though no doubt, some of his staff excelled in one language rather than the other. Most of the translators of the next generation received their training from Hunayn or his pupils, therefore he stands out as the leading translator, and some of his versions were afterwards revised by later writers."

http://evansexperientialism.freewebspace.com/oleary05.htm

Most of the translators of the next generation received their training from Hunayn and his pupils." One of the most famous medical students of Hunayn was the Persian Rhazi, who became the greatest doctor of that era. (Whipple, 1067, 27) Among surviving translations by Hunayn are the sixteen canonical works of Galen and seven books of Galen's anatomy, lost in their original Greek language. When Al-Mamun died in 833 his son Musta'sim succeeded him. Because of disorder in Baghdad, he transferred his court to Samarra. During this period scholarship was neglected, but in 892 when Al-Mutawakkil (847-61) came to power he restored interest in science and scholarship.

Hunayn did his best work during Mutawakkil's rule, but suffered because the new Caliph was, unlike Al-Mamun, a strict and orthodox Muslim. Hunayn students have left behind a list of books translated by him that included ninety-nine books of Jalinous in Syriac and thirty-nine books of the same author in Arabic, in addition to six books which his students wrote in Syriac and thirty more in Arabic. Both medieval Arab and contemporary European scholars have praised the quality of Hunayn's translations. Two of his best known medical books are "al Massael Fel alTeb" and another about optometry. The last was used as the authoritative textbook on eye diseases throughout the Islamic world. (Javiddon Mohsen 1352,167) The eleventh-century Razi and Ali ibn-sienna have mentioned it as their most important reference book. Another important book written by Hunayn is "Alashre Magalat Filain," which was considered lost until recently.

Hunayn was also admired for being virtuous. When he was appointed as Mutawakkil's (847–61) private physician, he was ordered to make a poison for killing an enemy. He refused and was imprisoned for a year for insubordination. Then he was brought before the Caliph and was threatened with death if he did not relent. When asked by the Caliph—who claimed he was simply testing Hunayn's integrity—why he refused to prepare the deadly poison, Hunayn replied:

"two things: my religion and my profession. My religion decrees that we should do good, even to our enemies, how much more to our friends. And my profession is instituted for the benefit of humanity and limited to their relief and cure. Besides, every physician is under oath never to give anyone a deadly medicine." (Hitti, Philip, 1970, 313)

Hunayn left behind three sons, Ishaq, Dawood, and Hakim. Ishaq was a great translator—as his father, specialized mostly in philosophical books—died in 910 AD. Dawood, a well-known doctor, was mentioned by Razi. Among Hunayn's other students was his nephew Habbish, who was a renowned court doctor for Motawakkil, in addition to being a translator. Some of the drugs he mentions in his books did not appear in the Greek books. Hunayn's grandson Hassan ibn-Ishaq, also a prominent translator (877), held a council of debate in Baghdad about religion, logic, and philosophical subjects. He was described by Bar Hebraeus not only as a "source of science" but also a "mine of virtue." (Inati Shams C., 2003, 45)

Harranian School; the Beth Qarah Family

During the ancient Assyrian period, Harran was an important center of astronomy and mathematics, which were used to calculate the movement of planets, the prediction of eclipses, and other astronomical events. It should not surprise us that such knowledge had survived a thousand years later in that city. Perhaps this was possible; because Harranians refused to convert to Christianity and planetary worship was still part of their religion, and such knowledge was a necessary part of their life. In fact, Qarah, the name of the forbearer of the family dates back to the ancient Assyrian period, a clay tablet from the reign of King Adad Nerari III (810-738) period informs us that "Qarah, son of Adda-Rahimi from Asihu" sold a piece of land to another person. During the early Islamic period Harranians were called Sabians, a name mentioned in the Koran, which they adopted to join the ranks of the tolerated people. At times they have been confused with the Sabians living in southern Mesopotamia. Like the Christian Assyrians Harranians spoke the Syriac language.

One of the first translators of the Harranian school of mathematic and astronomy is known by his Arabized name Al-Hajjaj ibn Yusuf ibn Matar (786–833). He is credited with having made the first translation of Euclid's "Elements" and one of the first of Ptolemy's astronomical work in Arabic. He translated "Almagest" in 827–28 from a former Syriac version. It was revised by Hunayn ibn-Ishaq and later by Thabit.
(Philip Hitti, 1970, 314) Al Hajjaj ibn Yusuf ibn Matar is considered to be the greatest geometrician of the Arab period.

"Thabit translated into Arabic seven of the eight books on conic sections of Apollonius and wrote earliest known work on the sundial." (Bertram Thomas, 1937,177) Syriac-speaking scholars are often described as merely the custodians of the Greek knowledge and the teachers of Arabs, but their personal contributions to the world of knowledge is often overlooked. For example, Thabit Bar Qarah made important mathematical discoveries such as:

"the extension of the concept of number to (positive) real numbers, integral calculus, theorems in spherical trigonometry,

analytic geometry, and non-Euclidean geometry. In astronomy, Thabit was one of the first reformers of the Ptolemaic system, and in mechanics he was a founder of statics."

Thabit also wrote about logic, psychology, ethics, the classification of sciences, the grammar of the Syriac language, politics, the symbolism of Plato's "Republic," religion, and the customs of the Sabians. Aside from the House of Wisdom, Al Mamun erected an observatory in Baghdad. At this observatory, Thabit took the length of the solar year, and his great grandson Battani who was much admired by the European of the Renaissance period *"calculated the first appearance of the moon, the inclination of the ecliptic, the length of the tropic, and sidereal year, and parallaxes."* (Bertram Thomas, 1937,181)

An important work by Thabit: "Kitab fi'l-qarastun" (the book on the beam balance) deals with mechanics where he proves the principle of equilibrium of levers. It was translated into Latin by Gerard of Cremona, it became a popular work on this subject.

"Thabit ibn-Qarah lead a team of Syriac-speaking translators of Harranians. They are credited with having translated most of the Greek mathematical and astronomical works including the writings of Archimedes (212 BC) and Apollonius of Perga (262 BC), plus they improved on the earlier translations. A medical compendium by Thabit included a discussion of general hygiene, causes, symptoms and treatment of diseases of skin and other parts of the body, infectious diseases, fractures and dislocations, the importance of climate, food, diet, and sex. Thabit had written about sixteen Syriac works, most were available up to the thirteenth century, but none exist today. In contrast, some of his 150 Arabic treatises have survived."

Bar Hebraeus has quoted from a Syriac work of Thabit ibn Qarah, where he praises the Harranians for their loyalty to the ancient religion and contribution to the world of science.

"When many were subdued to error through persecution, our fathers through God were steadfast and stood out manfully, and this blessed city has never been defiled by the error of Nazareth. He

goes on to attribute the world's science and civilization to the pagan inventors."

Sinan ibn Thabit, (880-943) succeeded his father; he was forced by the Caliph Al Qahir to embrace Islam. His two grand sons, Thabit (893) and Ibrahim (946), and one great grandson, Abu-al-Faraj, continued the family contributions to the world of science. The greatest of Bet Qarah family was Al Battasni, the grand son of Sinan (929). He was known as Alhategnius or Albatenius by the Latin authors. He became famous for his original astronomical work. Other luminaries of the Harran Sabians were Abu-Ishaq ibn Hilal AlSabi, secretary of both Al-Mufti (946–74) and Al-Tai (974–91), and perhaps Jabir ibn Hayan, who was an alchemist.

Prominence of the Christian Doctors

The dominance of the medical field by the Christian Assyrians is attested to by Assad bin Jani, an Arab doctor who blamed them for his inability to build up a clientele. He writes:

"In the first place, I am a Muslim, and before I studied Medicine, nay, before ever I was created, the people held the view that Muslims are not successful physicians. Further my name is Assad, and it should have been Saliba, Mara'il, Yuhanna or Bira [Christian Assyrian names], and my family name is Abu ul-Haris and it should have been Abu Isa, Abu Zakariyya, or Abu Ibrahim [Arabized version of christian Assyrian family names]. " (Elgood Cyril, 1979, 173-74.)

The following episode, described by Usam ibn-Munqidh, an Arab writer, compares the superiority of the Middle Eastern Christian Physicians to the doctors accompanying the crusaders; M. Harwign Derenbourg translated it to French during the Medieval times.

"At the request of the French Warden of the castle of Munytirs in Lebanon, Usama's uncle sent his Christian physician, Thabit, to treat the sick in the castle. On Thabit's arrival they showed him two patients, one a man with an abscess of the leg that had failed to heal; the second a woman with consumption. He treated the man

with poultices, the woman with diet and medication.

When both patients were improving rapidly a Frankish doctor intervened, saying that the treatment was wrong. He asked the man with the healing abscess if he preferred to live with one leg or die with two. The man said he preferred the first alternative. The doctor called on a soldier and told him to chop off the diseased leg with one blow of his axe. This soldier failed to do, but with the second blow he crushed the marrow of the bone and the patient died of loss of marrow and blood.

The Frankish doctor then turned his attention to the phthisic woman and after examining her, he declared that she was possessed of devil in her head. He ordered her head to be shaved and ordered her to return to her former diet of garlic and olive oil. When she grew worse he made a cruciform incision in her scalp down to the bone, rubbing salt in the wound. The patient expired soon after. Thabit then asked if his services were any longer needed, and receiving a negative answer he returned home." (Whipple, Allen, 1967, 30-31)

The Philosophers

During the late-ninth and the tenth centuries, logic was a virtual monopoly of a single school of logicians centered at Baghdad. The founders of this school belonged to a closely knit group of Assyrian Christians, including the teachers of Abu Baish Matta ibn Yunus and the teachers of these teachers." (Edwards Paul, 1972, vol.3, 526)

Abu Bishr Matta ibn yunus was a translator and commentator of the works of Aristotle. He was a Nestorian and a teacher at Dayr Qunna (monastery). He went to Baghdad during the Caliphate of Al-Radi (after 934) and taught Christians and Muslim student. The Jacobites made revisions to the existing translations of Aristotelian works or made new translations thereof. They have been credited with introducing Neo-Platonic speculations and mysticism into the Arabic culture.

During the late-tenth century, Jacobite Assyrian translators

were represented by Yahya ibn-Adi (d. 973) who was born in Tikrit and became one of the principle translators of books about philosophy into Arabic from the Syriac language. His translations of Aristotle energized the Aristotelian studies at the expense of the earlier prominence of psudepigraphic Neoplatonica. The only surviving text of Aristotle in his translation are "Posterior Analytics," considered the highest point of logic, and the "Metaphysics and the Ars Poetica. His commentaries were more or less extensive notes.
(Meisami, 1998, 517)

Yahya had once claimed that he copied a hundred leaves during a day and night on the average. In Baghdad, he had debating sessions with the Nestorians about the differences of theology between the two denominations. Except for Farabi, up to the tenth century the leading and most recognized logicians and philosophers in the Arab world not Arab Christians. The teacher of Abu Nasser al-Farabi (d. 950), who became an influential Arab Philosopher, were Yahya ibn Halilan (d. 920), the Jacobite philosopher, and Abu Bishr Matta ibn-Yunus, who was also the teacher of Yahya ibn-Adi. (Inati Shams C. Ed., 2003, p.42)

Arab philosopher Al-Farabi was called "The second teacher," in comparison to Aristotle being the first. It is said that he surpassed his Nestorian teachers, who for theological reasons were forbidden from studying logic beyond Aristotle's "Prior Analytics." He is credited with reinvigorating the philosophy by rejecting constraints that were stifling it. He was specifically concerned with religion and political aspects. (Nanji Azim, A., 1996, 193) He influenced the upcoming Muslim philosophers, including the famous doctor and philosopher ibn-Siena (Avicenna), who admitted that he found Aristotle's "Metaphysics" incomprehensible until he read Al-Farabi's "On the Goals of Aristotle's Metaphysics."

A few decades after the founding of Baghdad (762 A.D.), the major philosophical works of Aristotle and the Neo-Platonic commentators, the chief medical writings of Hippocrates and Galen, the main mathematical compositions of Euclid, and the geographical masterpiece of Ptolemy were translated into Arabic directly form the Syriac language.

Chapter 14

End of the Golden Age

Islamic extremism and applications of punishment directed toward the non-Muslims intensified during the Mutawakkil rule and by the end of the ninth century it reached its peak. In 850 AD Mutawakkil began to apply repressive laws to the Christians that already had existed, but were not enforced, and added his own disabilities.

"Christians were ordered to wear distinctive garments and were forbidden from riding on horseback. They were not allowed to go into market on Fridays. The graves of their dead had to be destroyed. Their children could not attend Muslim schools or to be taught Arabic and were commanded to nail a wooden image of the devil on the door of their house. Furthermore, a number of churches and monasteries were demolished." (Vine, 1937, 95)

These and similar practices have been used by the extremist Muslims during the last 1400 years to define the Christians and Jews as the children of a lesser God, to denigrate their social standing, to make them feel inferior, to minimize their opportunity for success, to impoverish them, to make Muslims feel superior to them, and to persecute them at will. Introduction of the Greek philosophy, which encouraged questioning the precepts of the government, religion, and life in general, angered the Islamic extremists and gave rise to resentment against Christians. They accused them of having introduced such knowledge to undermine faith in Islam. In reality Muslims were eager to learn philosophy at first, so that, they could argue the superiority of their religion over the others. Al-Tabari, who was a convert to Islam from Christianity, in his book, "Al-Din wal Dawla," or "Religion and State," rebuked Christians by reminding them that they were "dhimmis," meaning tolerated only to a certain extent. The Islamic schools that encouraged moderation were closed and the schools of Al-Sunna and Shariah took over. Often the agitated Muslim crowds rioted and destroyed churches and monasteries. In 884 the convent of Kalish in Baghdad was destroyed. Its gold and silver vessels were plundered and the wood of the building was sold.

"During the reign of Caliph Qadir, in 1015, Muslims sacked the houses of Christians in Baghdad and burned down or destroyed many of their churches. The Caliph issued a decree that all Christians should be forced to accept Islam and those who did will be rewarded. Many Christians accepted Islam. Some immigrated to the Byzantine territory, but the majority refused to yield, and they endured persecution. They were forced to wear wooden crosses weighing four pounds instead of their silver and gold. For unknown reasons, Qadir regretted his orders and rescinded his decree, allowed the converted Christians to retun to Christianity. Those who had left returned and the ruined churches were rebuilt." (Yohannan, 1916, 97-98)

Suha Rassam, in her book, "Christianity In Iraq," attributes several factors for the change in Muslim's treatment of the Christians: (1) the growth in the number of educated Arabs who were no longer dependent on the Christians for their education, and increased knowledge; (2) their scientific achievements to the superiority of Islam and the Arab mind, rather than contributions by the Christian scholars, and the enrichment of the Arabic language and its greater use due to the massive translations by the Assyrian scholars and the increase of Muslim population; (3) the Assyrian church had become impoverished because its highly educated scholars had abandoned it, and a great number of its adherents had converted to Islam. Great Christian centers such as Seleucia-Ctesiphon, Tikrit, and al-Hira had declined; and (4) the weakness of the later Arab rulers, and the rise in power and influence of the newly Islamized Turkic and Iranian factions. (Rassam, Suha, 2005, 88-9)

However Aubrey R. Vine, the author of "The Nestorian Churches," ascribes the reason for the oppression of Christians by the Muslim to the fact that Nestorians had become more influential in all walks of life, including wealth and power, which made Muslims angry and envious. Although Arabs were good warriors, the traditions and habits of the Christians made them superior in business and other affairs where education counted. (Vine, 1937, 101-02)

In this writer's opinion, the most important factor that contributed to the decline of the Golden Age of Islam was the rise of Islamic fundamentalism, which considered all new knowledge that did not originate from Quran, as threat to Islam. This mindset not only rejected all new ideas, also contributed to the continued persecution of non-Muslims, who were considered as threat, even when they were not.

Struggle For Survival

By mid-tenth century, the Arab dynasty had began to decline. The Abbasid Caliphs began to use foreign mercenaries to do their fighting and ensure their security. These men were mostly Turks, specifically trained to protect Caliph and his ministers. They were called "Mamluks," meaning "owned" or "slaves." As the Mamluks increased in number they gradually became the power behind the throne. Periodically, they were dispatched to establish a De facto Turkish control over territories in behalf of the Abbasid dynasty. Gradually the ruling power shifted from the Arabs to the Seljuk Turks, but the Islamic religion, which Arabs had brought to the Middle East, continued to remain the popular religious culture of the region. Turks were ferocious horsemen. Their coming to power shifted the balance of power against the Byzantine, and Emperor Romanus was unable to halt their advance into Anatolia. In 1071 the two armies met at Manzikert in Armenia, and the Byzantines were decisively defeated. Their defeat gradually led to the collapse of the Empire.

The Seljuk invasions resulted in widespread destruction of human life and property, and massacre and/or enslavement of some part of the population. Those who survived often faced starvation, because Turkmens usually destroyed crops and cut down fruit-bearing trees in the surrounding villages. In describing the plight of the Christians of Asia Minor during the following years, Matthew of Edessa wrote;

> "Toward the beginning of year 1079–80 famine desolated . . . the lands of the worshippers of the cross, already ravaged by the ferocious and sanguinary Turkish hordes. Not one province remained protected from their devastation. Everywhere, the Christians had been delivered to the sword or into bondage, interrupting thus the cultivation of the fields, so that bread was lacking. The farmers and workers had been massacred or led off into slavery, and famine extended its rigor to all places. Many provinces were depopulated; the Oriental [Christian] nation no longer existed, and land of the Greeks was in ruins."

(Stoneman Richard, 111,)

The launch of the crusading movement by the Pope in 1095 to recapture the Holy Land from the Turks proved disastrous for the Middle Eastern Christians, because it incited Muslims fury against them. They were systematically subjected to persecution, massacre, and expulsion because crusader's wars were seen as great threat to Islam, and Muslims deemed the local Christians as Crusaders' sympathizers and considered them as potentially subversive. The Crusaders' hopes in the region faded when Muslims captured the cities of Edessa, Antioch, and Acres that previously were under their control. Their populations, who were predominantly native Christians, were decimated.

The Mongol's Rule

The Mongols set out to invade Iraq in 1257. One Mongolian army, under the command of Baichu, crossed the Tigris at Mosul and marched down the west bank. Some thirty miles north of

Baghdad, they confronted the Caliph's main army and defeated it. The other Mongolian army led by Chingiz Khan's grandson, Hulagu, marched directly toward Baghdad and arrived there on January 18, 1258. Twelve days later Mongols began massive bombardment of the eastern walls of Baghdad. Al-Mustasim sent his vizier along with the Nestorian patriarch Makeekha to intercede with Dokuz Khatun, Halaku's wife, to save the city from the attack, but they were sent back without obtaining an audience. As the bombardment continued by the first week of February, the eastern wall began to collapse.

On February 10, the Mongolian army entered the city. The Caliph surrendered along with his army and chief officers. Once they laid down their arms, they were massacred. Indiscriminate massacres continued throughout the city. Women and children perished along with men. However, Christians who were all gathered in one church of Baghdad were spared, as Halaku had ordered. The fact that they all could take refuge in one church indicates that, by that time, their number did not exceed a few thousand. The kindness shown to the Christians, in contrast to the savagery inflicted on the Muslim population, undoubtedly played an important role in inciting persecution of the Christians in Mesopotamia and Persia in later decades.

In September 1259 Halaku led the Mongol's army out to conquer Northwest Syria. They went through Harran, Edessa, and Birejik, and crossed the Euphrates. By March of the next year both Aleppo and Damascus were conquered, followed by the usual brutal massacres of the Muslims and leniency toward Christians. Mongol's kindness toward Christians was partly due to the Nestorian missions in Turkestan, Mongolia, and China, which had succeeded in planting Christianity in the Far East. According to Vine:

"The religion of the Mongol khans was Shamanism, a primitive form of magic. Christian influences had been gradually affecting them for some centuries. The fact that so many men of special knowledge such as doctors, secretaries, and officials were Christians—unlike the Mongols who were a people of little culture—drove the Moguls to welcome Christians among them. Furthermore, undoubtedly, there was considerable Christian element among the

Mongols, including Halaku's wife and mother." (Vine, 1937, 14-46)

The Church of the East missionaries by the tenth and eleventh century had succeeded in infusing Christianity among the tribes of central Aisia, such as the Kerait, Uighurs, and due to intermarriage with the Kerait, the mothers of the Mongolian ruling class were often Nestorian Christians.

After Halaku's death in 1265, his son Abaka's rule began. He did not mistreat Muslims, but antagonized them by being kind to the Buddhists and the Christians, as did the succeeding Khans. Abaka was poisoned and died in 1282. Teguder—who converted to Islam—succeeded him, but was killed in 1284. Arghun came to power in 1284. The Buddhists and Christians breathed again. Though he was a Buddhist, he wished to forge an alliance with the Christians of the West. In 1285 he sent a letter to Pope Honorius IV inviting the West to join him in war against the Mamluke. In 1827 he sent an embassy to the pope led by a Nestorian prelate from China, but later he abandoned the whole idea.

His vizier, Sad Al-Daula, was an able Jew who repaired the treasury and established the administration of justice, based on law, to provide security to the oppressed. His Jewish religion earned many enemies for the king. In 1291 a group of emirs hostile to Sad Al-Daula and Arghun conspired to overthrow him, but they were all seized and executed. A month later, Sa'd Al-Daula was formally tried and put to death. His family was sold into slavery. Argun died a month later on March 10, 1291, at the age of thirty. His death led to pogroms against the Christians, Jews, and Buddhists in Tabriz and Baghdad. Marco Polo, who passed through Iraq and northeast Persia during Arghun's rule, mentions the Nestorians and Jacobites population in Baghdad, Mosul, and Tabriz, which he visited. He writes that in Mosul there are cloths made of silk and gold, which are known as muslins. In "The Travels of In Tabriz," he writes:

"The Muslim population oppresses those of other faiths by plundering them and subjecting them to all kinds of cruelties in order to convert them. He follows by stating that if they were not restrained by the governing power, they would even practice greater

outrages." (Marco Polo, 1958, 24-25)

Another Arghun followed Gaikhatu's rule, but soon Baidu replaced him. He was defeated and executed by Nowrouz. On October 4, 1295, Ghazan, who had converted to Islam, replaced him. His first decree was the destruction of all churches, synagogues, and Buddhist temples in Tabriz, Baghdad, and throughout the Il-Khan's domains. *"There was a great sorrow among the Christians in all the world."* wrote Bar-Hebrious.

"The persecutions and disgrace and mocking and ignominy which the Christians suffered at this time, especially in Baghdad, words cannot describe. Behold, according to what people say, no Christian dared to appear in the streets (or market), but the women went out and came in and bought and sold, because they could not be distinguished from the Arab women, and could not be identified as Christians, though those who were recognized as Christians were disgraced, and slapped, and beaten and mocked." (Boyle J.A. ed., 1968, 379)

Clergies and scholars were killed, and three major churches in Baghdad were destroyed. The trouble extended to Mosul, but the clergies were able to avert disaster by paying a bribe of 15,000 dinars. In 1297 a military force under the command of Aladean ibn-Jaja invaded the city of Amedia and took 12,000 Christian prisoners who were forced to convert to Islam. Those who refused were killed. As noted in the Wikipedia article about Islam; *"[the] Verse, or Ayah 256, of Al-Baqara, is one of the most quoted verses in the Islamic holy scripture, the Quran. It famously notes "there is no compulsion in religion."* However in reality, the humiliation and the persecution of non-Muslims by the Muslim extremists has been historically intended to convert them to Islam. It is surprising that they do not see the contradiction between their actions and the edict of the Holy book they claim to obey.

Wholesale Massacre in Arbil

In 1310 AD the Arabs and the Kurds attacked Assyrians of Arbil. Many died in the insuring conflict, and the surviving Assyrian population took refuge in the citadel. Kurds and Mongol mobs who were Incited by the local Muslim clergies destroyed Nestorian, Jacobite, and Armenian churches and extended their killing and looting to other Christian towns and villages in the region. Patriarch Mar Yav-alaha, along with the bishop of Arbil, desperately tried to defuse the situation but was unable to stop the carnage. Bishop Sliva escaped to the village of Bit-Sayadee, in the Plain of Nineveh, and from there he went to plead with Argon Khan for help. It was decided that Patriarch Yav-alaha would enter the citadel to inform the Christians that peace had been agreed on, but as soon as the gate of the citadel was opened to let him in the Muslim warriors forced their way in and eventually killed all who had taken refuge there. Vine writes:

"The change of Mongol's sentiments from favoring Christianity to becoming fanatical Muslims can only be described by assuming that they were led to the belief that Christianity was not a religion that ensured worldly success; therefore, they concluded that Islam was preferable in that respect. The complete defeat of the Mongols by the Mamluk Sultan of Egypt in 1260, at the battle of Ain Jalut, which was followed by the persecution of Christians in Damascus, served to underscore such presumption. Similarly in 1262, when the Muslims temporarily drove the Mongols out of that city, many Christians were slaughtered." (Vine, 1937, 149-150)

The Onslaught of Tamure

Tamure was a military adventurer who came to power by building followers and defeating other chieftains. In 1370 he made Samarkand his capital. Local Muslim elites of Samarkand and the Sufis were his spiritual advisers. From 1379 to 1402 he conquered most of the Eastern world to impose Sharia (Islamic laws) upon the region with the pretext that his enemies were traitors to Islam. He punished prominent Islamic cities in Persia, India, and Syria—killing tens of thousands in each and building pyramids of human heads wherever he went. He considered himself as the exterminator of the Christians. *"He followed Christians with relentless fury, destroyed their churches and forced them to accept Islam, otherwise they were put to death or doomed to perpetual slavery."* (Yohannan, Abraham, 1916,109)

Tamure's attacks against the Assyrian cities forced the population to take refuge in the mountains of Kurdistan. Some returned after the event, but others remained there until they were driven out by the Turks and Kurds in 1915.

Muslim persecution of the Assyrians by their Muslim neighbors in Iraq, Turkey, and Northwest Iran continued into World War I and beyond. Assyrians lost two-thirds of their population during the Ottoman Turk massacres between 1914 and 1918. Survivors were driven out of their historical homeland in Turkey, the highlands north of Mosul, and Northwest Iran, in Assyrians in Iraq were massacred.

1894-1896 Massacre of the Assyrians and Armenians by the Ottoman

Between 1894 and 1896, because of its territorial losses in the Balkans due to the Russian intervention and the rise of Armenian nationalism, Turkey began a policy of systematic extermination of its Christian citizens. By some estimates about 300,000 Christians were killed at that time. Although these wholesale killings are known as the "Armenian Genocide," a great percentage of Assyrians belonging to the Chaldean Church and the Syrian Orthodox Church were killed at the same time. Dispatches and reports from Gustave Meyrier, the Vice-consul of France in Diyarbakir, attest to this fact. His Report #2, dated February 9, 1895, p. 50, describes the situation of the Christians in the cities of Turkey as follows: *"The state of affairs affects all Christians regardless of race, be they Armenian, Chaldean, Syrian [orthodox,]* or Greek. It is the result of religious hatred . . ."In a letter from Paul Cambon to his mother on November 4, 1895, wrote:

"At Diyarbakir, they have been killing and looting since Friday. Our consul is locked in his house with 500 refugees, and from his window he watches policemen take up arms with groups of savage Kurds from outside the city, and Muslims from within. They are massacring all Christians without distinction." (de courtois Sebastien, 2004, 106) In a later report, on December 18, 1895, Gustave Meyrier wrote: *"At day, at sunrise, the carnage started and lasted until Sunday night."* Armed Turks were divided into groups going systematically from one house to another making sure not to disturb the Muslims. *"They kicked the doors, looted everything, and if the people were home, they slit their throats. They killed everyone they could find, men, women, and children, the girls were kidnapped."* (De Courtois Sebastien, 2004, 105.) The massacres continued way into 1896.

World War I Massacre of the Assyrians

The decline of the Ottoman Empire resulted in the coming to power of the Young Turks, who saw the World War I as another opportunity to rid Turkey of its Christian population, the indigenous people of the country. The massacres spilt over into the mountains north of Mosul and Urmia province in Northwest Iran. About 750,000 Assyrians in the three regions lost their life along with more than 1,000,000 Armenians and an unspecified number of Greeks.

Armenians are often cited as the only people who were persecuted in Turkey during World War One by the Turkey's official documents and the Western Press—because they had a larger population and were better known due to their trade contacts with the West, and because of their troubles with the central government. Western travelers often stayed away from the rural regions such as the Tur Abedin in Southeast Turkey, the mountain regions of Kurdistan, between Persia and Turkey, or the province of Urmia in Northwest Iran, where mostly Assyrians lived. Turks and Kurds, during the massacres, had no intention of making a distinction between the Armenians and the Assyrians who were considered the enemy of the state because they were Christians. If genocide means the systematic and planned extermination of an entire national, racial, political, or ethnic group, then Assyrian were subjected to such treatment during the massacres known as "The Armenian Genocide," but the Assyrian plight was mostly ignored in the West, though their massacres were described in the Blue Book published in 1916, by the British Government titled "The Treatment of the Armenians in the Ottoman Empire." Henry I Morgenthau, the American Ambassador at Constantinople, from 1913 to 1916, who brought to the attention of the world the plight of the Armenians, wrote:

"The story which I have told about the Armenians I could also tell with certain modifications about the Greeks and the Syrians [Assyrians]. Turks afterward decided to apply the same methods on a larger scale was inflicted not only to the Greeks but to the Armenians, Syrians, Nestorians, and others of its subject peoples."

(Henry I Morgenthau, 1918 Chapter XXIV)
The Assyrian authors also described what happened to their people in books such as "Death of a Nation" by Abraham Yohannan (1916); "The Rage of Islam: an Account of the Massacre of Christians by the Turks in Persia" by Yonan H. Shabaz (1918); "Shall this Nation Die?" by Joseph Naayem (1920); "The Flickering Light of Asia" by Joel Werda 1924. Bar Malik Esmaeil, Yagov. "Assyrians During the Two World Wars," in Syriac (1964).

Jean Naayem in his "Les Assyro-Chaldeans ET les Armenians Massacres Par les Turcs," Paris, 1920, writes: *"[I will] relate the details of the tragic martyrdom of the Assyro-Chaldeans from the Jezireh district on the Tigris [not far] from Midyat, "where more than fifty villages, whose names I know, villages for the most part fertile and flourishing . . . were completely sacked and ruined while the entire population was put to the sword."* (Sebastien de Courtois, p.162)

Turks and Kurds attack on Urmia

Urmia often pronounced Uremi is located in Northwest Iran in the Persian province of Azerbaijan. It had been an Assyrian stronghold since the early centuries of Christianity. The region, according to Syriac sources, had a series of Nestorian bishops between the fifth and seventh century. (Chabot, "Synodicon orientale," 665) The oldest standing building in the area is the Assyrian Virgin Mary Church, which may date back to before the seventh century AD. It is the oldest standing building in the area. According to one tradition, several Assyrians tribes from the Harkkiari Mountains arrived in the region in the twelfth century, and others came later. (Naby Eden, 1977, 239)

World War I was a conflict between sovereign nations trying to further their selfish interest. Turkey found it an opportune time to decimate not only its own Christian population, including Assyrians, of the country, but also the Assyrians of the Zagros Mountains, north of Mosul. Turks usually deny the fact that they committed genocide against Assyrians and Armenians by claiming that they were plotting against Turkey. The fact that Turks were also responsible for the massacre of the Assyrians and Armenians within the borders of Iran disproves their claim. Under "Jihad And Iran," David Gaunt writes:

Few weeks before Turkey officially allied itself with Germany and joined the war, in September 1914 a call for Jihad declared by an Ottoman Mufti was posted in an important Kurdish town of Sawuj Bulok, south of Urmia. On October 1, 1914, a large force of Beqzad Kurds under the command of their Turk officers massacred the Assyrian inhabitants of the Targavar and Margavar, the Persian district, adjoining Turkey's eastern boundary. Later they descended from the hills and began to plunder and burn the Assyrian villages on the shores of the Lake Urmia. Most of the Christians escaped and fled to the city, other towns, and larger villages. From the hills surrounding the city, every night one could see the flames and the smoke of villages on fire. Soon it became apparent that this was not an ordinary Kurdish raid, but a well-equipped army of thousands, organized by the Turks. The attacking forces surrounded the city of Urmia and were prepared to invade it, but the Russian guards stationed in the city were able to keep them at bay until a greater reinforcement arrived to drive them away.

In anticipating of future attacks, some Russian troops were stationed in the larger Christian villages. On October 9–12, another army of Kurds along with their Turkish officers came down the mountain and attacked the villages that had survived the previous onslaught. In Charrbash a small contingent of the Russian soldiers by their long range cannons was able to keep the attackers at a safe distance from the village during the day. The Kurds returned at night under the cover of darkness. They attacked all night long trying to breach the defenses, but were unsuccessful. When the enemy retreated in the morning, many dead were left behind, among them a high ranking Turkish officer along with a large quantity of spent German ammunition casings.

"On November 12, 1914, Sultan Mohamed V, in his capacity as Caliph, proclaimed holy war and appealed to the Muslim subjects of the Entente Powers to join in a common struggle with the Ottoman Empire. The Sultan's proclamation was immediately posted on government buildings, in Mardin, for instance on the courthouse door. This proclamation was confirmed in a fatwa issued by the Shaykh-ul-Islam on November 14. The fatwa directed the holy war against the enemies of Islam particularly Britain, France, and Russia. Sultan's proclamation was repeated on November 21, as an appeal to non-Ottoman Muslims particularly Iran to join in the Jihad. Major Shi'ite leaders in the holy cities of Najaf and Karbala also issued a fatwa of jihad." (Gaunt David, 2006, 62)

Massacre in Urmia

Urmia (Assyrian city of water) was among few regions where Assyrians as a community had survived in Persia until the twentieth century. They lived in the city of Urmia and 120 villages along the shores of a large salt lake. An Assyrian church of Mart Maryam (St. Mary) in Urmia, which still stands, is the oldest building in the region. Evidences indicate that it may have been built in the fifth or sixth century AD. Long before World War I, the Ottoman Turks and the Russians had often dominated the northwest region of Persia, known as Azerbaijan, at one time or another. Since mid nineteen century Russia had not only gained a de facto control of the Iranian provinces near its border also maintained a firm hold on the Shah by loaning him considerable amount of money which he used for his own enjoyment. During the Russian presence in northwest Iran Assyrians and Armenians enjoyed a respite from persecution they historically had suffered at the hand of their Muslim neighbors.

On October 29, 1914, after officially aligning itself with Germany, Turkish torpedo boats entered the harbor of Odessa, sunk the Russian gunboat Donetz, killing a part of the crew, and damaged two Russian dreadnaughts. They also sank the French ship Portugal, killing two of the crew and wounding two others. They then turned their guns on the town and destroyed a sugar factory. This led to the Russia's declaration of war Russia against Turkey.

Consequently, on December 30, 1914, when the Russian army stationed in northwest Iran was ordered to withdraw into Russia, the panic stricken inhabitants of the Assyrian and Armenian villages of Urmia, and Salamas, who feared that Russian withdrawal would result in the massacre of the Christians by the Muslims, abandoned their homes in the middle of the night, and followed the troops heading for DeJulfa, a hamlet on the Russian border. They left behind their homes, cattle, and all they had, taking with them only the minimum necessities they could carry. They had to contend with the freezing cold and the wolves. The weak and the sick were first to die. Parents became separated from each other, lost their children, and were unable to find them in the darkness and the masses of hurrying, frantic, and demoralized people. At night, the stop shelters in villages on the way were so crowded that many were unable to find a place to keep warm. They had to contend with the freezing cold and the wolves. At one place, seventy people were found frozen to death in the mud. After a perilous journey, according to a report dated March 1, 1915, by the Reverend Robert M. Labaree of the American Mission stationed in Tabriz, some 17,000 Assyrians had survived the ordeal and had been temporarily settled in the district of Erivan in Armenia.

As it was expected, on the first day of the year, thousands of Muslims were out with their swords, guns, and dangers eagerly searching for Christians to kill. The Muslim clergies in a meeting had decided to eliminate the local Christians, but they wanted the Kurds to do the actual killing and plundering because they suspected that the Russsian army may return and punish them. Special messengers were sent to several Kurdish chiefs representing thousands of warriors offering them the Christians as gift to do with them what ever they wished. Two days later, Kurdish Beqzad, Herki and Zaza tribes came from neighboring areas to invade the region. Some seventy villages in Urmia were plundered and destroyed, most of their inhabitants were killed. Those who survived took refuge in the American and French Missions. To quote Abraham Youhanan:

"Every incident turned upon a pillage or murder, rape or torture. The brutal creatures plundered the villages, killed the men, dishonored the women, sized the portable property, and returned leisurely home, conscious of having done a good day's work."

They proudly thought they had done Allah a favor as if he was powerless to carry out his own justice and needed the help of the criminally minded to heap death and destruction on helpless people. They did clearly contradicted the first statement of the Koran where Allah is described as kind and compassionate, but they were not. The massacres of the Assyrians began in October 1914 and continued until August 1918. Most of the Assyrians who managed to survive during the first year of the massacres did so by fleeing to Russia, or taking refuge in the French and the American missions in Urmia and Salamas. They all suffered grievously. In describing the plight of the surviving Assyrians, one American missionary who had witnessed the deaths and the destruction of the communities between January 1, 1915, and the end of May 1915, wrote:

"We had a service of thanksgiving in the church (at the American Mission) yesterday, the first time for many months, as it had been occupied by refugees. Thousands have lived in such terror and want; it is a wonder that many have not lost their minds. It has seemed sometimes as if our tears were all dried up and our emotions were dead, we have seen and felt so much. I suppose it is nature's way of saving brain and nerve. When I look at these poor wretched creatures and little children like skeletons, I find I still have some feelings left. It is estimated that 4,000 people have died from disease, hunger, and exposure, and about a thousand by violence. The suffering can never be told, nor is it ended. Hundreds, yes thousands, are destitute, and even if we empty our yard there is no one left but the missionaries to save them from starvation." (Diary of Missionary)

The massacre of the Christians of Iran by the Turks and their allies, the Kurds and Persian Azeri's, from October 1914 through August 1919 can only be described as a crime against humanity—the slaughter of the innocents. Non-Muslim citizens of Muslim countries historically have been prohibited from possessing weapons even for self-defense. Consequently, Christians of Iran were unable to defend themselves and were at the mercy of the greater population of the Turks, Kurds, and Persian Azeris, armed by the Turks with modern weapons.

Driving Christians out of their homeland and scattering them was a tactic used by the Turks as a mean of ethnic and religious cleansing. Talaat Pasha, Turkey's minister of the interior during World War I, had kept a notebook with essential data about the effect of his deportation orders. By May 27, 1915, a page in his notebook gives a total of 924,158 persons who were deported. The list however did not include Christians of Turkey and Northwest Iran who fled to Russia on their own. It is important to note that Turks and Kurds persecuted Armenians and Assyrians similarly because they were both Christian and were considered the enemies of Islam. Viscount Bryce in a preface to "Shall This Nation Die," a book about the Assyrian and Armenain genocide by Rev. Joseph Naayem, writes: *"It was the suffering of the Armenians that chiefly drew the attention of Britain and America because of their greater population, but communities such as 'Nestorian and Assyro-*

Chaldean' were equally subjected to extermination, even though Turkey has never alleged that they constituted any danger to that country. This fact was also attested to by other reports by the news media in the west, at that time."

http://www.aina.org/books/stnd.htm

The November 1916 "Current History Magazine" published by the *New York Times* confirmed this fact. Under the heading: "The Total of Armenian and [As]Syrian Dead," it states:

"The Armenians are not the only unfortunates; the [As]Syrians also have been decimated. There are many varieties of [As]Syrian Christians. Some lived near the Persian border and in ancient Assyria, and are known as Nestorians, or Assyrian Christians. Some of these living north of Mosul have been massacred. The Nestorian Highlanders, who, according to figures I communicate from a pamphlet now in press, claimed before the war to number 90,000, had to fight their way out to Persia in the Autumn of 1915, our committee fed them.

It also mentions the killing of the members of the Assyrians of the Syrian Orthodox Church and also the Catholic Assyrians, otherwise known as Chaldeans. By the end of the war, in the cities of Turkey, the villages of the Hakkari Mountains, and Northwest Persia, more than a million Armenians and 750,000 Assyrians, including members of the Chaldean and Syriac denominations, were killed in most cruel fashions. About the end of 1917, after three years of death and destruction, Assyrians of Northwest Iran in desperation began to defend themselves against a powerful enemy that was resolute to wipe them out. Defeat at every location led to the wholesale massacre of the Christian population.

On May 2nd 1915, after defeating the Turks in Caucasia, Russian army arrived in Urmia, the surviving refugees in the American and the French Missions were free to leave and return to their former villages. The return of the Assyrians to their battered villages was akin to the return of a defeated army engaged in many battles. The prosperous villages they had left behind were all in ruin. Some of the villages had been all wiped out and had no inhabitants left, entire families had disappeared forever. The survivors mourned the absence of one half to two-third of their original numbers. Aid from the United States and Russia made it possible for the very poor to receive ration, and the homeless to build humble shelters. (Werda Juel, 1924, 53-54)

Massacres of the Highland Assyrians

The highland Assyrians who lived in the fastness of the Kurdistan Mountains, far removed from the outside world, were in no position to threaten Turkey even if they wanted to. Hostile Kurds who had been often used by the Turks to massacre them surrounded them on all directions, making it impossible for them to have direct contact with the outside world. On the August 3, 1914, the Valli of Van, Tahsim Pasha, invited the religious and temporal leader of the community, Patriarch Mar Benjamin Shimon, to inform him that if Assyrians remained loyal to the Turks during the upcoming war they could expect military and financial help from Turkey.

Soon it became clear that this was a ploy, a telegraph from the Ministry of the Interior to the office of the Directorate of Public Security, dated early October 1914, indicates that Turkey had other plans in mind. Orders were given for the deportation and expulsion of Assyrians belonging to the Church of the East, especially those living on the border of Turkey and Iran, to provinces such as Ankara and Konya, where they should be dispersed exclusively among Muslim people, so that no more than twenty families would be settled in one area. The authorities were also instructed not to provide any type of aid or support for them.
(http://www.bethsuryoyo.com/articles/AssyrianDeportation/

These orders unleashed a bloody onslaught against the Assyrians of the highland and the Plain of Urmia. According to Surma Beit Mar Shimon, during the same month persecution of the Assyrians living in the highland near Iran's borders began. Some fifty Assyrian men of Gawar were taken to the local government center in Bashkalla and were murdered. The Turkish soldiers plundered Assyrian peasants of North Berwar district. Young men of Albag were killed, women and young children were taken captive, and houses were plundered. Assyrians of other villages such as Shamsadin, Norduz, Mar Bishu, and Iyil who were most loyal to the Turkish rule suffered the same fate.

Appeals for help from Tahsim Pasha remained unanswered. Soon it become evident that Turkey's promises to the Assyrians of Kurdistan were baseless. In mid-April 1915, a meeting was arranged between the Assyrian tribes, where it was decided that unless they began to defend themselves against Turkey's ethnic cleansing policies, they too, at no time would be wiped out. A month later, on June 11, a Turkish army led by Hidar Baq the Vali of Mosul together with troops from various Kurdish tribes equipped with artillery and up-to-date weapons began a coordinated attack against the Assyrian villages.

Mir Rashid of Barwer led a confederation of Kurds against Lizan and lower Tyrai. Arthosh Kurds and regular troops of Julmerk attacked Chumba and upper Tyrai. Agha of Chalbrought and his forces went against Slabekan, and Thuma and Sutu Agah of Ormar assailed Jilu and Baz. Despite being greatly outnumbered, Assyrians bravely defended themselves, but their antiquated flint guns were no match for the firepower of the mountain cannons and machine guns. The explosions of the cannons thundered in the mountains and the echo of their blast bounced back and forth from one mountain peak to another. The cannonballs striking the Assyrian defensive position shattered rocks into sharp nails flying in all direction killing and wounding anyone they struck. When the cannonballs blasted the rocks of a higher altitude, they unleashed an avalanche of rocks rolling down the slope and crushing anyone standing in their way.

One after another, Assyrians villages were defeated; their inhabitant men women and children were killed. Only those who managed to escape to the villages at the higher altitudes survived. After weeks of fighting, the Village of Qochanis was pillaged and burned; the Valley of Lizan was occupied as were the villages of the Sapna and Berwar Valley. Attacks on Jilu, Chumba, and Salabekan were repulsed, but not for long. Because the meager Assyrian supplies of weapons and ammunitions was dwindling, Mar Benjamin traveled to Albag to seek help from the Russians in Persia, but they were not able to help.

On June 27, a letter was received from Haider Baq the Vali of Mosul informing the Patriarch that the district of Tyari had been conquered, destroyed, and set on fire, as were the villages of Barwar, Sarzar, Dashton, and Darvanish. He also informed the Patriarch that unless he and his people surrender, his brother Hormuz, who was in his custody would be put to death. There was no reason to believe that if the Assyrians surrendered they would not be massacred. The Patriarch replied: *"My people are in my charge; they are all my brothers. How can I betray them for the sake of one?"* Upon the receipt of this letter Hormozd, was put to death. (Wigram, 1922, 368) During the five or six weeks of respite before the second round of attacks, Mar Benjamin Shimon twice appealed to the Russians for help—but it never arrived. The second assault began in the middle of August. This time the Barzans had joined the ranks of the assailants. (Wigram, 1922, 369) During these attacks, Tahoma, Baz, Jilu, and Tyari were ravaged. *"The churches and houses were burned, the fields were wasted, the trees cut down, the irrigation channels demolished, and the valleys were rendered uninhabitable."* (Wigram, 1922, 370)

The eldest son of Simko of Shakak Kurds had boasted that he would not rest until every Christian church in the land was destroyed. Though driven out of their villages, they were not about to give up. Instead they ascended to further heights, some 10,000 feet above the sea level, a place they called "Yailas," where their flocks and herds used to graze in the summer. It was still summer; the cattle were already there and the melting snow provided plenty of fresh water. Attempts by the Kurds to penetrate these strongholds were easily repulsed at the passible access paths. Assyrian raiders were able to descend into the valley from time to time to carry back small supplies of corn from the hidden granaries in the villages. Yailas provided excellent sanctuary, but because of extreme freezing temperatures during the winter living there would have been almost impossible. As they were dreading the arrival of winter, in October, Kurds and Turks were waiting to see them freeze or come down to be killed. (Wigram, 1922, p. 371)

To solve the desperate situation, Patriarch Benjamin Shimon, decided once more to ask for help from the Russians. He along with Malik Khoshaba of Lizan, and two guides descended the precarious heights, while travelling mostly at night, to evade the ever-present enemy and made their way down to Salamas. Again, Russians were in no position to help because they were preparing once again to withdraw. The local Russian commander advised the Patriarch to stay with him to save his life instead of returning to the mountain. This suggestion was promptly rejected by the Patriarch, who replied; *"I go back to my people, to live or to die with them."* (Beit Mar shimon. Surma 1983, 73)

By October 1915, the only viable option for the Assyrians was to find a way to break the blockade and lead the population to Urmia. Such an attempt would have been difficult, even without having to defend along the way some 25,000 noncombatants, mostly women and children. Defeat or surrender at any point would have meant the certain death of everyone, because there was no mercy, either among the Kurds nor the Turks. Assyrians had to pass through some of the most rugged and difficult to descend mountains. The only solace they had was in knowing that *"they had leaders who knew how to make the most out of the slenderest chances of survival."* (Wigram 1922, 372) The bulk of their enemy forces was blocking the direct routes to Urmia, among them were tribesmen like Nuri Beq, who had just completed the massacres of unarmed Christians of Urmia. They chose to go westward, hoping that no one would expect them to pass that way. To decrease the chance of being seen, they reduced the length of their line by divided their population into two different bands. If one band was caught and destroyed, the other could survive. They planned to cross a flimsy wooden bridge over the river Zab; and to make a wide turn northward to meet on the further side of Julamerk. From there they had to walk one day, to Albag, near Bashkalla, to reach Salamas north of Urmia.

"The Patriarch was leading one of the Columns. As they moved over a lofty mountain height near Julamerk, he was able to look down and see a small spot which marked the site of his own village of Qochanis. As he paused to gaze, a wistful sorrow filled his heart. From that distance he could only see the leafless trees surrounding

the village, but he remembered in the spring how luxuriously green the trees and the surrounding crops and even the encircling mountains were. Now it was an isolated place of ruined houses, blackened with fire. As he watched for the last time he sighed and said: 'when shall I ever drink the waters of Qochanis again?' His words were heard by three brave men who silently broke away from the line and burst past the Kurdish picket who tried unsuccessfully to stop them, and brought back a pitcher of water from the Qochanis spring." (Wigram, 1922, 274)

Before the two columns could reunite at Albag, they were confronted by a body of Kurds that had passed the Zab at another bridge to cut off their advance. An Assyrian detachment under the command of Khoshaba of Lizan defeated them and allowed the refugees to go on their way. Many men, women, and children lost their life mostly because of famine, and others in battle. Near Albag, Kurds once again confronted the Assyrians. Loses on both sides were great. Out of a population of 250,000 highland Assyrians prior to the war, only about 30,000 succeeded to arrive in Salamas to join the Assyrians of that region who had survived repeated attacks by the Kurds, the Azeri Turks, and Turkey's army. Wigram writes:

"It was not a beaten host that arrived . . . They had held their own against great odds, as long as resistance was possible; and when forced to retreat under appalling difficulties, they had brought away with them not only their women and children, but large proportion of their flocks and herds as well. They had indeed suffered heavy losses in the fighting and many women and children had succumbed to the hardships of the retreat. But their spirit was still unbroken, as they were yet distained, amply, to prove." (Wigram, 1922, 374-5)

It is important to note that Turks often justify their massacres of the Assyrians during World War One by claiming that it happened because Assyrians had allied themselves with the Russians, or the allies. Judging by how easily the Kurds under the direction of the Turks destroyed the Assyrian villages and killed thousands, it is obvious that they had no one to help them. In reality, long before world one Turkey was either directly involved in attacks against the Assyrians, or instigated the Kurds to do so. Such atrocities were seldom reported in the Western Media, but the little that was published indicates that they were a matter of rule rather than exception.

The London Times of June 4th 1904 in behalf of the Canterbury Mission to the Assyrians reported that three Assyrian villages in the district of Tergawar were attacked and destoryed by the Kurds in that year, a dozen men were burned alive, "and the crops remained unsown or un harvested. throughout the district." (The London Times, the Primate and Assyrian Christians", June 4,1904) .."*in Qudshanis (Hakkari), last winter, (1904) every [As]Syrian village but one in the neighborhood was raided of all their sheep by Kurds, and to these pastoral (As)Syrians the sheep were everything.*" Only the village where the missionaries lived was spared. (ibid) The Kurds continued to wreck havoc in Tergawar Slodoz territory for another two years and due to the lawlessness the fields remained unharvested. When the Persian troops were sent to establish order in the region in June of 1907 they were attacked by the Turkish military and forced to retreat. The pursuing Turkish troops entered the Christian villages of Mawana and Kurana burnt the houses, church, "*and killed most of the non-combatants*" Those who survived fled to Urmia appealing to the English Missionaries for food and shelter. (The London Times, "The Turco-Persian Frontier Incident", August 15,1907) In a letter dated August 2, 1907 Elizabeth Wend the daughter of a German missionary reported about the plight of the Assyrians of the Tergawar district who had been attacked and forced to flee into the plain of Urmi.

"*Our village, Charbash is now completely filled with people coming through, fleeing from Tergawar. Hundreds of people ...arrive starving....Yesterday morning the Kurds came [to their villages] and everyone who was not killed fled. They fled from there without bread, without clothes, with only their lives. Many hundreds have gone to the city to the Russian consul and more keep coming. The actual reason for the terribly rushed flight was the Turks came up behind the Kurds with cannons..."*

(E. Wendt. Source: Sonderuck des Evangelischen Vereins Zur Forderung der nestorianischen Kirche in Kurdistan (offprint from the Evengelical Association to sposor the Nestorian Church in Kurdistan). Lerbeck b. porta W. 1907. in G. Yonan Ein Vergessener Haolocaust (A Forgotten Holocaust) 1989. p. 67)

The number of the Assyrians who fled to Urmia seeking protection from the Russian consul in 1907 was estimated about 2,000 by the Assyrian publication Kokhva (The Star). (Kokhva, Urmia, Iran, Nov. 1907)

"Persia asked for assistance from the Russian Foreign Office on August 7, 1907 to help it resolve its conflict with Turkey saying that Turkey's invading troops were burning, slaying and had advanced some forty miles inside the Persian territory." (The New York Times, "Persia Appeals to Russia", New York Times, october 6, 1907) A report by Pastor Karl Robbelen in 1909 indicates that the Turmoil subsequent to the Turkish invasion continued not only in the mountainous districts but also in the plain of Urmia, the two regions where Assyrians predominantly lived. He wrote:

"Since spring (of 1909) the Kurds looting has been constantly increasing in intensity. The rich Baranduz region was the first to be devastated in this manner, the Urmia Region where our brothers live was next." (Pastoren Pera Johaness und Luther Pera im jahre 1909 an Hermannsburg (Circular Nr. 3) in G. Yonan Ein...P.75.)

Highland Assyrians in Persia

After Arriving in Persia, in Mid of September they were distributed in the cities of Salamas, Khoi and Urmia. During their exodus, they had lost some four or five thousand souls, mostly women and children; they had lost also all their earthly possessions. They were sad about their plight but were also grateful for the protection they were given in a strange country. However shortly after their arrival they fell victim to epidemic of fever followed by typhus. Thanks to the Russian medical service the disease was checked and was prevented from inflicted even thousands more. For as long as the Russians were in control of the Northwestern Persia, local Muslims did not dare to bother the Assyrians, but there was no doubt that Turkey army, and their allies the Kurds, will resume attacks against them. As a measure of self defense volunteers were organized to be trained by the Russian military to prepare for such possibility. The Persian authorities were informed that this step was not intended as a movement against the Persian government, but rather to discourage invasion by the Turkey's military and the Kurds. Meanwhile the Muslim population of the city had been supplied with arms and ammunition. Large number Muslim volunteers in disguise had arrived in Urmia, from the neighboring communities. A substantial military arrived in Urmia from Tabriz.

Early in February 1918 a number of Assyrians were killed at the western gate of the city. To quell the violence Mar Benjamin wrote a letter to Eshrat Homayoon the Governor of Urmia expressing gratitude to the Persian government for allowing the Assyrians of the highland to settle in that country. He Stated that Assyrians had no intention of harming the interest of Iran and were willing to defend it for foreign enemies. He promised that as soon as the war ended Assyrians of the highland would either return to their previous home, or go to another country. He requested that the Eshrat Homayoon put an end to the escalating killings of the Christians.

The letter was hand delivered to the governor by Agha Petrous who was in command of the Assyrian forces in Urmia, and a companion. Eshrat Homayoon's answer was that *"there is no way to stop the killings, that they will continue and in fact violence will grow even worst. The only solution to this problem is either for the Assyrians and the Armenians to disarm or leave Persia immediately."*

A meeting of the heads of the Assyrian and Armenian communities was assembled in Urmia to decide what to do. The majority consensus was that Christians could not disarm because that would lead to their wholesale massacre and their departure from Persia was impossible because roads were still covered with snow and ice and there was no safe place for them to go. In addition it would have been impossible to protect a large population of unarmed men, women and children on the open roads from the likely attacks by the Kurds, Turks and the Persians. (Bar Malik Ismail Yagov, 1964, 88) In a letter to Mukhti-Shams the governor General of Tabriz who was also the Crown Price of Persia, Mar Benjamin expressed the Assyrian good-will toward Persia and its government. He explained that the Assyrians of the mountains were forced to take refuge in Persia because of Turkish government intention to massacre them all. The weapons they carried were intended to defend not only the Assyrians against Turkey's attacks in Persia also to defend the Persian borders. "My people, therefore, rather than having the impossible political designs on the integrity of the Persian soil, as falsely reported to your Highness, in reality and by virtue of their precarious position, are the very protectors of that soil." (Joel Werda, 1924, 96)

Unable to disarm the Assyrians or to deport them the Persian Governor Arshad-elMoolk decided to assassinate the Assyrian leaders. He had sent Special Forces to assassinate Agha Petrous at his home. They arrived before the dawn and surrounded his house, shooting from all directions. The windows and walls of his home were literarlly riddled with bullets, but the general though surprised by the sudden attack, ordered his family to hide in the basement, and single handedly manned the machine gun he had hid on the roof, for such an occasion and succeeded in forcing the attackers to flee. (Joel Werda, 1924 p. 105)

All-out Attack Against Assyrians

The long awaited Persian attack against the Assyrians began on February 9th 1918. It started with shouts of Jihad followed by the rattling sound of weapons, explosions and thunder of cannons, which shook the Christian quarter. Fierce street to street fighting ensued and continued for three days. At the end the attackers were trapped on all sides in the main street of the Christian quarter, they were defeated, disarmed and allowed to flee. A meeting was arranged with the Muslim dignitaries to assure them that Assyrians had no intentions of harming anyone but will defend themselves. (Werda, 1924, 103-116)

Departure of the Russian Troops.

The October 17, 1917 Russian Revolution Marked the disintegration of Russian forces who were in the process of training an army of 2000 Assyrian volunteers in Urmia and Salamas to help them get ready to protect their communities from attacks. When the Bolsheviks took over Russia, the new government ordered the return of all the Russian troops from the Caucasian Front. The Russian troops stationed in Urmia revolted against their officer, whom they accused of being Royalist, and abandoned, the munitions, provisions, and weapons, which in most cases, were claimed by the Turks and the Kurds. With their departure Assyrians were left to fend for themselves against the combined armies of Turkey's military, stationed in the region, the Persian troops, and thousands of irregular Kurds, who were always ready to kill and plunder the Assyrians. The telephone service between Urmia and Tiflis, in Caucasia, were still working. Soon became evident that Russia, had given approval for the government of Georgia to become an independent Republic.

While the Assyrian National assembly was pondering the possibility of quitting Urmia and Salmas and to move the Christian population to the Caucasus, Capitan Gracy, a member of the British Mission in Caucasus, arrived at Urmia in December of 1917, and held a special meeting with Patriarch Mar Benjamin and others dignitaries, he "promised; money, equipment, munitions, reinforcements and self-government," if the Assyrians remain where they were. Assyrians at that time had some 10,000 sparsely equipped irregular fighters half of them under the leadership of Agha Petrous Eillia in Urmia and the rest in Salamas under the command of Malik Khoshaba of Tyari.

Mar-Benjamin wrote two letters to the Governor of Urmia and the Governor-General of Azerbaijan at Tabriz; to be communicated to the Crown Prince of Persia. In these two letters Mar-Benjamin declared that he harbored neither suspicion nor hostility towards the government or the inhabitants of the Persian Azerbaijan, and that he only wanted to defend his people, who had taken refuge on the Persian soil, against the attacks of the Kurds and Turks. He asked them hospitality for the winter, until the spring, when he would leave the country and go with his people to Russia or elsewhere.

Starting on February 8, 1918, even the Persian Army began attacking the Assyrians. A substantial military arrived in Urmia from Tabriz. A number of Assyrians were killed at the western gate of the city. To quell the violence Mar Benjamin wrote a letter to Eshrat-homayoon the Governor of Urmia, expressing gratitude to the Persian government for having allowed the Assyrians of the highland to settle in that country. He also stated; "Assyrians had no intention of harming the interest of Iran and were willing to defend it from foreign enemies." He promised that as soon as the war ended Assyrians of the highland would either return to their previous home or go to another country. He requested that the Eshrat-homayoon put an end to the escalating killings of the Christians. The letter was hand delivered to the governor by Agha Petrous and a companion. Eshrat-homayoon's answer was; "there is no way to stop the killings, they will continue, and in fact, violence will grow even worst. The only solution to this problem is for the Assyrians and the Armenians to disarm or leave Persia immediately."

A meeting of the heads of the Assyrian and Armenian communities was assembled in Urmia to decide what to do. The majority consensus was that Christians could not disarm because that would lead to their wholesale massacre, and their departure from Persia was impossible because the ground was still covered with snow and ice and there was no safe place for them to go. In addition it would have been impossible to protect a large population of unarmed men, women and children on the open roads from the likely attacks by the Kurds, Turks and the Persians. (Bar Malik Ismail Yagoo, 1964, 88)

In a letter to Mukhti-shams the governor General, of Tabriz, who was also the Crown Prince of Persia, Mar Benjamin expressed the Assyrian good will toward Persia and its government, he explained that the Assyrians of the highland were forced to take refuge in Persia because of Turkish government intention to massacre them all. The weapons they carried were intended to defend, not only the Assyrians against Turkey's attacks in Persia, also to defend the Persian borders. "My people, therefore, rather than having the impossible political designs on the integrity of the Persian soil, as falsely reported to your Highness, in reality and by virtue of their precarious position, are the very protectors of that soil." (Joel Warda, 1924, 96)

All-out Attack on Assyrians

Unable to disarm Assyrians, or to deport them, the Persian Government adopted a plan to assassinate the Assyrian leaders. Arshad-el-Moolk had sent Special Forces to kill Agha Petrous at his home. They arrived before the dawn and surrounded his house and began shooting, but the general although surprised by the sudden attack ordered his family to hide in the basement, and single handedly manned a machine gun, which he had hid on the roof for such an occasion. The windows and walls of his home were literarlly riddled with bullets but by climbing on the roof and using the machine gun against the attackers succeeded in forcing them to flee. (Joel Werda, 1924, 105)

The long awaited Persian attack against the Assyrians began on February 9th 1918. It started with shouts of Jihad followed by the rattling sound of weapons, explosions, and thunder of cannons that shook the Christian quarter. Fierce Street to street fighting ensued and continued for three days. At the end the attackers were trapped on all sides in the main street of the Christian quarter, they were defeated, disarmed and allowed to flee. A meeting was arranged with the Muslim dignitaries to assure them that Assyrians had no intentions of harming anyone but will defend themselves if attacked. (ibid pp.103-116)

Murder of Mar Benjamin

Capitan Gracy had advised Mar Benjamin to establish with Ismaeil Simko, the leader of the Shakak Kurdish tribe. On February 18th a letter arrived from Simko inviting Mar Benjamin to a conference to discuss a friendship pact. The Assyrian community council was convened and it was agreed that Mar Benjamin should accept the invitation. Later Agha Petrous and members of Mar Benjamin family suspected that this was an ambush and advised him to postpone or cancel the meeting but, he refused. These were desperate times and Assyrians needed any help they could get. Peaceful relations with Simko would have prevented future attacks against them by the Shakak Kurds. And since Mar Benjamin had promised the English to form an alliance with Simko, he was not about to break his promise, or to disobey the decision of the council. (Bar Malik Ismail Yagoo, 1964, 93)

A group of riders who took the Mar Benjamin's acceptance letter to Simko came back with glowing praises about how well they were treated which further eased the fears about the meeting. On Saturday March 3, 1918 Mar Benjamin along with one hundred guards arrived in Kohneh-Shahr where Simko had established his headquarter. The city was under the Persian government control and a group of dignitaries came out to welcome the Patriarch and his guards. He and couple of his men were led into the courthouse where the meeting would be held. Assyrian guards were positioned at the city gate, and various other points in the town. Five were stationed in the courthouse, outside the conference hall.

When an officer worried about the situation was able to get a glimpse at the meeting room, he found the participants were sitting around a table and eating lunch, the meeting ended in a friendly manner, and the Assyrian party returned to Khosrawa. Shortly later a messenger from Simko arrived with a message inviting Mar Benjamin to another meeting on the same day in Kohneh-shahr. Immediately a council meeting was arranged to discuss the new invitation. Since it was snowing and an important period of fasting was about to start most council members did not want the meeting to take place on that day but Mar Benjamin prevailed. The second meeting went well, Simko and his guards played their charade of friendship and respect successfully. At the end of meeting Simko followed Mar Benjamin in to the front yard and said a hasty goodbye and returned to the building. Within seconds a rain of bullets was unleashed on the unsuspecting Assyrians from the rooftops of various buildings within the compound. As Mar Benjamin began to step into his carriage he and many of his guards were killed, some were wounded and the rest scattered into disarray. Forty-seven on the Assyrian side were killed, among them were four Russian officers who had stayed with the Assyrians, rather than returning to their homeland after the Bolshevik Revolution. Forty-six were wounded, including Balkonin Gondratof, another Russian officer who was wounded in the foot but had jumped on a horse and had returned to Khoosrava in the district of Salamas to bring reinforcement. The body of Mar Benjamin and that of others were recovered and returned to Khoosrava at twelve at the midnight.

Assyrians owe a great debt to the dedicated Russian officers who stayed with them to help them out during their most tragic years of their life. Balkonin Gondratof who became the commander of the Assyrian troops in 1918 had been at war for most of his adult life, he was wounded at various parts of his body but had survived them all, those who knew him well, described him as brave, dedicated and very intelligent.

It was feared that Patriarch's brother David, who had accompanied Mar Benjamin to the meeting with Simko, had also been killed. No one knew what had happened to him, since the day before. On Sunday, early in the morning Mar Benjamin's sister, Surmi Khanim dressed in black, and in mourning for her brothers, sent invitation to the Assyrian tribal chiefs and Agha Petrous inviting them to a meeting to discuss the Assyrian response to this tragedy. Soon an Armenian arrived from Kohne-shahr bringing with him a message from David, who told him that he and five other Assyrian soldiers were hiding in the Armenian church in that town and was asking for help before the Iranian authorities find out their location. Some of the bodies of Assyrians, who had been killed the day before, still remained in that town. Balkonin ordered four hundred troops under the leadership of Malik Shimzideen of Teyari and Malik Oshana of Tkhumi to go to Kohne-shahr and rescue the stranded troops to bring back the bodies of the Assyrians killed on the previous day. As if to add insult to injury, on Monday the 5th March, Simko's forces attacked Christian villages of Patvar and Malham in Salamas which were populated by the Assyrians and the Armenians. The Assyrian troops stationed in the area were able to repel the attacks and chase away Simko's fighters.

"The Sixth of March 1918, the day of Mar Benjamin's funeral, the city of Khoosrava was filled with sorrow. His body was carried in a casket on the shoulders of clergies. Followed by priests and bishops, then came the Russian officers who had so selflessly and faithfully served the Assyrians. After them came about two thousand Assyrian fighters. They were followed by what it seemed like, the entire population of the town, walking behind his casket in rows, on two sides of the street. As he was being taken to the Armenian Church of Mar Sarkis for the funeral services, the scent of incense mixed with the singing of the clergies and the ringing of the church bells filled the streets. The whole crowd was crying, not only for his death, but also for others who had died. They were crying for their shattered dreams and the many others that would die before this nightmare was over. He was put to rest in the backyard, on the Southside of the church." (Bar Malik Esmaeil Yagov)

The death of Mar Benjamin was great blow to the Assyrians. He was not only the head of the ancient Church of the East but had also led highland Assyrians and had helped them from being slaughtered despite impossible odds. Although most of the Urmia and Salamas Assyrians no longer belonged to his church and did not consider him as the father of their faith but they trusted his leadership and were willing to follow his advice. Though he was not a warrior but the highland warriors followed his every command and all respected his decisions. Even Agha Petrous who was against clergies' participation in the political and military matters respected him and had a good working relation with him.

Assyrians had no standing army, troops came together when there was an eminent danger of attack by the Turks or the Kurds. In such situations volunteers were willing to participate to the extent that they trusted and admired their leaders to lead them out of the precarious plots their vengeful enemies had planned for them. Paulus a younger brother of Mar Benjamin was chosen as his successor and a strong force was mustered to avenge Mar Benjamin's death.

Exodus from Urmia

After Mar Benjamin's death, starting in April 1918, Turkey's troops poured into Urmia and Salamas to attack all the Assyrian communities from all directions. During a period of six weeks Turkey's regiments, together with their Kurd allies, attacked Assyrians fourteen times, from various positions. In all these cases Assyrian militias were able to defeat the attackers.

But on June 21st 1918 Turkey military with the help of the Kurds succeeded in defeating the Assyrian defenders of Salamas. It was deemed necessary to evacuate some 35,000 Assyrians and Armenians from Salamas to bring them to Urmia. Along the way the Shakak Kurds under the command of Ismail Simko massacred several thousands of refugees. The atrocities in the plain of Urmia and Salamas continued for another three years. It will take great volumes to describe the inhumanity inflicted on the defenseless Assyrians in the cities of Turkey, Mountains of Zagros (Kurdistan), Urmia, and elsewhere during the entire World War One.

On June 21, 1918, after repeated attacks by the Turkish armies and their allies, the Kurds and Persian Azeri forces defeated the Assyrian defenders of Salamas. Their defeat led to a panic flight toward Urmia, some thirty miles to the south. Along the way, the Shakak Kurds, under the command of Ismail Simko, massacred several thousand of the refugees. Assyrians knew Simko and his tribe as Kurds who inflicted various massacres on them. Also in March 1918, he invited Mar Benjamin Shimon, the temporal leader of the Eastern Assyrians, for peace talks, but he assassinated him, at the behest of the local Persian authorities. His murder left Assyrians demoralized, divided, and without effective leadership. At Salamas, the Turkish commander Ali Ihsan Pasha ordered the killing of the remaining unarmed Christians including men, women, and children—except for the young ladies and girls who were carried off by the Persian Azeri, Turks, and Kurds.

About a month after the fall of Salamas, after four years of constant attacks against them by the regular Turkey's army and their allies, Assyrian defenders in Urmia were defeated, on July 30, 1918. The panic stricken people began to flee, leaving behind all they had. Since the enemy had blocked the way to Russia, their only escape option was southward where they hoped to find Agha Petrous, who with some troops had gone to receive weapons from the British.

About 60,000 Assyrians and Armenians fled from Urmia on the evening of that day. Along the way, they were pursued and attacked by the combined forces of the Turkish 6th and the 12th divisions, and thousands of irregular Kurds plus the Persian (Azeri) troops under the command of Majid-ul-Sultan. They followed the fleeing population, determent to kill as many of them as possible. When Majid-ul-Sultan succeeded in cutting off the retreat of some refugees and murdered a couple thousands of them, he sent a telegram from Miandab to Tabriz bragging that he had sent 2,000 infidels to hell. His dispatch was published on the following day in the "Tidjaddad," the official organ of the social democratic party at Tabriz. In Sahin-Galla he had encircled another 3,000 refugees, but the timely arrival of the brave Colonel Ezaria Tamraz and a handful of Assyrian riders spoiled his plans and forced his troops into retreat. Evidently Father Ghiwargis at Batoum took Majid-ul-Sultan into custody, but there are no details about how and what happened to him. Colonel McCarthy, a British officer who witnessed the plight of the fleeing Assyrians, later wrote:

"Never shall I forget that retreat from Urmia, when I met the panic-stricken people on the Nidjar road, and never do I want to see anything like it again. . . Apart from being harassed by the enemy, every known disease seemed to attack these unfortunate people and hundreds died from typhus, dysentery, smallpox and exhaustion. It was a common thing to see children, abandoned on the roadside, the parents probably dead. Wherever they camped for the night, the ground next morning was littered with dead and dying. What these

unfortunate people suffered few can realize. Some 10,000 were cut off by the Turks and no one heard of them since."

Only 35,000 Assyrians and 15,000 Armenians made it to the Baquba refugee camps in Iraq after passing through Hamadan. By this calculation, 10,000 Assyrians and Armenians died along the way. It is odd that during World War One the British military was capable of arming and supplying its forces all over the Middle East, but it was incapable of delivering few machineguns and ammunitions to the Assyrians, at a hundred miles distance. However, it expected the besieged Assyrians to withdraw half of their forces, from the battlefield, to go and get them, which led to events that decimated the Assyrians.

The Last Assyrians in Urmia

The following official U.S. archives document describes the plight of a typical Assyrian family during those tragic events. In response to an inquiry by Mr. Musey Benjamin, an Assyrian resident of the United States, who had inquired about the whereabouts of his father, Yonan Benjamin, and the rest of his family in Urmia, the American Consul in Tauriz, Iran, replied as follows:

Your Received, Consular Bureau, Dept. of State, Sept 22 1920)
No, 154.
AMERICAN CONSULATE,
Tabriz, Persia, July 10, 1920.

Subject: Whereabouts and welfare of Yonan Benjamin.

THE HONORABLE
THE SECRETARY OF STATE,
WASHINGTON.

"SIR:

"I have the honor to report, in reply to the Department's telegraphic instruction of October 17, 1919, and written instructions Nos. 163 (File No. 391/19) and 173 (File No. 391.9115 B 43/-) of September 4, 1919, and April 3, 1920, respectively, as follows:

"Yonan Benjamin is said to have died in the village of Gulpashan, Urumia, Persia, on or about July 24th, 1918; or about one week before the general exodus of the Christian population of the Urumia region on the advance of the Turkish forces. Aswa, the wife of Yonan and mother of Musey Benjamin, together with Yonan's daughters-in-law Sonam and Anna, the latter the wife of Musey, are reported to have been transported with numerous other Christian women of Urumia to Salamas by the Turks, and to have died at Salamas in the summer of 1918, as a result of the hardship and exposure to which they were subjected. Yonan Benjamin's daughter Marguerite is said, to have been abducted, by the Kurds, and her whereabouts or fate are unknown. Abram, the grandson of Yonan and son of Musey Benjamin, is reported to have fled from Urumia at the time of the Christian exodus, and to have died at the village of Tazakand near Hamadan, Persia, in the summer of 1918. It is reported that the late Yonan Benjamin's house and vineyards at Urumia have been destroyed and devastated by the local Muslims."

They proudly pose over the corpses of innocent Assyrians whom they hunted down and killed in cold blood.

"*All property of the former Christian inhabitants of the Urumia region, is at present, either vacant or occupied by the Persian Muslims, and all personal possessions of the Christians remaining after the Turkish withdrawal from that region have also been stolen or destroyed by their Muslim neighbors. No Christians have resided at Urumia since the withdrawal of the Christian remnant after the massacre of the refugees at the American Mission in Urumia by the Persians on May 24th, 1919, as reported by this Consulate to the American Legation at Tehran.*

It has been impracticable to obtain the information necessary for a prompt reply to this and similar inquiries, for the reason that the families of the Urumia Assyrians, and others having such information, are scattered, and considerable delay is occasioned in communicating with such persons; more particularly since postal communication with Tabriz during the past year has been uncertain and not infrequently interrupted."

I have the honor to be, Sir,

Your obedient servant,
    Gordon Paddock
Consul."

In his book "Shall This Nation Die?" Joseph Naayem, similarly describes the testimony of the priests and bishops of the Chaldean Church, who had survived, and told about what happened to the Assyrians in Urmia, who for one reason or another were unable to escape, on July 30, 1918.

"*When the commander of the Fourth Corps Turkish army, Salah-Eddin Pasha, arrived in the city he granted three days and nights of killing of the helpless Christians by the Turks, Kurds, and the Persian Azeri. Every night the sound of the carts carrying off the bodies to be thrown into mass graves could be heard. Some 16,000 Assyrians were massacred at that time. The Persians and the Kurdo-Turks carried off hundreds of women and young girls. The*

Persian soldiers of Arshad-Homayoun dishonored the Sisters of the French school at Urmia, who took refuge in the church of the Mission, among other women. Dr. D. Israel and a few others were hanged by the order of the Turkish Commandant, Kheiri Bey. Turks shot to death the wounded in the American hospital. One clergy reported fourteen members of his family, including his mother, were murdered or died of typhoid and other epidemics.. His sister's family including her son John, her brothers-in-law, James, Lazarus, Nicholas, Thomas, and Issa, her cousins, Paul Warda, Joseph Basile, Mary, and her aunt Rachel, were killed in her presence. She was taken captive by the Turks and was later transferred from Salamas to Urmia with others. Only those who took refuge in the French Mission were left alone.

Jean Djoumma, a Chaldean Assyrian who had returned to Khosrawa when it was safe to do so, in a letter to Abbe Decroo in Tauriz dated May 3, 1919 wrote:

"You know all the horrors suffered by our Christians during the massacres! Our women were burned alive, others were sawn to pieces, and men, women, and children were crucified or hacked to death. So great indeed were the horrors that the barbarous Turks were astonished to find at Urmia Muslims were more barbarous than themselves, Bishop Thomas Audo, a French missionary, and Mar Dinkha were led naked through the streets of Urmia before being martyred. My heart is torn, and I cannot tell you all the cruelties and the different tortures invented by the Muslims for our thousands of martyrs." (Naayem)

Form Hamadan to Baquba

The region, presently known as Northern Iraq, or Kurdistan, has been historically the homeland of the ancient and Christian Assyrians. Historical evidences show that during the periods of persecutions Christian Assyrians often fled their homes in the Plain of Nineveh and took shelter in the inaccessible mountains north of Mosul, located on the borders of Turkey, Iran and Iraq.

From there they also descended into Turkey, and the Plain of Urmia in northwest Iran. In 1831, When Yukhana Hurmizd, the last patriarch of the Church of the East in the Plain of Nineveh, united his church with the Roman Catholic Church, those who were unwilling to abandon the faith of their forefathers had no choice but to leave the region and join members of their denomination in the highlands of Hakkari and the Plain of Urmia, because they were being persecuted by their brethren who had become Catholic and were now called Chaldean. Therefore, Assyrians who lived in Iraq, before World War One were primarily members of the Chaldean and the Syrian Orthodox Churches. In other words, the Assyrians from the highland and northwest Iran, who arrived in Iraq, in 1918, had returned to their ancient homeland.

After passing through Hamadan Only thirty-five thousands Assyrians and fifteen thousands Armenians made it to the Baquba camps near Baghdad where the British had established tents to house them. They took good care of them, and later their able-bodied men were recruited into military force and others were employed to help with the tasks related to the war. Later, some Assyrians were recruited to serve as members of a militia force, which became to be known as Levies. It was organized by the British to ensure Iraq's security. Its members at that time consisted primarily of Arabs, Kurds and Turcoman.

When, in 1919, the British commanders of the Kurdish Levies were murdered at Amedyia, two battalions of Assyrian Militia, under the command of General Nightingale were used in a retaliatory action against the Kurds of the region, and their revolt was broken. Thereafter, the British continued to use Assyrians as protectors of Iraq, to put down successive rebellions by the Arabs and the Kurds. In April 1920, the British government formally announced its desire to establish Iraq into an Arab state, and received a mandate from the League of Nations, at the Remo Conference, to do so.

When the news of the mandate reached Iraq, in May of 1920 a group of Iraqi nationalists met with the British administrator Wilson, and demanded independence for their country, but their demand was rejected. In response, the grand mujtahid (an authority in Islamic law), of Karbala, Imam Shirazi, issued a fatwa and jihad against the British, by declaring that Islamic rules forbid the Muslims from being ruled by non-Muslims. Due to the instigations by the Turks, revolts erupted in Mosul, in July 1920, and from there they spread further south. Arab and Kurd members of the Levies deserted their force because of pressure from their communities. But the rebellions were crushed with the help of the British troops from Iran and India. By some estimates British lost 20,000 soldiers at that time. In a conference held in Cairo, to plan for Iraq's future, it was decided to use the Levies to relieve the British and the Indian forces, but the Arab could not serve as Levies because they would be enlisted in an Iraqi Army that was to be established soon. Consequently, Assyrians alone were to serve as Levies.

In 1920 a large number of Assyrians had made their way to their ancestral valleys in the Hakkari district. They continued to live there undisturbed until September 1924.

Starting in April 1921, British officers, Capitan MacNary and Captain Renton traveled to the Hakkari villages to enlist Assyrians but their efforts were far from successful. Assyrians declined to join until the British promised to ensure their return to their homes in the highland. However within two or three months, two hundred had joined, largely through the persuasion of Dr. Wigram, who had served as an Anglican missionary among them in the Hakkari. He undoubtedly promised that Britain would do its best to fulfill their wish. Finally an Assyrian force of 6,000 strong under the British command, led by General David d' Mar Shimon, and other Assyrian officers was trained and equipped during the years 1922-1923. Turkey's threat against the province of Mosul was always imminent.

The Assyrian troops were used successfully against Turkey's regular army and the Kurds, to save Iraq from total disaster. However, instead of earning the appreciation of the Muslim population, this increased their hatred of the Assyrians, they resented attacks by Christians against their Muslim brethren, and viewed the Assyrians as instrument of the British imperialistic policy.

In praising the Assyrian Levies role in protecting the Iraqi borders, Sir Percy Cox the British administrator of Iraq between October 1920- March 1922, wrote:

"In justice to the Assyrians it must be added that during the first three months of this year, when a Turkish attack was always a possibility, they have proved their strategic value on the Iraq frontier. In March, over 2,000 Assyrians enlisted in the Levies, within three weeks. It is far from improbable that this instant response on the part of a people whose qualities as fighting men are renowned was the main reason which induced the Kemalists [Turks] to abandon their projected attack."
(http://www.aina.org/books/tat.htm)

In 1924 Turkish forces arrived at the Assyrian occupied villages in Hakkari, and in retaliation for the use of the Assyrian Levies against them, they burnt and plundered the villages and forced about 8,000 men women and children to flee southward, who arrived as refugees in Amadiya within Iraq's territory. They were easily driven out of the region because most of their able-bodied men had been conscripted as Levies and were not present to defend their people, also the British had made no plans to protect them.

1924: The Mosul Affair

Immediately after the armistice Turks withdrew from the Mosul district and the British occupied it. At the Lausanne conference Turkey contended that Mosul was unjustly given to Iraq, and insisted that it should be returned to it. The British failed to bring up the requirement of settling Assyrians in their former home or demand any form of concession from the Turks on their behalf. Instead, in April 1924 Britain informed the Iraqi Government that it intended to demand from Turkey to hand over the former Assyrian territory of Hakiari to Iraq, and explained that Iraq would benefit from this because it would have the war hardened Assyrians guarding its northern frontier which would promote their ties of friendship and gratitude with the Arab state. But in return, Iraq should be willing to help the Assyrians, who were not yet settled, to be able to acquire some uninhabited land in the northern districts. In addition British asked the Iraqi Government to provide local autonomy to them similar to what they had enjoyed under the Turkish rule, before World War one. Iraqi government agreed to such conditions.

Up to the 1925, the northern frontiers of Iraq were undecided; the Turks argued that the entire Vilayet of Mosul was theirs. Hennery Conway Dobbs, the British High commissioner in Iraq in May 1924 published in the Assyrian press in Mosul the following statement;

"The British Government being interested in "safe guarding the interest of the Assyrian people, and because of the service they provided to the allied cause during world war one, and their future relations with the Iraq State, has decided to press for the extension of the Iraq frontier beyond the present borders to include the lands previously occupied by the Assyrian tribes of Tiyarai, Tkhuma, Jelu and Baz. [The region of Hakkiari] *"There are more than sufficient deserted lands, the property of the 'Iraq Government' to the north of Dohuk in Amadiya and northern hills upon which the latter class of persons [scattered Assyrians other than the tribes mentioned] could be permanently settled."*

A few days earlier on May 19th the Constantinople conference was formed to decide the frontier between Turkey and Iraq and to settle the Mosul problem. The British proposed the possibility of extending the Iraqi frontier beyond the Mosul Vilayet to include the former Assyrian territory in Turkey, lost after world war one. Sir Percy Cox the British representative explained that his government considers the solving the Assyrian future that formerly had lived in the Kurdistan Mountains as an important issue. He stated that:

"His Majesty's Government has decided to endeavor to secure a good treaty frontier, which will at the same time admit of the establishment of the Assyrians in a compact community within the limits of territory in respect of which His Majesty's Government hold a mandate under the authority of the League of Nations, .." (Lamsa George, 1926, 123)

As it turned out this was a negotiation ploy by the British to ask for far more than the Mosul Vilayet so that Turkey would be willing to settle for less. In response, on May 21s, Turkey's representative Fethi Bey replied; *"Turkey is willing to allow the Assyrians,"* (whom he called Nestorians, *"to return to their former territory, provided they did not repeat the errors which they committed with foreign encouragement, at the beginning of the Great War."* (Ibid p.124) Instead of negotiating an agreement with Turkey which would have allowed the Assyrians of the highland to return to their former home, where they could live in peace and enjoy some form of self government, Henry Cox, immediately rejected the idea by claiming that Assyrians will not accept such offer. He did not even bother to consult with the Assyrian leaders to find out what they wanted. As the disagreement continued the Turks and the British agreed to refer the question to the League of Nations.

On September 3, 1925 in the meeting of the league council Turkey insisted that its present border should be moved further south to include the Mosul Vilayat. British representative responded by saying:

"Such partition would involve the very maximum of hardship and injustice to all parties concerned. It would exclude from Iraq the great Arab center of Mosul as well as the bulk of the Assyrian population which wishes to remain in Iraq, and not become part of Turkey." He further added; *"ceding Mosul to Turkey would lead to an immediate panic and flight out of Mosul, into Iraq, of the Assyrian population."*(Progressive Assyrian, 6, 5, 2, 1998, 7)

In the spring of 1925 The British delegation brought along Lady Surma to a decisive meeting to underscore its point that the Mosul Vilayet should be given to Iraq in exchange for the lost Assyrian territory in Turkey. Though Turks insisted that they will welcome the Assyrians to return to their homeland, "and Turkey will pay for their resettlement expenses and grant them full autonomy" the British insisted that Assyrians could not live under Turkey's rule. This meant that Britain was not interested in negotiating any possibility of returning Assyrians to their former home and would rather trade their land in exchange for the annexation of Mosul to Iraq.

After the Constantinople conference Turkey amassed its troops on the border of Iraq, threatening to occupy the province of Mosul. Since the Iraqi army was not ready for confronting the Turks, 2000 Assyrian levies were sent to the north to stop the invasion.

"A League of Nations official admitted that 'both politically and from the military point of view, the Assyrians were largely responsible for the annexation of Mosul to Iraq rather than Turkey." (Dadesho O. Sargon, 1987, 102-03)

The British use of the Assyrian levies to prevent Turkey from invading Iraq and using Assyrians to justify the annexation of Mosul to Iraq inflamed the ire of the Turks against them. In retaliation, in the spring of 1925, Turkey instructed the Kurdish chiefs in Kurdistan to massacre the Chaldean Assyrians who lived in their territory, and those who refused to comply were executed. (Lamsa George, 1926, 130) Consequently "The 62nd regiment of Turkish infantry was dispatched by the Angora Government to drive out the Chaldean Assyrians out of that territory." (Ibid p.130) The British Colonel Amery reported the atrocities committed by Turkey against the Assyrians to the League of Nations but when the Commission asked to enter Turkey to investigate the matter its request was refused. A report by Colonel Amery stated:

"Turkish soldiers under the command of officers occupied the villages and obtained delivery of all arms, imposed sever fines, demanded women, pillaged houses, and subjected the inhabitants to atrocious acts of violence, going as far as to massacre... During the deportations several persons fell ill and were abandoned. Others died of starvation and cold because they were not permitted to carry food and clothing when obliged to leave their homes. Even after the forced exile some of the survivors were still being held in Turkey's labor camps." (Ibid-p. 131)

The Turkish delegation as usual blamed the victims to justify their being massacred. It claimed that the Nestorians had attacked the Turks with the help of the British government. However in this instance the victims were Chaldean Assyrians (Catholic) and not

Nestorians who lived in the mountains as serfs of the Kurdish chiefs. (Ibid p.132) On September 24 the council appointed General Laidoner of Estonia to investigate the incident. After interviewing the refugees he reported:

"In the district of Zakho there are at present some 3,000 deported Christians and every day isolated groups continue to arrive in Iraq. These refugees come from the villages situated in the zone between the Brussels line and the line claimed by the British Government [further north which included Hakkiari]; there are also some who have come from the villages situated north of the latter line..." (Progressive Assyrian, 1988,7)

Before these deportations some members of the council were considering to divide the disputed territory between Turkey and Iraq but Turkey's behavior changed their mind. According to Toynbee; "This incident had decisive effect on Unden, the council's rapporteur, who previously was in favor of a compromised solution, but if the Chaldeans who are Assyrians, but religiously were united with Rome, were persecuted by Turks, it was possible that Assyrians living in northern part of Mosul vilayet would have been subjected to a similar fate if the council had adopted a compromise by granting part of Mosul to Turkey." (Ibid-p. 7) Consequently the leagues decision meant that Assyrians, not only could not return to their previous lands also the matter of their being settled permanently in Iraq was not yet resolved.

In the spring of 1925 The British delegation brought along Lady Surma to a decisive meeting to underscore its demand that the Mosul Vilayet should be given to Iraq in exchange for the lost Assyrian territory in Turkey. Though Turks insisted that they will welcome the Assyrians to return to their homeland, "and Turkey "will pay their resettlement expenses and grant them full autonomy." But the British representative insisted that Assyrians could not live under Turkey's rule. This meant that Britain was not interested in negotiating any possibility of returning Assyrians to their former home, but had brought up this issue so that it could barter their homeland in exchange for annexing the Mosul province to Iraq.

A commission was formed by the League of Nations, to resolve the conflict between Britain and Turkey over what to do with Mosul. Its members included a Swedish diplomat who was known for his Anti-British views; a Hungarian who was fanatically pro-Turkish; a Belgian Colonel of Artillery; and a Russian Jew. The British high commissioner protested the moral reputation of some members of the commission by saying; "This is the sort of privilege we get for having to pay through the nose to support the League of Nations, which, as one might say, bites the hand that feeds it." (The Assyrian Atrocities, The Saturday Review, January 6, 1934 p.7) On July 16th 1925 due to the instigation by the Turks the commission rejected the possibility of allowing the Assyrians to return to their former home for the following reasons.

1- The question of restoring Assyrians to their former homes north of Mosul vilayet was not brought up in the Lausanne Conference and the British only raised it on April 1924 at the Constantinople conference.

2- Assyrians without cause had risen against their lawful government therefore "it was not fair to take from Turkey a territory which indisputably belongs to her, in order to settle a people who deliberately took up arms against its sovereign." (Stafford p. 86)

The two reasons cited as justification to not allow Assyrians to return to their former home were unjustified. The issue the commission had to decide was not whether this matter had been previously brought up or not. Its duty was to decided the future of a people who had been massacred by Turkey and driven out of their homeland. The reason this issue was not brought up previously was because Assyrian representatives were not allowed to participate in the serves and the Lausanne conferences, which was another injustice that was perpetrated upon them by the British.

The commission assertion that Assyrian rose against their lawful government is totally false. The massacre of the Assyrians by Turkey's army and its Kurdish allies began in October 1914, months before the World War One, and culminated into a massive attack against their villages in June of 1915, in the highlands of

Hakkiari, which resulted in their being massacred and driven out of their homeland. Turkey's systematic massacre of its Christian citizens including Assyrians between 1914 and 1918 was well documented.

Concern for the safety and security of the Assyrians was often cited as justification for annexing the Mosul province to Iraq. In arguing the necessity of attaching the Mosul Vilayet to Iraq the British representative on September 3, 1925 stated "if the region is handed over to the Turks: "from the racial point of view and the wishes of the inhabitants, any such partition would involve the very maximum of hardship and injustice to all parities concerned. It would exclude from Iraq the great Arab center of Mosul, as well as the bulk of the Assyrian population which wishes to remain in Iraq."

He further added; *"if Mosul is given to Turkey: "there would be an immediate panic and flight into Iraq of the Assyrian population".* (The Progressive Assyrian, June 1988, 7)

To bolster its negotiation position Britain once again requested that the Iraq frontier should be extended further north to include the former Assyrian homeland in the highlands. The last request was just a bargaining chip, which England knew would be rejected by the Turks but would make it easier for the League to decide in favor of giving Mosul to Iraq.

Consequently on December 16, 1925 the League of Nations passed a resolution declaring the Brussels Line as the permanent border between Iraq and Turkey. This meant that the Assyrian homeland of Hakkiari, would remain part of the Turkish territory, Assyrians would not be allowed to return there, and the Mosul would become integrated into the British controlled Iraq.

As for the Assyrians, the commission recommended that they should accept the promise of the Turkish delegate at Constantinople, which would have allowed them to return to their former home, and would have guaranteed a complete amnesty and local autonomy to live in safety. This was nothing more than a pie in the sky comment. Turkey's promise to allow the Assyrians to return to their former homeland was predicated on the possibility of allowing Mosul to become part of Turkey, but the British had spent years not to let that happen, even if they had to sacrifice all the Assyrians to make sure that Britain controlled its oil resources. After this meeting the League of Nations asked the Permanent Court of International Justice to suggest an advisory opinion. The court decided:

"The so-called Brussels Line was considered the most desirable. It believed that if they had extended the northern frontier to cover territory desired by the British for the Assyrians they would have to enter into a long struggle to dislodge the Turks...If they had extended southward (Turkey's border to include Mosul) they would have jeopardized the lives of thousands of Christians and pro-Iraq Muslims..."

It is important to note that the pledge of the Iraqi government that it would provide land for the settlement of the Assyrians in northern Iraq, with some sort of independence played an important role in shaping the Frontier Commission's decision, as described in the following letter from Sir Henry Dobbs to Gertrude Bell.

"...IN order to reassure them (the Assyrians) as to their future, two successive Iraqi cabinets, those of Jafar Pasha and Yasin Pasha, officially pledged the government of Iraq to provide lands in Iraq for those Assyrians who might be dispossessed of their original homes by the decision of the League of Nations and to devise a system of administration for them which would assure to them the utmost possible freedom from interference. It can hardly be doubted that this liberal attitude on the part of the government of Iraq had its influence on the deliberation of the Frontier commission." (Frederick 2006, 159)

The fact that the British officials were not willing to remind the later governments of Iraq about such promises attest to their duplicity and reveals their collaboration with the Iraqi government in preventing Assyrians from being settled in homogeneous communities, an issue that ultimately resulted in their being massacred.

However, According to Stafford, since the territory occupied by the Assyrians before the war was not assigned to Iraq therefore it was not possible to find land in that country, to settle them in homogeneous communities and granting them a measure of autonomy. (Stafford, 1935, 87-88) It is odd that there was not enough land in Iraq to settle 30,000 Assyrians as an intact community even after the annexation of the Mosul Vilayet to Iraq, which provided it untold oil riches, for a long time to come. The entire population of Iraq at that time was only 3 millions population, yet presently accommodates a population of twenty five million people. Stafford later writes even if the Assyrian homeland was included in Iraq it is doubtful that Iraq would have allowed a semi independent enclave within its border, if Stafford was right, then British officers, the Iraqi government, and the League of Nations, all along lied, to the Assyrians that they would be settled in homogeneous community and with some sort of self-rule, and when they were reminded of it they were mercilessly massacred.

On June 5, 1926, Great Britain, Iraq and Turkey entered into a treaty in Ankara to resolve the status of Mosul. Turkey officially agreed to the Brussels Line as its border with the kingdom of Iraq. In return, Article 14 of the Mosul Agreement stipulated that Iraq shall hand over ten percent of its oil-revenue to the Turkish Republic for a period of twenty-five years.

The 1933 Semail Massacre

When in 1932 Britain decided to terminate its mandate over Iraq, fifteen years before its legal term, Assyrians were in panic because for 15 years they had suffered, mental, physical, and spiritual grief and were disheartened by the British government's refusal to fulfill its promises to help them return to their homeland in Turkey or to have them settled in Iraq as a homogeneous community.

The League of Nations had mandated that Iraq's minorities should be protected, and the British had also promised economic and social equality for minorities such as the Assyrians and the Kurds, but the British government's political maneuvering before the end of mandate made it impossible to ensure such possibility. When in 1929 the British Government signed a new Anglo-Iraqi treaty that described the British rights in Iraq, it did not include provisions to protect Iraq's minority rights. (Rayburn Joel, www.foreignaffairs)

The premature announcement of the British to allow early Iraqi independence prompted the Sunnis to stonewall to secure specific minority rights, and instead made it possible for the various Iraqi factions to prepare for a civil war as soon as the British left. (Ibid) At that crucial moment Assyrians could not have remained silent because otherwise they were about to be scattered among their enemies and there woul have been no one to help protect them. For as long as they could remember their Muslim neighbors, especially the Kurds, who had subjected them to all sorts of atrocities including being massacred and uprouted from their homeland. Without a secure region where they could live in peace, future persecutions would have scattered them in every direction, as it had often happened in the past.

A letter dated July 31, 1933, by Rev. Dr. John B. Panfil, an American who lived in Mosul, corroborates such fears:

"The Assyrians were promised and hoped for a special treatment if they were to remain in Iraq. They joined their little force with the Allies and fought on the side of the British Army in Persia and Iraq. The long and bitter experience of the past has proved to them that they cannot live in villages of Kurds without a special arrangement. They knew that they couldn't expect much assistance from Muslim Government in case of difficulty. They knew that in the last incident of Yagov, the Government actually armed the Kurds against them. They were told that they would have to give up their arms before anybody else. The government appointed five new leaders from different tribes, gave positions and salaries to oppose the patriarch.... The Assyrians could not resign themselves to be persecuted unjustly...."
(Dadisho, 1987, 132)

To find a solution to the problem, patriarch Mar Eishay Shimon traveled to Geneva on September 10, 1932, to warn the High Commissioner that there were reasons to believe that soon after the British withdrawal the massacre of the Assyrians would follow. Since the British government had succeeded in making Mosul part of Iraq and secure a contract to exploit its oil resources the British representative at the meeting did his best to defend the Iraqi government by stating

After examining the petition of the Assyrian community the Permanent Mandates Commission recommended that the Iraqi government should provide "the Assyrians with opportunities for settlement in a homogeneous group that would satisfy their economic needs." Sir Francis Humphreys responded by saying: "Never before there had been such tolerant and civilized Muslim state as Iraq," and he proposed that it should be admitted to the League of Nations as an independent state, and further stated that: "in any case the moral responsibility for any mishap would be upon Greet Britain." Iraq was accepted into the League of Nations on October 3, 1932, without having solved the Assyrian settlement problem. Patriarch remained in Geneva and addressed the sixty-ninth session of the Council's eleventh meeting where he urged its members to fulfill the Council's obligations to the Assyrian nation. Consequently, the Council asked five of its members to study the Assyrian petition, and make a decision accordingly. After deliberation the group of five underscored the need to settle Assyrians in homogeneous community in Iraq, with a local autonomy (Aprim A. Frederick 2006, 151). It also stated that Assyrians through the special survey of the League of Nations approved the joining of the Mosul Vilayet with Iraq because they believed that the British mandate over Iraq would be far longer than twenty-five years. In response to this decree the Iraqi government agreed to hire a foreign expert to help in the settlement of all unsettled Iraqis: "including Assyrians ...under the suitable conditions and so far as it may be possible, in homogeneous units, without prejudicing the rights of the present population."

The legalistic language of the promise left plenty loopholes for government to use as excuse not to implement it. The 'foreign expert' hired by the Iraqi government was the British Major Thompson who undoubtedly with the help of the Iraqi government decided to scatter Assyrians in a wide area throughout northern Iraq, "from Dasht Bazar Gair bordering the Persian territory, through the heart of Kurdish populated region, and on to the north of Amadiya, This area was infested with malaria and other diseases, and the appropriate part of the land could hardly accommodate several hundred families. The Assyrians would have been in the middle of an area of Kurdish unrest and revolts." (Aprim, 2006, 152)

In other words, The Iraqi government was giving Assyrians the choice between being scattered amongst greater Muslim populations or to leave Iraq. To explain why Assyrians insisted on being settled in homogeneous communities Malek Yusuf writes:

It was difficult for a group of ten or twelve Assyrian families to live in a village far away from other Assyrians. Clannishness may have been part it, but security was of greater concern. They did not expect to engage in armed conflict with their neighbors but since their Muslim neighbors had often persecuted them they worried about such possibility. Furthermore, as a small minority living in a Muslim country they had little chance of enjoying what can be considered as fair justice during the periods of social, economic or legal conflicts. They believed they could enjoy greater security, racially, culturally and religiously if they lived as a compact group geographically. (Malik Yusuf, 1935)

Meanwhile, months before Mar Eishay Shimon's appeal to the League of Nations Iraqi politicians and media were promoting extensive propaganda against Assyrians Iraqi nationalists and politicians were publishing articles, in the Iraqi press to justify a future attack against them. There were specific calls for the extermination of the Assyrians simply because they asked to not be scattered among predominantly Muslim population. Shortly after patriarch Eishay Shimon's return to Iraq, he was arrested and deported to Cyprus without any trial. This was instigated by the British major Wilson, the administrative inspector of Mosul who sent a secrete telegram to the Iraqi officials in April 1933, advising them to:

"Ask Mar Shimon to come to Baghdad to discuss matters with the government. Detention to follow, forth with! This should eliminate the danger of seeing Mar Shimon installed in his summer

residence at Sar Amadiya; the consequence of such move will be against the Iraq interest.... Iraq government runs the risk of seeing the Assyrians proposing a scheme on lands near or bordering the Syrian frontier." (Dadesho, O. Sargon, 1987, 129)

This implied that Assyrians were involved in a secret conspiracy against the Iraqi government, which was not true. This served to further cause Iraqi's distrust of the Assyrians' intentions. The exile of Mar Shimon brought the matter of the Assyrian settlement to a final standstill. The British and Iraqi government hostility against the supporters of Mar Shimon convinced them that there was no future for the Assyrians in Iraq, especially when they were told if they don't like the way they are being treated in Iraq they could go and live in another country. Yagov bar Malik Ishmael and four other supporters of Mar Shimon decided to explore the possibility of moving their families to Syria. In his book titled; "Atturaye o Tray Plashi Twilaye," (Assyrians and the Two World Wars) Yagov provides detailed information about the incident that was used as excuse by the Iraqi army, in August of 1933 to massacre unarmed Assyrian men women and children.

On July 14, 1933, at night, Yagov together with four other ex-Levies, namely: Benjamin Marogil, Malik Loko, Makko, and Mooshi began their travel to Syria. Near the village of Peshkhabor they found the French border guards and asked their captain about the possibility of settling their families in Syria. Captain Larist contacted the French Ambassador in Beirut for such permission. While they were waiting for an answer, on July 17th, Makko wrote a letter to Gashisha Ghiwargis a priest friend of his in Iraq and explained the reason for their travel to Syria. He had explained that they are waiting for the permission to stay in Syria and as soon as they get it they would also work to get authorization for Assyrians who wish to leave Iraq and settle in Syria to do so. On July 19th Malik Yagov and his friends who were waiting for a response from the French Ambassador in Beirut learned that 900-armed Assyrians who had arrived in Syria had been detained by the French troops. In answer to the question, why they did not wait for Yagov and his friends to obtain permission for them to arrive, the priest explained that as soon as the Iraqi government had learned about the travel of Yagov and his friends to Syria the Iraqi press began a campaign of hatred toward the Assyrians, to incite the entire country against them. The Iraqi government also began to find excuses to punish the supporters of Mar Shimon.

To explain the reason for their travel to Syria Yagov and his friends sent a letter to the Internal Minister of Baghdad On July 25th stating that they left because in a meeting with the government officials in Mosul they were told that anyone who wishes to leave Iraq is free to do so. The letter also assured the minister that they had no intention to engage in conflict with the Iraqi army unless they were forced to do so. Malik Yagov, his friends and the leaders of the newly arrived group, signed the letter.

On the same day the French, captain Larist informed them that the request of Yagov and his friends to settle in Syria had been approved, but before they were allowed to stay in Syria each faction had to separately relinquish its weapons. However, soon there was meeting between Captain Larist and the governor of Dohuk who informed him that the Iraqi government had promised that it had no ill will against the Assyrians who had traveled to Syria and they are free to return to their villages. Though Yagov explained that this was a trap, Captain Larist had no authority to allow them to stay, he explained that France would not jeopardize its relation with Britain for their sake. This meant that the even the British government was involved in forcing them to return to Iraq. The Iraqi officials also sent a letter to the French government demanding the disarming the Assyrians and their return to Iraq. The letter stated that Assyrians would be allowed to enter Iraq peaceably. Meanwhile the entire Iraqi army was amassed along the Syrian border on the Iraqi side.

British officials had been well aware of how often Assyrians were massacred in Turkey and Iran by their Muslim neighbors, for the slightest of excuses. They should have known well that by forcing the French government to drive the Assyrians who had gone to Syria back into Iraq they were not only causing their death, but also the death of thousands of other Assyrians who would be massacred if there was a battle between the Iraqi army and the returning Assyrians, but they did not seem to have cared.

The departure of the 900 Assyrians to Syria gave Iraq an opportunity to solve its Assyrian problem without bloodshed, but Iraqi officials and the British were determined to teach Assyrians a lesson for having dared to remind them of the promises that were made to them in return for safe guarding Iraq's integrity and serving the British interest. But the British and the Iraqi government wanted the Assyrians who had gone to Syria to return so that Iraqi army would have an opportunity to show its military might. But as Joel Rayborn put it:

Iraqi army of the 1930's, was the most dangerous kind: It was easily the most powerful institution in the country; too strong to be checked by other groups and free from any real constitutional constraints, it also was too weak to actually defend the country from outsiders. (Rayburn Joel, www.foreignaffairs) On August 5th 1933 at 3 p.m. the Assyrian group in Syria arrived at the bank of the Tigris River. Yagov observed an Iraqi plane dropping leaflets to inform the Iraqi Army of their arrival. Three Assyrian volunteers were sent to the other side of the river to test the intentions of the Iraqi army. As soon as they stepped on the Iraqi side an Iraqi soldier knelt down and shot at them. This action began a battle that lasted until 3 A.M. when the Iraqi army was defeated and forced to withdraw. (Bar Malik Ismael, 1964, 230) The governmental agencies broadcasted the news of the battle throughout the country. Assyrian fighters were falsely accused of having mutilated the dead Iraqi soldiers to incite public hatred against them and Assyrians in general.

After the retreat of the Iraqi army from the border, its soldiers together with Arab Shammar tribes, Kurdish tribes, and other local fanatics who were armed ahead of time committed wholesale massacre of the defenseless Assyrians who were promised by the local government that they would be protected by the Iraqi army if they handed over their weapons, and they complied. Instead men women and children were massacred with rifle, revolver and machine gun. Groups of Assyrians were tied up and shot down by the regular and irregular troupes of the Iraqi army. Priests were killed and their bodies mutilated. Women were violated and killed. Priests and Assyrian young men who refused to convert to Islam were killed instantly. The rapacious armed and instigated by the Arab officials carried away the cattle and belongings of the Assyrians with impunity. Assyrian children while hanging on to their parents were driven to the butcheries and shot to death. Pregnant women had their wombs cut and their babies destroyed. The British flying officers could do no more than take photographs from the air, while those in the service of the Iraqi government were prevented from visiting the massacre zones. Even the English officer Stafford in his Assyrian Tragedy attests to this fact. He writes:

"A cold-blooded and methodical massacre of all the men in the village then followed, a massacre, which for the black treachery in which it was carried out was as foul a crime as any in the bloodstained annals of the Middle East. The Assyrians had no fight left in them, partly because of the state of mind to which the events of the past week had reduced them, largely because they were disarmed...Machine gunners set up their guns outside the windows of the houses in which Assyrians had taken refuge, and having trained them on the terror-stricken wretches in the crowded rooms, fired among them until not a man was left standing in the shambles. In some other instances, the blood lust of the troops took a slightly more active form, and men were dragged out and shot or bludgeoned to death and their body thrown on a pile of dead. (Stafford 1935, 174-178) Sixty-five out of ninety five Assyrian villages were either destroyed or burnt to the ground."

To give the ordinary citizens a chance to celebrate the bloodshed, the population treated murderers of unarmed Assyrians as heroes; Triumpal arches in the city of Mosul were set up. "Decorated with melons stained with blood and daggers stuck into them. This delicate representation of the head of slain Assyrians was in keeping with the prevailing sentiment." (Aprim 2006,176) This was also an indication how effective the Iraqi propaganda had been in portraying the Assyrians as the enememies of Iraq. To this day the Iraqi government has denied any responsibility for the Semail massacre, instead, it blames it on an Assyrian revolt, which is not true.

The British treatment of the Assyrians has been condemned not only by Assyrians as betrayal, but also by the fair-minded British writers. In an article published in the "Near East And India", Wigram wrote: "When return of the Assyrians to their former home seemed impossible we promised them "either an enclave, or arrangements for safe and decent existence" (Curzon, House of Lords, 17/12/19) and the league of Nations promised them "all their old rights, including autonomy and the right to pay their tribute through their Patriarch," This was the clause included in the awarding the Mosul province to Iraq." (Turko-Irak frontier, C. 400. M. 147. 1925. V.II p.90)

Now these promises have not been kept, and we have said in exchanged that Assyrians must be settled somehow, and we have accepted service from them on that understanding. Finally, we left the land before our time, with promise still unfulfilled, and we blame the Assyrians for ingratitude."

He further writes that Mar *"Shimon is blamed for this but he asked for no more than " him to use his temporal power to keep "the Assyrian Levy loyal to their duty when they shared the general duty of their people."* (Wigram, W. A., 1933,.969)

The Saddam's Rule

After Iraq's defeat in Kuwait, Shias in Southern Iraq and Kurds in the north launch a popular uprising against the Baghdad regime. Within two weeks, 15 of Iraq's 18 provinces weree free of government control. But when it became clear that the U.S. will not support the rebellion, Saddam's forces crushed the revolt throughout. Iraq Consequently Hundreds of thousands of Kurds and Assyrians were driven into the mountains between Iraq and Turkey. In response to humanitarian plees, U.S. troops move into Northern Iraq in response U.S. established the "Operation Provide Comfort". A No-fly zones in Northern Iraq.

An article in The newsweek issue of June, 17, 1991 p. 33, accurately described the plight of the Assyrians in northern Iraq as followa:

"Like the Kurds they traditionally live in mountainside villages, most of stone houses with flat earthen roofs. And as with Kurdish villages, most of their settlements has been destroyed by the Iraqis. Unlike the Kurds, they speak Syriac an ancient tongue descended from the Aramaic....They are Chaldean Catholics and Nestorians, members of some of Christianity's oldest sects, marooned in the hostile land."

"In northern Iraq- the ancestral homeland they share with the Kurds, Saddam's wrath fell on the Christians as much as their Muslim neighbors, and they fled together to the borders of Turkey and Iraq. "Everyone talked about the Kurdish refugees", said a Nestorian priest who returned recently from a Turkish refugee camp, but many of us were Christians." Relief workers complained that in the undisciplined melees at the camps in the first week the Christians often had a harder time than the Kurds. Less numerous and without Kurds powerful tribal organization, they often lost in the scramble for relief supplies."

"But when Saddam set out to decimate the Kurds, the Christians suffered alongside them. When an Assyrian civil engineer in Duhuk was drafted to begin destroying villages in [so-called] Kurdistan, his first assignment was a place called Babok- his own home village. "They did' t care if we were Christians or Kurds," he said. "They wanted to destroy all of us."

The article goes on to say that Chaldeans are Eastern rite Catholics who recognize the Pope in Rome as their patriarch. The Nestorians are followers of sect begun with st. Nestor, thrown out of the Catholic Church. "Both sects however consider themselves ethnic Assyrians."

"Some of the Christianity's most ancient monuments were demolished. In the village of Deri, a 12th-century monastery was reduced to rubble in 1988 by Iraqi Army sappers. Monks from the monastery have since moved to a small cave high in the mountains, where they live as hermits still." A forth century Catholic Church of St, Mary in Amadiay along with a Christian village nearby were destroyed.

The Newsweek article ends by saying; "They [Christian Assyrians] are people the world has by and large forgotten, and they know it. Now thy hope that a more democratic Iraq might one day grant them a treasured wish. "With freedom, we might be able to publish something more than just prayer books in our own language" said father Khoshaba, whose name means Sunday. Even Father Sunday's modest goal, however, seems far away in Saddam's Iraq."

Illegal confiscation of Assyrian lands in northern Iraq under the Kurdish Regional Government continues to be one of the most challenging issues confronting the Assyrians presently living in that region. Many Assyrians, who fled the country due to the ongoing terror against Christians of Iraq, have lost their lands to illegal Kurdish settlers. A flagrant example being the resolution promulgated by the Kurdish Parliament in the city of Arbil in October of 2002 entitled "General Conditions for the Ownership of Illegally Obtained Lands" which deals with formal transfers of illegally appropriated Assyrian lands to Kurdish squatters who have inhabited Assyrian towns prior to and until January 1st 2000. The Kurdish Regional Government has yet to implement appropriate measures in guaranteeing Assyrian refugees and their right to return to their ancestral homelands.

2003 United States' Invasion of Iraq

In retaliation for the U.S. invasion of Iraq, Starting in 2003, Assyrians suffered various forms of persecutions in that country. The Islamic fanatics conveniently accused them of sympathizing with the Crusaders; they were subjected to various forms of violence; including kidnapping, beheading, rape, and demand to convert to Islam, otherwise leave the country or be killed. Seventy some of their churches were bombed, Christian businesses were torched and their owners were murdered. Members of the families were kidnapped for ransom, they were tortured and killed even when ransom was paid. Consequently, up to a million Assyrians had no choice but to abandon all they had and to flee their homeland to other parts of the Middle East or to immigrate to the West. Such atrocities continued even after the departure of the United States' troop.

A horrific act of terrorism against the Assyrians took place on October 31, 2010, when suicide bombers from the Islamic State of Iraq, massacred 58 parishioners in a church during a bloody siege in Baghdad. The youngest of the victims was a three years old boy who went around and beged the terrorists to stop the killings. This was widely publicized but was one of countless assaults on their schools, churches and neighborhoods. The central government was either incapable of protecting them or was unwilling to do so. The 1.4 million Assyrian population of Iraq, before 2003 now numbers less than 400,000. A hundred thousand Assyrians are internally displaced. Most of them fled to the relative safety of the autonomies Kurdish region. Even there they suffer from chronic unemployment because they do not speak the Kurdish language, and jobs are scarce, especially since they are being discriminated against.

Iraq's society has been in political, societal and religious turmoil since the end of Baathist regime. While battles for the religious future of Iraq have continued between Shiites and Sunni, at the same time, their fanatics have decimated the Assyrian community.

Assyrians Today

The World War One massacre of the Assyrians by the Ottoman Turks in southeast Turkey and Persia followed by the Semail massacre in Iraq not only decimated three-forth of the Assyrian population, also uprooted the survivors from their historical homelands and scattered them to the four corners of the world. Their social, religious and educational institutions were destroyed, and were rendered a people without a country and impoverished, The loss of their homelands where they had lived in predominantly since before Christianity and their being scattered far from each other, has undermined their linguistic, religious, historical, and communal elements that had united them and had helped them survive for the last 2,600 years. Despite the fact that the homeland of the Assyrians has been governed and dominated by Muslims who have historically subjected them to various forms of persecutions they have managed to preserve their religion, language and their Assyrian identity which is a testimony to their endurance and perseverance, however their scattering in many countries of the world, especially in the West and the fact that in the future they no longer be able to live in homogeneous communities where they can preserve their language and way of life threaten their continued existence. It has been a misfortune of the Christian Assyrians that their homelands has been located on the crossroads of foreign invasions and they have been surrounded on all sides by neighbors that have been hostile to their Christian religion. Furthermore, they have practiced the pacifist form of Christianity that encourages turning the other cheek, which has made them easy target for the countless persecutions and massacres they have suffered. Their Muslim rulers have historically forbidden them from carrying weapons, even for self-defense. Their three major Christian denominations, i.e., Church of the East, the Syrian Orthodox Church, and the Chaldean Church not only, have been hostile towards each other, they have also discouraged the rise of secular leadership to help their people during the periods of strife and uncertainty. The clergies of the Chaldean have gone as far as claiming the name of their Church as the ethnic identity of its members and the Syrian Orthodox Church clergies since 1952 have identified their members as Arameans to promote the identity of their denomination, and to set apart their members from the followers of the two other churches, they justify such decision by quoting the opinions of the misguided western writers who have questioned the Assyrian identity of the Christian Assyrians. However, their assumed identities have caused further confusion about who they are. Therefore when Western journalists report about the persecution of their followers they identify them as Christians rather than their ethnicity.

Despite the fact that during the last few years hundreds of thousands of their population has been driven out of its historic homeland there has been no meeting between the leaders of the three denominations to come to an agreement about how best to help their people, and to provide intelligent leadership for their members. Normal Communication between the three communities is essential to ensure their future survival.

The reluctance of the clergies of the three denominations to unite with each other to bring their people together contradicts the teachings of Christ who implored his Apostles to be known by their love for one another, and others. As the saying goes "We are only as strong as we are united, as weak

as we are divided." J.K. Rowling, *Harry Potter and the Goblet of Fire*

The first step to achieve unity among the three major Assyrian communities, i.e. members of the Church of the East, Chaldean Church, and the Syrian Orthodox Church is to unite under the name Assyrian, which has been historically proven to be the identity of the Christians of Mesopotamia based on the evidences presented in this book. We have plenty to learn from the Armenians and the Kurds both of whom presently have their own internationally recognized homeland because they did not allow religious or tribal factionalism to tear them apart, and to live at the mercy of their enemies.

During the United States' invasion of Iraq Kurdish troops occupied northern Iraq and declared the region as Kurdistan (the land of the Kurds). Since then they have strived to Kurdify the Assyrian history and geography by expanding their territory into the Assyrian villages in the Plain of Nineveh. Even that has not brought together the clergies of the three denominations. In desperation some Assyrians have asked the Iraqi central government to declare the Plain of Nineveh an Assyrian Administrative Region; where with the government's help they can take care of their own security, and create a more prosperous life for its residence, but so far, Iraqi government has shown no interest in such idea.

Bibliography

Abdalla, Michael. "Assyrian Loyalty and Devotion to Medical profession: Three Centuries of Bakht-Isho's Family Service to Mankind." JAAS, XVI, NO.2, 2002.

Al-Gorani, Ali Sidi. "From Amman to Amediya."

Aprim A. Frederick. "Assyrians From Bedrkhan to Saddam Hussein," 2006

Aprim A. Frederick. "Baghdeda (Modern Qara Qosh or a Thriving Assyrian Village." @Zindamagazine.com

Armajani Yahya. "Middle East: Past and Present.", New Jersey : Prentice-Hall: 1970.

Arsanos Benjamin. "Poorgana'd Iran, Kha Egbal Koomta, (Syriac) Deliverance of Iran, from a Black Misfortune." Tehran, Iran 1953.

Associated Press Writer. "Artifacts Show Rivals Athens and Sparta." Yahoo News, December 5, 2006.

Atwater Donald. "The Christian Churches of the East." Volume I, Churches in Communion with Rome, Milwaukee: The Bruce Publishing Co., 1945.

(Austin H.H. "The Baqubah Refugee Camp, An Account of Work on behalf of the Persecuted Assyrians" Faith Press, 1920.

Aydin, Edip. "The History of the Syriac Orthodox Church of Antioch in North America: Challenges and Opportunities." Saint Vladimir's Orthodox Crestwood, New York May 8, 2000.

Bacon Edward. "Digging for History, Archaeological Discoveries Throughout the World, 1945to 1959." New York 1960.

Badger Percy George. "Christians of Assyria." 1869.

Barkho L. Y. "The Assyrians In No Way Had Been Obliterated from the Surface of the Earth." Associated Press report reprinted in Nineveh Magazine, Vol. 7 No. 3& 4, 1984.

Bar-yakoub, Afram www.aina.org/ata/20100111165243.htm 2012.

Benjamin Yoab. "A Comparative Study of 'Abdisho's Paradise of Eden and the Makamat of al-Hariri." Journal of the Assyrian Academic Society, Vol. VIII, NO.1.

Beth Mar Shimon Surma. "Assyrian Church Customs and the Murder of Mar Shimon," (Syriac), Mar Shimon Memorial Fund, 1983.

Bertram Thomas. "The Arabs." New York: Doubleday, Doran and Co., 1937.

Blockley R.C. "The History of Menander the Guardsman Liverpool, Francis Cairns, Ltd., 1985.

Bournoutian George. "Armenians and Russia (1626-1796): A Documentary Record." Coasta Mesa, California: Mazda Publishers. Inc.,1998.

Boyle J. A. edit: "Cambridge History of Iran." 1968.

Brackman Arnold C. "The Luck of Nineveh: 'Archaeology's Great Adventure. "McGraw-Hill Book Company, 1978.

Brock Sebastian. "Syriac Dialog, An Example of the Past." JAAAS, Vol. 18, no. 1, 2004.

Brock, Sabastian Aprim the Syrian. "Hymns On Paradise." St Vladimir's

Seminary Press, 1990.

Bruce F. F., editor. "The New Testament Documents: Are They Reliable?" The Inter Varsity Fellowship, sixth edition, 1981.

Bryce Tervor, "The Routledge Handbook of people and places of ancient Western Asia, 2009, 205.

Budge, E. A. trans., 1932. "The Chronography of Gregory Abul-Faraj" 1225–1286. Vol. 1. Reprint, Amsterdam: Philo Press, 1976.

Burgess Henry. "Ephraem Syrus, Repentance of Nineveh." trans. Robert B. Blackader, Samson Low Son and Company, 1853.

Burn Robert Andrew. "Persia and the Greeks, the Defense of the West 546-478 BC," Minerva Press, 1962.

Bury, J. B. "A History of the Roman Empire, From Arcadius to Irene (395 A.D. to 800 AD).," New York: Macmillan And Co., 1889 pp. 249-252.

Carcton W. "The Acts of Sharbil: Ancient Syriac Documents Relative to the Earliest Establishment of Christianity in Edessa, and the Neighboring Countries." London, 1864.

Carter, Harry, trans. "History of Herodotus." The Heritage Press, New York, 1958 Vol. I.

Chabot, J.B. "Chronique de Michael le Syrien." Culture et Civilization, Tome Premier, Paris, 1899.

Dadesho O. Sargon. "The Assyrian National Question at the United Nations," 1987.

Dio Cassinus. Earnest Cary trans."Dio's Roman History." Book LXVIII, William Heinemann London 1955 p. 411.

Collins, Robert. "The Medes and Persians, Conquerors and Diplomats." McGraw-Hills Book Company, 1972.

Conway John, translation of Herman Bengston editor. "The Greeks and the Persians." Del Publishing Co., 1963 (Cowley A., ed., trans. The Aramaic Papyri of the 5th Century B.C., Oxford 1923.

Cook, Crone Patricia, Mikhail. "Hagarism, the Making of the Islamic World." Cambridge University Press 1977 paper back edition 1980.

Dalley Stephanie. "Nineveh After 612 BC." Alt-Orientanlishce Forshchungen #20, 1993.

Dalley, "The Legacy of Mesopotamia." Oxford University Press, 1998.

de Courtois Sebastien, translated by Vincent Aurora. "The Forgotten Genocide." Gorgias Press, 2004.

De Kelaita Robert W. "On the Road to Nineveh, a Brief History of Assyrian Nationalism 1892-1919." JAAS, Vol. VIII No. 1, 1994.

Dolabani, Yuhanon, Som_Nynawai, Al-Hikma, 4, 1, Jerusalem: 1930.

Drijvers, H. J. W. "Bardaisan of Edessa." Studia Semetica Neerlandica, 6; Assen: Van Gorcum, 1967.

Drijvers, H. J. W. "Cults and Beliefs at Edessa." Leiden, E. J. Brill 1980.

Dual R. Ishoyahb Patriarche, Liber Epistularum, Louvain: CSCO, 1962)

Dunlop D. M. "Arab Civilization to AD 1500." D.M. Dunlop, New York 1971 p.220

Edwards Paul, edit. "The Encyclopedia of Philosophy." Macmillan Publishing Co., Inc. & The Free Press, 1972 vol. III.

Elgood Cyril. "A Medical History of Persia and the Eastern Caliphate" APA-Philo Press Amsterdam, 1979.

Elias, Joel, J.. "The Genetics of Modern Assyrians and Their Relationship to Other People," www.atour.com/health/docs/20000720a.html

Eyre & Spottiswoode. "A Chronicle of the Carmelites in Persia." London 1939 Vol. 1.

Fagan Brian M. "Return to Babylon." Little, Brown & Co., Canada, 1971.

Fiey, J. M. "Assyriens" ou "Araméens," L'Orient Syrien 10 (1965).

Fiey. "Assyrians or Arameans?" The Syrian East, Volume X 1965.

Fiey, J.M. "Assyrie Chretienne Impimerie Catholique." Beyrouth, 1959.

Frank Irene M, and Brownstone David. "The Silk Road: A History." Facts On File Publication New York, 1986.

Gaunt David. "Massacres, Resistance, and Protectors: Muslim-Christian Relations in Eastern Anatolia During World War I." Gorgias Press. 2006, 62).

Ghiwargis Odisho Malko, trans. Yuel A Baba. "We are Assyrians." JAAS, Vol. XVI, No. 1, 2002 p.84.)

Ghiwargis Odisho Malco. "We Are None Other Than Assyrians." (Syriac) , Journal of Assyrian Academic Studies, Vol. XVI NO. 1, 2000.

Gibbon. "Decline and Fall of the Roman Empire." chpt. 47, note.

Guest Edwin. "Origions Celticae (a Fragment) and Other Contributions to the History of Britain," kennikat Press 1971.

Heinrichs. "The Modern Assyrians – Name and Nation." in Semetica: Serta philologica Constantino Tsereteli dicata (Silvio Zamorani), p. 103) cited in 83.

Herodotus, trans. George Rawlinson, "The Persian Wars," 1942.

Hitti, Philip. "History of the Arabs." Princeton University, 10th edition, Mac Millen St. Marin's Press 1970.

Honggeng, GUO. "The Assyrian Intelligence Activities During the Assyrian Empire." JAAS, Vol. 18 No. 2, 2004.

Horace Leonard trans. "The Geography of Strabo." New York, Putnam's Sons, Vol. VII 1923.

Horatio Southgate. "Narrative of a Visit to the Syrian [Jacobites] Church." 1844.

Hourani Albert. "A History of the Arab Peoples." the Belknap Press of

Harvard University press, Cambridge Mass. 1992.

Ibn Wahshaya. "The Christian Remember," A Quarterly Review. Vol. XLI. Jan-June, 1861, 262.

Inati Shams C. Inati edit. "Iraq in History, People and Politics." Humanity Books, 2003.

www.upi.com/Science_News/2009/08/12/Iron-Age-cuneiform-tablets-found/UPI-66011250080173/ Aug. 12, 2009.

Ishaya, Arian. "Intellectual Domination and the Assyrians." Nineveh Magazine, Vol. 6 No. 4 (Fourth Quarter 1983), Berkeley, California.

Jammo Sarhad. "The Two Branches of Eastern Church." Bayn-Al-Nahrayn 95/96, Baghdad 1996.

Javiddon Mohesen trans: of Ceril Lloyd Elgood, Persian translation. "History of Medicine in Iran." Sherikat Egbal, 1352 Tehran Iran.

Jenkins Philip "The Lost History of Christianity, the Thousand Year Golden Age of the Church in the Middle East, Africa, and Asia--and How it Died." Harper One, 2008.

Joan Oates. "Babylon." Thames and Hudson, 1979.

Joel. J. Elias. http://www.atour.com/health/docs/20000720a.html 2012.

Jones H.L. Jones Translation of "Geography of Strabo."New York 1916.

Joseph, John. "Assyria and Syria: Synonyms?" JAAS, 11, (2).

Joseph John. "Nestorians and their Muslim Neighbors." Princeton University Press 1961.

Justinus Marcus. "Epitome of the Philippic History of Pompeius ,"Trogus Tran. John Selby Watson. (London: Henry G. Bohn, 1853].

Koodapuzha Xavier. "Faith and Communion in the Indian Church of Saint Thomas Christians." Oriental Institute of Religious, Studies, Kerala, India, 1982.

Kubie Nora Benjamin. "Road To Nineveh: The Adventures and Excavations of Sir Austen Henry Lanyard." 1964.

Kulia Shmoeil. "safar d' Gasha Sleevo all Shmaya." (Syriac) Tehran, Iran, Young Assyrians' Literary Association, 1962.

Lamsa George, and Emhardt William, The Oldest Christian People 1926.

Layard, Austin, Henry. "Popular Account of Discoveries at Nineveh." Harper & Brothers Publication, New York 1852.

Layard Austin, Nineveh and Its Remains." New York, 1853, Vol. II.

Layard Henry Austen edit. H.W. F. Saggs, "Nineveh and Its Ramians." Frederick A. Praeger, 1969.

Lecick Gwendolyn. "Mesopotamia: the Invention of the City." Penguin Books, 2001.

Macqueen James G, "Babylon." London 1964.

Malech G. D. "The Syrian Nation and the Old Evangelical-Apostolic Church of the East." 1910.

Malek Yusuf. "The British Betrayal of the Assyrians." Lebanon 1936.

Meisami Julie Scott, and Paul Starkey, "Encyclopedia of Arabic Literature." vol. II Toutledge 1998.

Marcellinus Ammianus. "The History of Ammianus Marcellinus." 1939.

Mar-Emmanuel E.J., "Aturaya: Kaldaya gav siami d avahati d eidta d Madenkha: (Syriac) The Assyrian: Chaldean Expressions in the Fathers' Writing of the Church of the East." The Diocese of Canada, The Assyrian Church of the East, 2003.

Mar Saka, Ishaq. "The Syrians: Faith and Civilization." Aleppo archdiocese publications, Syria, 1983.

McCullough W. Stewart. "A Short History of Syriac Christianity: The Rise Of Islam." Scholars Press, Chicago1982.

McGinnis John, and Matney Timothy. "Archaeology at the Frontiers: Excavating a Provincial Capital of the Assyrian Empire." JAAAS, Vol. 23 No. 1, 2009.

Macintosh
http://www.quillandquire.com/google/article.cfm?article_id=1188 2

De dea Syria, 1, etc.; cf. Millar. "The Roman Near East." pp. 454-55

Moffett, Samuel, Hugh. "A History of Christianity in Asia." Harper San Francisco, 1992, Vol. I.

Morgenthau, Henry I. The Murder of a Nation." 1918 Chapter XXIV.

Naby Eden. "The Assyrians of Iran: Reunification of A "Millat." 1906-1914", Int, J. Middle East Stud. 8 1977.

Nafissi Saeid. "Masiheyat Dar Iran." (Christianity in Iran) Persian, Tehran 1964.

Nanji, Azim A. editor. "Muslim Almanac." Gale Research Inc. 1996.

http://news.blogs.cnn.com/2011/06/10/now-we-know-how-they-babbled-in-babylon/

Nettleton Fisher Sydney. "The Middle East History." Alfred. A. Knopf, New York 1969.

Oates, David. "Studies in the History of Northern Iraq." London 1968.

Oates, Joan. "Babylon." Thames and Hudson, 1979.

Ohannes and Sossie, Hannessian. "Shirak's, English–Armenian

 Dictionary." 1999.

Olsmtead, A.T. "History of Assyria." The University of Chicago Press 1968 third edition.

Olmstead, A.T, "History of the Persian Empire. "University of Chicago Press, 1970

Parpola Simo. "National and Ethnic Identity in the Neo-Assyrian Empire, and Assyrian Identity in Post-Empire Times." JAAS. Vol. 18, No. 2, 2004.

Parpola Simo. Helsinki, Assyrian Identity In the Ancient Times and Today, www.nineveh.com/parpola_eng.pdf

Parpola Simo. Assyrians after Assyria, Journal of Assyrian Academic Society, 12,1, 16.

Parpola http://www.forumbiodiversity.com/showthread.php/31567-quot-Sons-of-God-The-Ideology-of-Assyrian-Kingship-quot

Patton, Douglas, Badr alDin Lu'Lu. Atabeg of Mosul. 1211-1259, Seattle; University of Washington Press1991.

Parry, O.H. " Six Months in a Syrian Monastery, 1895.

Pierre Briant (ed.), Dans les pas des Dix-Mille: Peuples et, pays du Proche-Orient vus par un Grec Actes de la Table Ronde internationale, organisée à l'initiative du GRACO, Toulouse, 3-4 février 1995. Toulouse: Presses universitares du Mirail, 1995.

Pinker, Aron. "Nahum, the Prophet and his Message," Jewish Bible Quarterly, Vol. 33, No. 2, 2005.

Potts T. editor, "Archaeology of the Near East," Blackwell publishing Ltd. Vol. I, 2012. P. 1015.

Prichard James B. editor. "The Ancient Near East, An Anthology of Texts and Pictures", Princeton university press 1950.

Progressive Assyrian, "Assyrian case for Autonomy", 6, 5, 2, 1998.

Qais Sago, translation of Fadel Pola. "El Qosh -From Senncherib to Liberation", Assyrian Star, Fall 2003 Vol. LV, No. 3.

Rabban. "Chaldean Rite." Catholic Encyclopedia, 1967.

Rassam Hormuzd, "Asshur and the Land of Nimrod", Cincinnati: Curtis & Jennings, New york 1897.

Rawlinson George, Herodotus, "The History of the Persian Wars." 1942.

Rassam, Suha. "Christianity in Iraq." Gracewing, 2006.

Radner Karen, State Archives of Assyria, Volume XV (2006).

Richard Diebold Center for Indo-European Language and Culture (www.utexas.edu/cola/centers/lrc/eieol/armol-4-R.html).

Roberts Alexander. "Ancient Syriac Documents: The Writings of the Fathers, Down to AD, 325." Edinburgh, 1869.

Rollinger, Robert. "The Terms 'Assyria' and 'Syria' Again." in JNES 65 no. 4, 2006.

Rosenfield, John M. "The Dynastic Arts of the Kushans. University of California Press, 1967.

Roux Georges."Ancient Iraq." George Allen & Unwin LTD, 1992.

Runciman Steven. "A History of the Crusades." Vol. I Cambridge University Press, 1996.

Sabro a publication of Syrian Orthodox Church of America, Nov-Dec. 2000.

Saggs, H.W.F. "The Might that Was Assyria." London, Sidgwick & Jackson 1989.

Segal J.B. "Edessa The Blessed City." Oxford at the Clarendon Press, 1970.

Segal J.B. "The Planet Cult of Ancient Harran, in E. Bacon (ed) Vanished Civilizations." 1963.

Seibt W, "The Creation of the Caucasian Alphabets." Prof Werner Seibt, Tbilisi. September 8th, 2011.

Sharaf Khan Al Bidlisi, "Sharafnameh." in Persian, Cairo, 1596.

Sharaf Khan Al Bidlisi, trans. Jamil Rozbeyati, Al-Hajah Publishing house, Baghdad, 1953.

Smith George. "Chaldean Account of Genesis." Wizards Book Shelf,

Minneapolis 1977.

Soane, Bannster. "To Mesopotamia and Kurdistan in Disguise: With Historical Notices of the Kurdish Tribes." 1912.

Soylemez MM. "The Jundishapur School: Its History, Structure, and Functions." Am J Islamic Social Sci. 2005.

Southgate Horatio. "Narrative of a Visit to the Syrian [Jacobites] Church." 1844.

Stafford R. S. "The Tragedy of the Assyrians." G. Allen & Unwin 1935.

Starr Chester G. "Early man: Prehistory and the Civilizations of the Ancient Near East." New York: Oxford University Press.

Stoneman Richard. "A Traveler's History of Turkey." 1998.

Sukumar Sen, "Old Persian Inscriptions of the Achaemenian Emperors." University of Calcutta 1941.

Tacitius, Cornelius. "The Annals and The Histories." Edit. Ronert Maynard Hutchis, Encyclopedia Britannica, 1952.

Tallqvist K. "Assyrian Personal Names." (Helsinki, 1914).

The Progressive Assyrian, Case for Assyrian Autonomy, June 1988, vol. 5 no.7.

"The Travels of Marco Polo", The Orion Press / New York, 1958.

Thomas of Maraga. "The Book of Governors." Budge, E.A. Wallis Ed. London, 1893.

Time-Life Books. "Time Frame AD 200-600, Empires Besieged." Time-Life Books Inc. 1988.

Toynbee, Arnold J. "A Study of History" 1954, vol. vii, p. 654 n. 1, Also see George Rawlinson, "The History of Herodotus", ed. Manuel Komroff (New York, 1956.

Tsereteli Konstantin. "Assyrians in the Correspondence of Irakli II, King of Georgia." Journal of The Assyrian Academic Society, Vol. VIII, No.2, 1944.

Vatican archives, Rome 1902, pp. 69-100; 604-610. XII. (Archiv. Vat. Secr Archiv. de Castello, Armad. VII, caps.

Vine, Aubrey R. "The Nestorian Church." reprint London Independent Press, LTD 1937.

Walker t. Joel. "The Legend of Mar Qardagh." University of California Press, 1968.

Warda, William. "Assyrian Heritage of the Syrian Orthodox Church."

http://christiansofiraq.com/joseph/reply2.html

Warner Rex trans., Anabasis. "The Persian Expedition." Penguin Books 1972.

Wellard, James. "Babylon." Schocken Books, New York 1974.

Whipple Allen O. "The Role of the Nestorians and Muslims in the History of Medicine." 1967.

Wiesehofer Josepef. "Ancient Persia From 550 BC to 650 AD." I.B. Tauris, 1969.

Wigram W.A. "The Assyrians and Their Neighbors." G.Bell & Sons, London 1929.

Xavier Koodapuzha. "Faith and Communion in the Indian Church of Saint Thomas Christians, Oriental Institute of Religious Studies." Kerala, India 1982.

Yana, George (Bebla). "Ancient and Modern Assyrians." Xlibris Corp, 2008.

Yana George V. (Bebla). "Myth vs. Reality." JA A Studies, Vol. XIV, No. 1, 2000 p. 80.

Yohannan Abraham. " Death of a Nation." G.P. Putnam's Sons 1916.

Young, William G. "Patriarch, Shah and Caliph." Christian Study Center, Rawalpindi, Pakistan, 1974.

Yousif, Ashur, Nineveh Magazine, Volume 15, No. 4, 1992.

Abgar O' Kama.. viii, 168
Abu-al-Faraj 168
Achaemenid 22, 30, 160, 172
Adiabene.vii, 35, 36, 37, 39, 57, 58, 109, 110, 113, 123, 131, 132, 140, 150, 154, 165, 166, 167, 169, 171, 174, 184
Ahikar .... vii, 62, 93, 94
Akitu 33, 83, 90, 140
Al Atturaye 72
Al Hajjaj ibn Yusuf ibn Matar 213
Alexander the Great .. 131, 152, 164, 166
Algosh 101, 147
Alkosh .... viii, 24, 147, 148, 155, 156
Amadiya 185, 258, 269, 270
Amenius Marcelenius ... 39
Anatolia vii, 46, 76, 77, 100, 164, 193, 220, 285
Ancient and Christian Icons vii
Ankawa .... viii, 148, 199
Anushirwanviii, 181, 184, 185, 187, 188, 191, 192, 193
Anushzad 188, 189
Arab Conquest of Mesopotamia . viii, 196
Arabs .14, 16, 17, 25, 37, 38, 39, 40, 49, 51, 55, 58, 110, 113, 114, 115, 125, 128, 154, 159, 182, 184, 189, 190, 196, 197, 198, 199, 201, 202, 203, 204, 205, 206, 213, 219, 220, 225, 256, 282, 285
Aramean ..vi, 28, 31, 33, 44, 46, 48, 73, 74, 78, 89
Arameans26, 27, 28, 32, 33, 35, 37, 38, 39, 41, 42, 43, 44, 45, 47, 79, 279, 285
Arbela..15, 16, 90, 131, 141, 154, 160, 165, 166
Arbil.. vii, ix, 15, 36, 38, 47, 58, 69, 108, 131, 132, 136, 140, 148, 154, 155, 164, 169, 171, 225, 276
Archaeological .... vii, 109, 138, 139, 282
archaeological discoveries 25, 138, 169
Armenians ..... vi, 25, 48, 54, 61, 62, 63, 64, 65, 116, 117, 168, 175, 193, 226, 227, 228, 229, 231, 233, 234, 242, 245, 249, 250, 251, 252, 256, 280, 282
Ashur.vii, 29, 30, 33, 41, 48, 49, 70, 71, 75, 76, 77, 79, 82, 83, 86, 102, 103, 107, 108, 120, 127, 131, 136, 139, 140, 141, 142, 143, 147, 151, 152, 158, 159, 160, 163, 187, 293
Ashuraya 108
Ashurbanipal ... 15, 30, 101, 128, 158, 159
Ashuri 64

Ashuriyun 64
Assyrian Christianity
.... viii, 132, 151, 167
Assyrian homeland 26
Assyrian Levies 258
Assyrian Nationalism .vii, 67, 71, 284
Assyrian Scholars...... ix, 205
Assyrian Surnames.. vii, 100
Assyrian Traditions.vii, 81
Ba Nuhadra.viii, 149, 150
Babylon ...... vi, xi, 25, 29, 31, 32, 38, 41, 50, 58, 61, 69, 82, 83, 94, 101, 102, 103, 108, 127, 129, 131, 140, 157, 158, 159, 160, 161, 162, 163, 164, 165, 168, 169, 172, 177, 209, 284, 286, 287, 288, 292
Babylonian ... 23, 29, 30, 32, 38, 43, 44, 79, 82, 83, 88, 94, 95, 121, 127, 129, 130, 134, 136, 141, 157, 158, 159, 160, 162, 163, 164, 165, 169, 187, 200
Baghdad .... viii, 35, 59, 60, 114, 126, 130, 155, 172, 191, 198, 200, 204, 205, 206, 207, 208, 210, 211, 212, 214, 216, 217, 219, 222, 223, 224, 256, 269, 271, 274, 277, 286, 290
Baghdida .... viii, 149
Bait Lapat 69
Bakht-Eisho family 207

Baqofa 150
Baquba.ix, 96, 98, 252, 255, 256
Bar Hebraeus 212, 214
Barsoum 72, 73, 74, 76
Bartella...viii, 149, 151, 155
Beth Aramaye .... vi, 41, 42, 43, 185
Beth Atturaye 41
Beth Lapat 173, 181
Beth Qarah Family .213
Bishops of Nineveh..vii, 112
Bit Akitu 83
Brigadier-Gen. Austin.. 96
Burial Practice ..... vii, 84
Carmelites missionaries vi
Chaldeans 13, 14, 19, 24, 56, 57, 59, 69, 105, 118, 145, 150, 158, 169, 228, 234, 275
Charbash 240
Christian Cemetery in Najaf viii
Christian Doctors ...... ix, 215
Church in Karbala ..viii, 198
Cyrus.29, 30, 160, 161, 162, 176
Dair Mar Mattay 93
Darius .29, 30, 84, 161, 162, 164, 166
Dur-Sharrukin 40, 145
Edessa/Urhay ...viii, 81, 83, 100, 179, 189

Esarhaddon..102, 103, 128, 158
Eski Mosul Dam Basin ....vii, 139
Eusebius ...57, 59, 131, 132, 168
Fast of Nineveh ..vii, 116
Fiey....27, 28, 31, 35, 36, 37, 39, 40, 41, 42, 46, 47, 95, 99, 101, 103, 110, 112, 113, 149, 284, 285
Genetics of the Assyrians....................vi
Georgia.64, 65, 68, 244, 292
Georgians..............vi, 64, 65
Golden Age ix, 218, 220, 286
grammar.44, 183, 204, 209, 214
Hamadan.ix, 252, 253, 255, 256
Harran...vii, 29, 38, 39, 77, 79, 108, 127, 128, 129, 130, 152, 158, 160, 163, 165, 170, 172, 187, 202, 210, 213, 215, 222, 290
Harranians...108, 128, 130, 213, 214
hats..................iv, 95, 96, 98
Huns..............185, 187, 190
Ishtar......15, 33, 49, 90, 108, 110, 128, 129, 131, 140, 142, 143, 147, 152, 163, 169
Islamic extremism.......218
Jacobite Assyrians .vii, 64, 70, 102, 136
John Joseph.13, 27, 34, 36, 39, 61, 67, 89, 117

Jundi-Shapur viii, 16, 190, 191, 202, 204, 205, 208
Jundi-Shapur Academy .... viii, 190
Karmales viii, 39, 43, 105, 151, 152
Khosro Anushirwan....188
Khosro Parviz .. viii, 112, 149, 192, 194, 196
Khosroabad.....................60
Kirkuk.......38, 69, 108, 112, 136, 145, 155, 165, 171, 195
Kurds..vi, 14, 25, 38, 56, 61, 65, 70, 91, 125, 150, 154, 197, 225, 226, 227, 229, 230, 232, 233, 235, 236, 237, 238, 239, 240, 241, 242, 243, 244, 245, 247, 249, 250, 251, 253, 254, 256, 257, 267, 274, 275, 280
Layardiv, 13, 15, 22, 40, 41, 51, 57, 58, 67, 95, 104, 107, 113, 114, 147, 150, 152, 287
Malabar Christians......56, 111
Mar Behnam iv, vii, 17, 85, 91, 92, 93, 104, 146
Mar Benjamin Shimon 235, 237, 250
Mar Ephraim iv, 72, 79, 85, 104, 116, 117, 119, 133, 175, 183
Mar Qardagh 89, 292
Marutha.................176, 177
mathematic..................213

medicine 175, 183, 188, 189, 190, 191, 192, 202, 203, 204, 205, 208, 212
Mesopotamia v, viii, 12, 15, 16, 18, 19, 20, 25, 27, 28, 33, 35, 37, 38, 39, 43, 44, 47, 49, 50, 51, 55, 64, 72, 73, 81, 88, 90, 92, 108, 110, 111, 113, 114, 119, 120, 122, 124, 125, 131, 132, 133, 134, 140, 141, 143, 146, 150, 158, 163, 164, 165, 166, 167, 168, 169, 170, 172, 173, 176, 179, 180, 183, 185, 190, 196, 199, 200, 201, 209, 213, 222, 280, 284, 287, 291
Mongol.....ix, 125, 154, 221, 222, 225
Mosul..vii, ix, 35, 39, 40, 41, 47, 61, 68, 69, 74, 84, 92, 93, 98, 102, 112, 113, 114, 115, 124, 125, 126, 131, 132, 139, 145, 146, 149, 150, 151, 152, 153, 154, 155, 221, 223, 224, 226, 227, 229, 234, 236, 237, 255, 257, 267, 268, 269, 271, 273, 274, 289
Nabu.. 33, 43, 110, 140, 141, 143, 169
Nader Shah............ 148, 155
Narses 131, 168
nationalism.. 49, 67, 68, 89, 226
Naum Faig 71

Nergal . 33, 49, 83, 129, 140, 142
Nestorian scholars 190, 206
Nestorius .. 58, 88, 175, 176, 179, 180, 182
New Year festival.... 33, 83
New Year in Edessa vii, 83
Nimrod.... 15, 50, 51, 79, 82, 89, 107, 110, 121, 129, 289
Nineveh i, iii, iv, vii, viii, 12, 13, 17, 19, 20, 21, 22, 23, 24, 29, 30, 31, 35, 37, 38, 41, 47, 50, 57, 59, 60, 61, 75, 78, 79, 80, 82, 83, 84, 85, 89, 92, 93, 99, 104, 106, 107, 108, 109, 110, 111, 112, 113, 114, 115, 116, 117, 118, 119, 120, 122, 123, 124, 125, 127, 128, 131, 136, 138, 139, 140, 141, 143, 145, 146, 147, 148, 149, 150, 151, 153, 154, 155, 157, 160, 165, 166, 185, 187, 194, 195, 198, 225, 255, 280, 282, 283, 284, 286, 287, 293
Nineveh After the Fall ....vii, 106
Nisibin .. vii, viii, 16, 39, 69, 77, 90, 112, 127, 132, 133, 134, 135, 136, 145, 160, 165, 167, 172, 173, 175, 178, 181, 183, 184, 190, 191, 192, 195, 202
Odisho Bar Yohannan Bet Maron 56, 57

Ottoman Turks ix, 15, 149, 231, 278
Parthian Rule.... viii, 165
Persian... viii, xi, 12, 22, 23, 28, 29, 30, 31, 32, 33, 43, 47, 48, 59, 60, 62, 64, 84, 89, 90, 94, 95, 98, 103, 111, 132, 133, 134, 135, 136, 148, 149, 155, 160, 161, 162, 163, 164, 165, 166, 169, 170, 171, 172, 173, 175, 176, 177, 178, 179, 181, 182, 183, 184, 185, 186, 187, 188, 190, 191, 193, 194, 195, 198, 202, 204, 205, 211, 229, 233, 234, 240, 241, 242, 243, 244, 245, 246, 247, 250, 251, 254, 269, 285, 286, 288, 289, 290, 291, 292
Persians ...vi, 14, 16, 25, 28, 29, 31, 40, 44, 46, 59, 64, 103, 110, 131, 132, 133, 134, 135, 145, 146, 152, 163, 171, 172, 173, 176, 177, 187, 188, 193, 194, 195, 196, 197, 202, 243, 245, 254, 283
philosophers......36, 94, 190, 207, 208, 210, 217
Plain of Nineveh ..256, 280
psychology 73, 214
Romans .14, 37, 43, 57, 112, 132, 133, 134, 135, 145, 165, 166, 172, 173, 174, 176, 178, 191, 193, 194, 195, 196

Russian......ix, 66, 103, 226, 230, 231, 234, 238, 240, 241, 242, 244, 248, 249
Russians .vii, 66, 231, 237, 238, 239, 242
Saddam .....ix, 17, 145, 149, 274, 275, 276, 281
Sassanian Rule viii
satrap ....vi, 26, 31, 136, 163
Satrapy 160
school in Nisibin 183
Seleucid Dynasty.... viii, 164
Tamure.....ix, 136, 225, 226
Telkaif.................. viii, 153
Tergawar 240
Thabit....210, 213, 214, 215, 216
Theological Disputes .... viii, 179
Tikrit38, 108, 126, 145, 151, 159, 217, 219
Translation into Arabic ix
Tur Abedin vii, 77, 78, 79, 83, 227
Turks ix, 14, 25, 55, 71, 154, 197, 220, 221, 226, 227, 228, 229, 230, 233, 234, 235, 237, 238, 239, 241, 243, 244, 245, 249, 251, 252, 253, 254, 255, 257, 258
Urmia .ix, 18, 54, 60, 65, 67, 68, 80, 99, 146, 227, 229, 230, 231, 232, 234, 235, 238, 240, 241, 242, 244,

245, 249, 250, 251, 252, 254, 255, 256
Walker 15, 16, 89, 90, 91, 292
Wigram ....xi, 39, 40, 41, 68, 69, 104, 114, 237, 238, 239, 257, 273, 274, 292
Wise Men................ 120, 169
World War I Massacre ....ix, 227
Xenophon 21, 22, 23, 25, 124, 136, 194

Xerxes .. 29, 30, 32, 162, 163, 164
Yazdegerd I 176, 177
Yuhanna ibn-Masawayah ix
Zakho ...... viii, 27, 136, 153, 154
Zoroastrian 30, 89, 152, 173, 176, 177, 178, 188, 189

www.ingramcontent.com/pod-product-compliance
Lightning Source LLC
Chambersburg PA
CBHW060111170426
43198CB00010B/854